Treating
Suicidal
Clients &
Self-Harm
Behaviors

Assessments, Worksheets & Guides for
Interventions and Long-Term Care

Meagan N. Houston, PhD, SAP

Copyright © 2017 by Meagan N. Houston

Published by
PESI Publishing & Media
PESI, Inc
3839 White Ave
Eau Claire, WI 54703

Cover: Amy Rubenzer
Editing: Hazel Bird
Layout: Amy Rubenzer & Bookmasters

ISBN: 9781683730842

Printed in the United States of America.

PESI
Publishing
& Media
www.PESI.com

"Finally! A hands-on resource which provides practical interventions for the assessment, intervention and management of suicidal and NSSI behavior. Dr. Houston's approach to suicide and NSSI prevention is timely, relevant and culturally sensitive. The level of detail and precision in which this delicate topic is discussed makes it clear why Dr. Houston is an authority on the topic of suicide and NSSI. This gem will benefit neophyte and seasoned clinicians alike!"

Jasmine Ross Burton, PhD
Licensed Psychologist
Essence Psychological Health Services

"Dr. Houston is a consummate professional and presenter, and her years of experience shine in this must-have resource. Working with personality disorders and challenging clients, and managing suicidal issues as well as non-suicidal self-injury on a routine basis, this book will quickly become an indispensable tool."

Daniel J. Fox, PhD
Licensed Psychologist
Award-winning author of *Antisocial, Borderline, Narcissistic & Histrionic Workbook*

"Dr. Houston has graciously and tirelessly given mental health professionals and their clients a priceless, clinical gift. Irrespective of your clientele, clinical setting or academic training, *Treating Suicidal Clients & Self-Harm Behaviors* answers questions, details treatment strategies and provides practical tools. Dr. Houston has thoroughly researched the challenges clinicians face with suicidal and self-harming clients, and provides a comprehensive, one-stop resource. Her book identifies and addresses the fears and inadequacies of clinicians, and empowers them to confidently and compassionately work with these challenging clients. The mental health community and the clients we serve will benefit from Dr. Houston's work for years to come."

Verdi R. Lethermon, PhD
Retired Director, HPD Psychological Services Division

"As a licensed psychologist with over 20 years of experience, I still become a bit nervous when dealing with a client who might be suicidal. Dr. Houston's book provides an excellent roadmap for conducting an in-depth assessment of a potentially suicidal client and then gives very practical information about how to intervene during this type of crisis. I work in a setting where we frequently have clients who express suicidal ideation and I supervise a number of students and interns each year. This book will surely become a favorite reference for my students, as it is clearly written, easy to understand, and has several sections that are directly related to the setting that I am in. It is also wonderful to have an up-to-date book that addresses the complications of suicide and modern technology, such as the impact of social media or working with clients through teletherapy. The checklists and worksheets are very useful and convey information in a way that is helpful for both the clinician and the client. This is the kind of book that I wish that I had available to me as a new clinician; however, I know that even seasoned clinicians can definitely benefit from this comprehensive work."

Nicole Dorsey, PhD
Licensed Psychologist
Training Director, Harris County Juvenile Probation Department, Texas

"Dr. Houston's book is impactful, powerful, and practical. It is easy to understand, with bullet points and clear explanations. She offers many resources and tools to use while working with suicidal and self-harming clients. A useful tool for therapists to use with parents of teenagers who engage in non-suicidal self-harming behaviors or contemplating suicide. Dr. Houston walks readers through assessing for suicide and the post suicidal interview with worksheets and step by step guides. This is a great and useful therapeutic tool."

Susan Beach Barris, PhD
Drug Abuse Program Coordinator

"This is a comprehensive and practical guide for clinicians of all experience levels. Dr. Houston reveals herself to be one of the foremost experts in the assessment and treatment of suicidal and self-harm behavior, both by providing the most up to date resources and tools, as well as offering specific examples of her clinical experience. What I find particularly helpful is the information on safety planning and special populations, the latter of which includes risk checklists for each group. Even more, what is likely the most unique aspect of this book is Dr. Houston's inclusion of technology factors and tools, which is what I am most looking forward to implementing into my own practice. These include mobile apps and web resources, as well as information on cyber-bullying and online communities promoting NSSI behavior. Finally, emphasis on clinician self-care is apparent throughout as necessary component to working with high-risk cases. Whether you are a graduate student, or a seasoned clinician, you will find this workbook a necessary addition to your library."

Scott M. Forbes, PhD
Licensed Psychologist,
Veterans Healthcare Administration

"Dr. Houston provides an excellent overview of assessment for suicidality from all angles. This book is an excellent teaching tool for new clinicians that provides a comprehensive overview of all factors to consider in conducting thorough and extensive evaluations for suicide risk. It also serves as an excellent resource and reference for experienced clinicians who want to make sure they are reviewing all relevant factors in their assessments, even reviewing specific factors related to a variety of special populations, to include LGBT, military vets, college students and more. Dr. Houston provides a comprehensive approach to treating suicidal clients, including ways of managing your own anxieties and concerns along the way!"

Kevin Correia, PhD
Clinical Psychologist

"This workbook takes a practical, well-informed, and nuanced approach to working with clients who engage in suicidal and self-harm behaviors. The worksheets and clinical examples make this a particularly useful guide for trainings. Of note are the several diversity variables and the Internet/social media, and how these may impact our clients' experiences and our treatment choices. Both novice and experienced clinicians will benefit from this resource!"

Cecilia Sun, PhD
University of Houston, Counseling and Psychological Services

"Dr. Houston has written a remarkable workbook for helping professionals of all skill levels. Houston's thoughtfulness regarding clinical responses will bridge traditional academic and experiential learning in a paramount manner, ultimately progressing the prognosis of our clients. This will be my training tool for novice and expert helping professionals alike. This is a significant guide for the helping field."

Charles Helm, PhD
Correctional Psychologist
Federal Bureau of Prisons

"It is with great pleasure and enthusiasm that I write this endorsement for Dr. Meagan Houston's workbook. Simply put, I found it very informative. She provided wonderful ideas that help professionals maintain their sanity when dealing with suicidal patients. It contains information that can really be useful and it is written in a dynamic, entertaining way. Her workbook highlights her skills and translates state-of-the-art research and knowledge into relevant, accessible, practical gems for the clinical as well as non-clinical. Dr. Houston is always knowledgeable, experienced, entertaining, and engaging and I highly recommend her workbook for trainings/conferences."

CDR Scarlet Lusk-Edwards, RHIA, MPH, PhD
United States Public Health Services, Federal Bureau Of Prisons

"Every good clinician has or does experience some sense of uneasiness or anxiety when thinking about potentially suicidal clients or when dealing with suicidal clients or those who engage in self-injurious behavior. Experience, consultation, and great resources help allay those concerns. Dr. Houston's workbook is one of those references that every clinician should possess--from graduate student to veteran counselor. Dr. Houston has created a thorough, practical guide for professionals of all experience levels. Although assessing suicide risk is extremely unpredictable, use of this workbook can improve clinical judgment and confidence when managing these at-risk clients. From etiology to initial assessment, crisis intervention, and long-term treatment, this workbook includes critical data and useful worksheets to assist mental health professionals in one, comprehensive resource."

Edwina L. Martin, PhD
Licensed Clinical Psychologist

"As a clinician who has experience in the educational and private settings, addressing suicide, suicide prevention, and self-harm behaviors has become a rising hot topic. Within Dr. Houston's workbook she was able to capture the "who, what, when and how" when it comes to identifying and supporting these populations. Dr. Houston also presented the information in a format that is easily applicable, ready to use and able for clinicians to translate across service settings. "

Stephanie S. O'Neal, MA, LPC, LSSP
Licensed Specialist in School Psychology

"*Treating Suicidal Clients & Self-Harm Behaviors* is what the field of mental health needs! Dr. Houston did an extraordinary job at tackling suicide topics from A to Z. Every clinician needs this workbook in their library as it gives great direction on how to handle specific clients."

Patrice Douglas, MFT
Clinical Therapist

"This workbook breaks down suicidality in a way that's easy to understand, along with various techniques that can be applied. I found the various checklists helpful as they broke down each population and specific warning signs in an easy to remember format. It not only explained what to do - but how to do it - with specific questions to ask a client to further and more effectively assess their risk, and the best interventions a therapist can provide for any given specific situation. This is a workbook that is practical for all levels of practitioners!"

Jessica Corey, LPC
Mental Health Clinician

"Dr. Houston's workbook is very beneficial to anyone working in the mental health field. In my role as a chief psychologist in a correctional environment, current and past suicidal behaviors are one of the major risk factors I assess. Dr. Houston's workbook is very concise in describing suicidal risk assessments and she does a great job differentiating between short-term and long-term treatment. She also gives a phenomenal explanation of Non-Suicidal Self-Injury (NSSI). Dr. Houston's workbook is a valuable resource for a novice or senior clinician."

David A. Freeman, PsyD
Clinical Psychologist

"Having been an independent practitioner for almost 25 years and in the field for considerably longer, I rarely find practice manuals interesting. However, Dr. Houston's approach allowed the reader to glean information at their own level of expertise and interest. Dr. Houston structured the material so that the reader is left feeling progressively more knowledgeable and at ease. Finally, structured evaluations that are valid and user friendly."

Vonceil C. Smith, PhD
Clinical Psychologist

"This is a must-have toolkit! The book is a nice mix of scientific literature, theory, and application. In addition to all the practical activities and worksheets, I also appreciate the attention to special populations when working with this important topic."

Summer Rose, PhD
Licensed Psychologist

This book is dedicated to my wonderful and supportive husband, Gabriel U. Bright, and to my amazing parents, Robert Lee and Rosemary Houston. Gabriel, I love you for all that you are and for all that you come with. Mom and Dad, I am me, because you are you. Thank you again for all of your motivating words and unwavering faith! I pray that God continues to guide my path on this journey. That he continues to afford me the opportunity to help those who have chosen this honored and privileged profession of helping others. I hope this workbook will be used to diligently provide effective and professional services to clients in need and to ultimately **just stop one suicide**. If we can do that as mental health professionals, we are fulfilling our purpose!

table of contents

Meagan N. Houston, PhD, SAP, has specialized in providing suicide treatment in a wide variety of settings and populations for over a decade. She has experience in high-risk settings where the application of suicide prevention, assessment, and intervention occurs daily. Dr. Houston treats clients who present with a variety of psychological and behavioral disorders that lend themselves to acute and chronic suicidality. She emphasizes the use of empirically-based approaches when conducting suicide risk assessments.

Dr. Houston is employed full time with the Houston Police Department Psychological Services Division, where she is responsible for providing an array of psychological services to active duty and retired police officers and their family members, in addition to civilian employees and their families. She also provides a variety of training at the Police Academy, including Stress Management, Intermediate Use of Force, and other core classes. In addition, she also maintains a part-time private practice in Houston, Texas, where she provides a wide range of psychological services, national consultation and training to various agencies on suicidal behavior, suicide risk assessment, self-harm behaviors, social media and contagion.

Previously, she worked in the federal prison system, and she filled the dual roles of Prison Psychologist and Federal Law Enforcement Officer, and she provided a variety of psychological services to both inmates and correctional staff. She frequently conducted training with correctional and executive staff and served as the Mental Health Expert on the Hostage Negotiation Team for several years, working closely with officers and special response teams. She has also provided psychological, psycho-educational, and chemical dependency programs in private practices and college counseling centers, and has provided geropsychological services to nursing homes and rehabilitation facilities.

who this workbook is for and how to use it

One of my first difficult clients cut himself for years and had multiple suicide attempts with lingering suicidal ideation. I had never worked with this kind of client and I was scared. Talk about sink or swim! I thought I was asking the right questions about previous attempts, current ideation, family history . . . all of those things they teach you in class. I was consistent with treatment and I provided structure and boundaries. It was working!

Then, I got "the call." Two days after I'd last seen him, he'd attempted suicide. He'd cut his throat and was in the hospital with 289 stitches . . . on my watch . . . under my care. It was my worst nightmare!

Where did I go wrong? I missed the subtle cues—the ones that may not necessarily be taught in the classroom but that are critical for successful outcomes. Since that time, I have learned to be creative in treating my suicidal and non-suicidal self-injurious (NSSI) clients by personalizing strategies. I've developed a successful suicide risk training program that has saved lives, and I've built an integrated assessment instrument that has become the standard of care for my organization. I've effectively put these principles to work with many at-risk groups, including kids and adolescents, veterans and military personnel, LGBTQI individuals, the elderly, police personnel, and prison populations.

HOW ABOUT YOU? ARE YOU PREPARED?
DO YOU HAVE THE BEST TOOLS TO FIGHT THESE BATTLES?

Did you notice the flower on the front cover? Its delicate, looks to be thriving and healthy, but if you look closely, it's not perfect. Subtle changes are happening, that can go unseen if we don't remain vigilant. The presence of suicide and self-harm can also be elusive in the same way, lurking right underneath the surface of what appears to be "normal" and blooming.

Treating suicidal clients and those who engage in self-destructive behaviors is not easy. There is no one right way to do this. Many clinicians feel confused or helpless in the face of the severe behavior or consequences associated with these types of clients. Clinicians become fearful, anxious, uncertain, or overly cautious when treating these clients and at times these feelings can lead to countertransference, negatively affecting treatment. We are not always prepared for the complexity of concerns associated with working with clients who present with suicidal behaviors, and this lack of preparation hinders our ability to provide adequate and effective care to our clients. Working with these types of clients can be intimidating, not only for the fledging practitioner but also for those of us who have continued to provide mental health services to clients who consistently present with suicidal behaviors.

Given the intricacies that affect our clients' choices to live or die, it is difficult to pinpoint just one effective tool or technique that will "fix" this problem. Each client will be in a different place with respect to intensity of suicidal ideation, intention, planning, and even attempting. And clients typically do not fit into nice, neat categories.

This workbook is designed to help clinicians understand the underlying etiology, varying life factors, and mental health concerns that influence suicidal and self-destructive behaviors. It is designed to assist mental health care providers in thinking critically about their clients' presenting concerns and understanding how cultural, environmental, social, and genetic factors play an enormous role in why our clients are thinking, feeling, and behaving in maladaptive ways. This workbook has been created to help you identify those subtle factors that may be key in the prevention of suicide for a client.

As a result of the integral complexity of the presentation of suicide, there are multiple approaches a clinician can use to assess, manage, and treat suicidal clients and clients who engage in NSSI behaviors. This workbook is designed to provide assistance to the treating clinician who may feel impeded, frustrated, or out of options when working with this multifaceted group of clients.

Topics/Areas that will be covered include:

- Discussing suicidality with a client.
- Assessing for suicidal potential.
- Understanding suicide prevention with special populations and the mental health diagnoses that have the highest risk for suicide.
- Using multiple therapeutic approaches, including interpersonal therapy, crisis management, cognitive–behavioral therapy, and dialectical behavioral therapy.

Chapter 1 | Suicide:
What You Need to Know

WHAT IS SUICIDE?

The Centers for Disease Control and Prevention define suicide as "death caused by self-directed injurious behavior with an intent to die as a result of the behavior." The dictionary *Merriam-Webster* defines suicide as "being or performing a deliberate act resulting in the voluntary death of the person who does it" ("Suicide," 2015). No matter the definition, suicide is an occurrence that is preventable, when our clients allow us to help. However, we need to be articulate in our conversations in order to accurately interview, assess, and manage suicidal clients and clients who present with suicidal behavior. We also need to recognize and acknowledge our own fears, anxieties, and possible lack of training in the application of management strategies for these behaviors.

Suicide is a topic that most people view as anxiety-provoking, taboo, and scary. It is a very real topic and, yes, it is frightening, but there are things about suicide that clinicians know that clients are unable to see due to their constricted and, at times, hopeless and helpless worldview. It is a phenomenon that must be addressed candidly and openly and it is an issue that will be found in every clinical and non-clinical setting.

Suicidal behavior can look like many things. It can look like self-destructive behavior (e.g., frequent drug use, driving recklessly, and/or placing oneself in dangerous situations), it can take the form of non-suicidal self-injury and "accidental suicide," or it can present as more blatant self-harm behavior (e.g., cutting, taking medication in excess, or swallowing objects). Suicidal behavior can be impulsive at times or it can be more rational and well planned.

IMPULSIVE SUICIDE

An impulsive suicide often involves the combination of a precipitating event, diminished coping ability, and feelings of helplessness, hopelessness, shame, guilt, burdensomeness, and feeling trapped. A precipitating event can include issues such as notice of a terminal illness, death of a loved one, loss of a job or financial stability, the break-up of a relationship, failing grades, or rejection. These events, typically, can make the risk of suicidal behavior imminent in the upcoming hours, days, weeks, or months. These events are typically sudden and involve crisis types of reactions. Drugs and alcohol are typically involved when a suicide is impulsive, as these substances lower inhibition, increase impulsivity, and compromise rational thinking and decision-making capabilities. Impulsive suicides are seldom accompanied by the classic warning signs, such as prior suicide attempts, diagnosed mental illness, or drug and/or alcohol abuse. The act is sudden and unrehearsed, and is thus especially more common among adolescents and young adults, who are already biologically primed to be more impulsive.

Clinical studies about impulsive suicide have varied, but some common characteristics of those who complete this type of suicide have indicated the following:

- **Gender**: Typically male.
- **Age**: Adolescents are at increased risk.
- **Emotional immaturity**: There is a diminished ability to think through consequences.
- **Mental illness**: Increased prevalence for psychosis and alcohol and/or drug abuse, but not for depression.
- **Method**: Considered medically severe. Jumping into a body of water or throwing oneself into oncoming traffic from a certain height (jumping off an overpass into traffic) are highly correlated with impulsive suicides.
- **Other factors**: A history of aggressive behavior or of previous impulsive suicidal behaviors (cutting, other self-destructive behaviors, and a history of poor decision making).

RATIONAL SUICIDE

Rational suicide has been defined as suicide in which there is a reasonable choice to die by a terminally ill person; it is also the ending of one's life for considered reasons as opposed to emotional or psychological reasons. Those who support rational suicide argue that there is a need to respect an individual's autonomy, meaning their right to be their own person or being able to act according to their own beliefs or desires without interference from others. The "right to die" is often viewed as an expression of the most extreme form of autonomy, which is the right to choose the time and manner of one's own death. Another view that supports the concept of rational suicide involves the ability of an individual to make a rational assessment of the utility or "benefit" that is gained by ending their life. Proponents of this view argue that suicide can provide escape and freedom from painful and hopeless disease. This view emphasizes the importance of quality of life rather than "just living."

Physician-assisted suicide describes the process of facilitating a patient's death by providing the necessary means and/or information to enable the client to perform the life-ending act (e.g., the physician provides sleeping pills and information about the lethal dose while being aware that the client may commit suicide). This type of suicide is usually reserved for individuals who are currently living with terminal illnesses that are progressive and debilitating. As of September 2015, physician-assisted suicide is legal in California, Montana, Oregon, Vermont, and Washington State.

COMMON ELEMENTS OF SUICIDE

A common **purpose** of suicide is to seek a **solution**. Those who are contemplating suicide usually feel as if they have exhausted all possibilities when attempting to solve problems. Typically, suicide is conjured when experiencing a stressful situation for which they have no coping ability or when attempting to navigate a situation that is out of their control.

A common **emotion** in suicide is **hopelessness** or **helplessness**. Research demonstrates that hopelessness and helplessness are typically accompanied by feelings of shame, guilt, burdensomeness, inability to cope, and intermittent insomnia. This combination of symptoms can increase one's suicide risk, and the imminence of suicidal behavior should be assessed when these elements are present. These symptoms are also prevalent in most mental health diagnoses, including depressive disorders, anxiety disorders, bipolar disorders, psychotic disorders, eating disorders, trauma and other related stressor disorders, obsessive–compulsive disorders, and even substance-related mental health disorders.

A common **stressor** in suicide is a **frustrated psychological need**. Frustrated psychological needs vary and are subjective. These needs could include the need for belongingness, financial needs, relationship needs, esteem needs, or safety needs. These needs are typically not being met and most individuals feel as if there are road blocks and other factors, out of their control, impeding the satiation of these needs. The intensity of this frustration varies for each individual and in relation to the most recent issue or precipitating event.

A common **goal** of suicide is **cessation of consciousness**. When suicide is being contemplated, individuals are typically seeking peace, homeostasis, and psychological and emotional congruence. They are seeking to end their existence in order to cease experiencing psychological and emotional pain.

A common **stimulus** (or information input) in suicide is **intolerable psychological pain**. This type of pain is, again, subjective, similarly to frustrated psychological needs. Intolerable psychological pain refers to the inability to attain symptom relief from everyday functioning. This pain has been described as chronic and pervasive and is typically severe in intensity. It can be caused by various factors, including relationships, self-loathing and self-worth distortions, and feeling as if there is no end or logical solution to managing the pain.

A common **internal attitude** in suicide is **ambivalence**. Ambivalence refers to the indecisiveness that accompanies suicidal behavior at times. Ambivalence is a **good** thing! When our clients remain ambivalent, they are uncertain about suicide and are more willing to discuss the issue. It becomes problematic when our clients move away from ambivalence and move closer to a sense of resolve about suicide. When resolve occurs, our clients do not typically give any indicators or warning signs about suicidal ideation or potential attempts.

The common **cognitive state** in suicide is **constriction**. When our clients are contemplating suicide, they tend to view the world through a narrow lens and begin experiencing "tunnel vision" about their current situation. Feelings of hopelessness and helplessness begin to manifest themselves cognitively when this type of thinking occurs. Clients may view prior efforts as useless and future orientation as futile. This is why it is so important to instill hope and provide alternatives to the various situations clients experience.

The common **action** in suicide is **escape**. When our clients are contemplating suicide, many of them are seeking to escape, flee, avoid, and/or seek a resolution to the problem they are experiencing. They want to be free of their current situation and are desperate to end their psychological, emotional, and at times physical pain.

The common **interpersonal act** in suicide is **communication of intention**. Many completed suicides and attempted suicides communicate pain, agony, and desperation. Whether this communication involves writing a suicide note, writing another text, verbal communication, or behavioral communication, the sender is attempting to express intolerable inner psychic turmoil to a receiver.

The common **consistency** in suicide is a history of **unhealthy lifelong coping patterns**. Most clients who present with suicidal ideation, intent, or a plan typically report a history of poor coping skills and becoming easily overwhelmed. They present with poor distress tolerance skills and poor emotion regulation skills.

Chapter 2 | Identifying At-Risk Clients:

DSM-5® Diagnoses at Increased Suicide Risk

A new feature of the DSM-5 is a specific section labeled "Suicide Risk," which is included for select diagnoses. This emphasizes that individuals with these disorders may be at an increased risk for suicidal ideation, intent, or planning.

SCHIZOPHRENIA SPECTRUM AND OTHER PSYCHOTIC DISORDERS AND SUICIDE

When working with clients who present with schizophrenia or other psychotic disorders, it is important to remember that these individuals, while not always dangerous, may present with suicidal ideation, intent, or planning. These ideas may be influenced by delusional content, feelings of paranoia, feelings of grandiosity, or feelings of invincibility. When an individual is experiencing actively psychotic symptoms, the risk for suicide increases, as cognitive and affective impairment influence the person's behavior.

When inquiring about suicidal ideation, intent, or planning with an actively psychotic individual, it is first important to remain calm and aware of their presentation. Are they agitated, restless, paranoid, or distrustful? If the client is presenting as agitated, it is most important that you first attempt to contact another clinician (if possible) and that you **do not** touch the client or physically approach the client. Continue to use your active listening skills and remain proactive in managing your safety. You can attempt to engage the client in deep breathing or other de-escalation techniques.

It is also important to assess for the presence of auditory and/or visual hallucinations and to inquire about the details of these hallucinations. Such details are important, because you want to know whether the client is experiencing derogatory and/or command hallucinations that are encouraging the client to harm him/herself or others, or whether the visual hallucination is dangerous or prompting of harmful behaviors.

Disorders with increased suicide risk

- Schizophrenia
- Schizoaffective Disorder (bipolar or depressive type)
- Substance-/Medication-Induced Psychotic Disorder
- Psychotic Disorder Due to Another Medical Condition

Schizophrenia and Suicide Risk

- Research has indicated that 20–40% of individuals diagnosed with schizophrenia attempt suicide.

- Clients may act impulsively and without warning. During a psychotic episode, a client can present with unpredictable and sporadic behavior. This behavior cannot always be predicted or anticipated. It is important to keep this information in mind when conducting a suicide risk assessment (SRA) or engaging in treatment with an actively psychotic patient.

- Clients may be influenced by hallucinations and/or delusions. The client may be experiencing derogatory and/or command auditory hallucinations, or other hallucinations (tactile, visual, and/or olfactory) that sway their actions and behavior. The delusions may also cause sporadic and dangerous behavior.

- Depersonalization can also occur. This causes loss of reality; thus, during a psychotic episode, the client may not recognize that their behaviors are dangerous or life threatening.

- Cognitive disruptions may affect decision making.

- Paranoid ideation may influence behavior.

- Non-compliance with treatment increases suicide risk. The treatment of this disorder can be overwhelming for clients, as it involves a variety of methods including psychotropic medication management, intensive outpatient and/or inpatient treatment, and case management.

- There may be mood disorder symptoms (symptoms of depression, anxiety, agitation, irritation, frustration, or being easily overwhelmed).

- There may be a lack of family or social support. Most individuals diagnosed with a psychotic disorder have difficulty establishing and/or maintaining relationships with others. They are typically estranged from their family and friends and can be ostracized from their communities. The stigma associated with psychotic disorders also plays a role in seeking help and discussing their symptoms with others. The stigma associated with this disorder is also reported to increase suicide risk, as many feel helpless and hopeless and also experience clinical levels of other mood disorder symptoms.

Clinician Safety Measures

- Position yourself closest to the nearest exit (e.g., door, entry way, hallway, window).

- Remain cognizant of any object in your office that may be used as a weapon against you and/or used by the client against him/herself (e.g., scissors, pens, pencils, staplers).

- Continue to remain calm and use a low and even tone when discussing provocative topics with the client.

- Do not use patronizing language or present as aggressive toward the client.

- Attempt to inform colleagues about the client prior to client's arrival. Do not provide treatment to the client when alone in the office.

- Contact law enforcement authorities when warranted—for example, if the client remains non-compliant or aggressive, or continues to refuse treatment or hospitalization.

- Remain empathic with the client when they are presenting with paranoid or delusional content.

Other Characteristics of Schizophrenia

- The client may demonstrate flat affect, inappropriate affect, (e.g., laughing when telling a traumatizing story or being angry when discussing a seemingly benign event).
- Depersonalization or derealization, which may be present, is an abnormal sense of self-awareness. It can consist of a reality or detachment within the self regarding one's mind or body, or being a detached observer of oneself. Patients feel they have changed and that the world has become vague, dreamlike, less real, or lacking in significance.
- Anxiety and phobias may be present.
- During a psychotic episode an individual may present with poor decision making, poor reality-testing, and poor problem-solving ability.
- Client may demonstrate aggression or hostility.
- Non-compliance with treatment is common with this diagnosis. Many individuals who suffer from a psychotic disorder are typically non-compliant with treatment, including psychotropic medication management, case management, and/or individual therapy.
- The onset of psychotic symptoms typically occurs during the late teens to mid-thirties.

Schizoaffective Disorder and Suicide Risk

- Presence of a major depressive episode or manic episode increases suicide risk.
- There may be hallucinations and/or delusions, particularly if these symptoms are derogatory and/or commanding in nature.
- Social isolation also increases suicide risk, as lack of social support has been correlated with increased risk. Given the intensity, severity, and frequency of their psychotic episodes, these individuals typically have difficulty establishing and/or maintaining relationships with others. There are also feelings of shame and guilt that are associated with this diagnosis, and this leads to isolating behaviors and remaining withdrawn.
- Suicide risk is increased due to impulsivity and poor decision making related to symptoms of schizophrenia, and these symptoms are often exacerbated by the presence of mood disorder symptoms.
- Those with this diagnosis are often non-compliant with their treatment regimen, specifically during an active psychotic episode.
- Increased occurrence of suicidal ideation occurs as a result of the combination of psychotic and mood disorder symptoms.

Individuals who have received this diagnosis are experiencing the symptoms of psychosis in addition to mood disorder symptoms. These mood disorder symptoms can include manic, hypomanic, mixed, and/or depressive symptoms. This mood disorder component exacerbates psychotic symptoms and can increase suicide risk. When working with these clients, it is important to thoroughly assess the presence of psychotic and mood symptoms, as this diagnosis is often misdiagnosed as a mood disorder with psychotic features (e.g., major depressive disorder with psychotic features). This is important because these two diagnoses are treated and managed differently.

When assessing for suicide risk, it is very important to attend to the intensity and duration of the psychotic and mood disorder symptoms. The likelihood of suicide increases during a depressive episode, wherein the client is experiencing feelings of hopelessness, helplessness, guilt, shame, worthlessness, loneliness, and sadness. During these episodes, suicidal ideation and/or morbid ideation can occur. The client may also be isolating him/herself from others and may be withdrawn. This may further diminish social support, creating an increased suicide risk.

Working with these clients involves patience, empathy, diagnostic skill, clinical competence, and knowledge of the available resources in your community (hospitals, psychiatry services, indigent services, etc.). You should also practice the clinician safety measures listed in the section on schizophrenia.

Other Characteristics of Schizoaffective Disorder

- There is an increased risk for developing a major depressive disorder or bipolar disorder symptoms following actively psychotic phases.
- There may be co-morbid substance-related disorders, including alcohol use disorder, cocaine use disorder, opioid use disorder, and/or amphetamine use disorder.
- Onset of symptoms typically occurs during the late teens to early adulthood (ages 16–30).
- This disorder is often misdiagnosed as bipolar disorder with psychotic features or major depressive disorder with psychotic features. This misdiagnosis increases risk for suicide and other socio-environmental risks, as the above-mentioned disorders involve a different type of treatment planning when compared to schizoaffective disorder.

Psychotic Episode Due to Another Medical Condition and Suicide Risk

- The chronicity of the medical condition could increase suicide risk. The medical condition could be terminal in nature and/or progressive (e.g., HIV, Huntington's disease, multiple sclerosis, or Parkinson's disease).
- The presence of mood disorder symptoms (including depressive and anxiety symptoms) can also cause elevated suicide risk.
- After a while, chronic pain becomes debilitating, draining a person's energy and diminishing their motivation. These individuals sometimes attempt to limit social contact with others in an effort to reduce stress and to decrease energy expenditure. Eventually, many people with chronic pain develop depression-like symptoms: lack of interpersonal interaction, difficulty concentrating on simple tasks, and the desire to simplify their life as much as possible, which often manifests as seeking isolation and quiet.
- Sleeping often makes the pain less intrusive, and that combined with the exhaustion that pain induces causes some pain sufferers to develop hypersomnia; alternatively, at times, pain can have the opposite effect and may cause intermittent insomnia. The combination of the above issues may increase risk for suicide.
- Impaired decision-making ability may increase suicide risk.
- Unpredictable nature of onset of symptoms increases suicide risk.
- Access to medical care may be limited or nonexistent to clients; thus, the medical condition may go untreated and worsen, possibly increasing suicide risk.

It is important to understand the medical condition causing the psychotic symptoms when working with your client. The medical condition could be terminal or progressive and this could increase suicide risk. It is also important to remain aware about the use of medications associated with the medical condition, as interaction effects could influence the presence, frequency, or intensity of suicidal ideation, intent, or planning. The concept of "rule-outs" (a term commonly used in outpatient care to eliminate a suspected condition or disease as the cause of the client's symptoms) should be practiced when managing this condition, and it is always important to consult with other health professionals to provide the most adequate care.

Other Characteristics of Psychotic Disorder Due to Another Medical Condition

- Treatment for the medical condition could include the use of innumerable medications and other treatments (e.g., chemotherapy, radiation, or interferon treatment). Psychotic symptoms could be side effects of certain treatments or medications. Additionally, interaction effects between the various medications may cause the development of acute psychotic symptoms.
- The medical condition may cause delusions and hallucinations.
- The client may experience transient or recurrent psychotic episodes.
- Psychotic symptoms may be contingent upon the course of the medical condition.
- The onset of symptoms typically occurs within older age groups due to the likelihood of such individuals developing conditions and/or the likelihood of their pre-existing medical conditions worsening.

BIPOLAR AND RELATED DISORDERS AND SUICIDE

Bipolar disorder is a mood disorder that involves high "highs" and low "lows." Individuals with this diagnosis experience manic, depressed, and mixed mood disorder symptoms. During a manic episode, clients are typically non-compliant with medication use and therapy approaches. Several of the medications used to treat this diagnosis are administered in high doses and have unpleasant side effects. Those diagnosed with this disorder also tend to enjoy manic phases, in which they feel creative, outgoing, charismatic, grandiose, and motivated; have an increased energy level; and experience an expansive or elevated mood.

These individuals may present as grandiose, feel indestructible, take dangerous risks, use illicit substances, and require minimal sleep. These risky behaviors can include compulsive gambling, risky investing, or spending without regard for one's true financial state (e.g., buying a car when you can't possibly make the payments). Clients may also engage in high-risk behaviors that may be hypersexual, such as making inappropriate sexual advances; spending a great deal of money on phone sex, being involved with internet pornography, or hiring prostitutes; or having affairs. This combination of symptoms increases suicide risk, as cognitive and affective functioning are compromised. "Accidental suicide" is possible due to the impulsive and risky behaviors and as a result of the intensity of manic symptoms.

When conducting a suicide risk assessment (SRA), the individuals adamantly deny any current suicidal ideation, intent, or plan and may present with a flight of ideas and/or with rapid or pressured speech. They may report an elevated or expansive mood and thus it is critical to thoroughly assess their behavior and to obtain observable information from those familiar with them about any drastic or dangerous changes in behavior. They may be resistant to feedback or lack insight about their mood state.

It is also possible for these clients to be experiencing actively psychotic symptoms during a manic and/or depressive episode. This makes it pertinent to assess for any auditory and/or visual hallucinations.

Depressive episodes are typically moderate to severe. The intensity of these symptoms increases the likelihood of suicidal ideation, intent, and planning. However, clients tend to be more amenable to psychotropic medication management and are more compliant in treatment while in this state.

Disorders with increased suicide risk

- Bipolar I Disorder
- Bipolar II Disorder
- Cyclothymic Disorder

Bipolar and Related Disorders and Suicide Risk

- There is a 15% rate of suicide among individuals with bipolar disorder. This rate is about 30 times higher than that of the general population.
- As in the general population, women attempt suicide more often than do men.
- Contrary to the general population, women are more likely to complete their attempt; thus, the rate for suicide deaths is slightly higher for women than for men who have been diagnosed with bipolar disorder. There are several theories about the reason for this statistic, for example: (1) This diagnosis causes tremendous relationship difficulty and those diagnosed with this disorder typically have a limited social support system. Research indicates that social interactions are more important to women than to men and thus lack of these relationships places women at an increased risk for completed suicides. (2) Research has indicated that women tend to be diagnosed with bipolar disorder more often than men and thus may be overrepresented within this group. (3) Women tend to use more lethal means then men when experiencing a manic episode (e.g., use of a firearm, jumping from a bridge, hanging).
- Individuals diagnosed with bipolar disorder are twice as likely to commit suicide as those suffering from major depression alone.
- Research has demonstrated that individuals become suicidal during bipolar depressive episodes and/or rapid-cycling bipolar disorder.
- When suffering from psychotic symptoms of delusions and hallucinations during a bipolar episode, clients are more susceptible to suicide attempts
- At least 50% of people with bipolar disorder experience suicidal ideation.

Other Characteristics of Bipolar I Disorder

- Many individuals diagnosed with bipolar disorder remain non-compliant with or resistant to treatment, specifically psychotropic medication management.
- 90% of individuals experience recurrent episodes of mania.
- 60% of manic episodes occur immediately before a depressive episode.
- The onset of these symptoms can occur throughout one's lifetime.
- Clients may become physically assaultive or aggressive during a manic episode, specifically if psychotic or paranoid symptoms are present.
- There are detrimental consequences to behavior.
- Clients may experience poor judgment.
- Clients may experience rapid mood shifts.

- Clients may have unpredictable behavior, including indulging excessively in high-risk behaviors.
- Clients may experience loss of insight and objectivity.

Bipolar II Disorder and Suicide Risk

- Impulsivity is present, which increases suicide risk.
- Severity and duration of depressive symptoms increase suicide risk.
- The presence of a substance use disorder increases suicide risk.
- Medication non-compliance also contributes to an increased risk.

Clients diagnosed with bipolar II disorder are at an increased suicide risk as a result of the duration and intensity of their depressive symptoms. Many clients who have been diagnosed with this disorder report intense feelings of helplessness, hopelessness, worthlessness, guilt, shame, and loneliness as well as intermittent insomnia. These symptoms often lead to more frequent and enduring periods of suicidal and/or morbid ideation. Clients often report feeling as if they have no purpose and question their existence. Once their depressive symptoms decrease and are reported to be milder in severity, they are better able to manage these ideations and are not as likely to act on these thoughts.

Hypomania differs from mania in that individuals typically "enjoy" the feelings associated with a manic episode, whereas a hypomanic episode is not pleasant. Clients typically report being easily agitated, irritated, frustrated, and provoked to anger. They report periods of restlessness, intrusive ideation, rumination, and racing thoughts. They may report excessive energy and cleaning tirelessly. They typically isolate themselves from others, become withdrawn, and have a limited social support network.

Other Characteristics of Bipolar II Disorder

- Clients tend to report a heightened sense of creativity.
- The onset of symptoms typically occurs in the mid-twenties.
- The onset of this disorder typically begins with a depressive episode.
- 5–15% of individuals with this disorder experience multiple mood episodes.

Cyclothymic Disorder and Suicide Risk

- Recent onset of mixed states and the recent onset of mania or depression increase risk for suicide.
- Rapid cycling involves feelings of hopelessness, helplessness, and being easily overwhelmed.
- Severe anxiety often develops due to the sporadic nature of this disorder.
- An inability to attain treatment (e.g., as a result of a lack of insurance or a lack of medical care) can affect the condition, for example by leading to non-compliance and/or lack of insight into the severity of the condition (by the client).
- The presence of panic attacks increases suicide risk, as this can be a debilitating symptom.
- Pronounced agitation increases suicide risk.
- Severe insomnia increases suicide risk.
- Recent alcohol abuse increases suicide risk.

- Loss of pleasure in normally pleasurable activities (e.g., eating, socializing, or sex) may also increase risk.
- Recent or anticipated loss of a job, loss of a personal relationship, financial loss, or criminal or legal proceedings may increase the likelihood of a suicide attempt.
- Acute psychosis, especially featuring command hallucinations, paranoid fears of punishment, or delusional guilt, may increase risk.
- Co-morbid substance use disorder diagnosis may increase suicide risk.

Clients diagnosed with cyclothymic disorder often report pervasive feelings of helplessness and hopelessness as a result of the unpredictable nature and difficulty of managing this diagnosis. They describe feeling as if these symptoms are out of their control, and some clients even develop symptoms of agoraphobia and panic. Individuals who develop these two specifiers are at times isolated, are withdrawn, have limited social support networks, avoid interactions with others, or plan activities around the panic attack. This causes an increase in suicide risk, and the presence of panic and agoraphobic symptoms should be assessed when working with these clients. Helplessness and hopelessness are pervasive symptoms of this disorder, increasing the risk for suicide.

Other Characteristics of Cyclothymic Disorder

- Symptoms typically begin in early adolescence or early adult life.
- Individuals diagnosed with cyclothymic disorder have a 15–50% chance of developing bipolar I disorder or bipolar II disorder.
- In children, the mean onset of these symptoms is 6.5 years of age.

DEPRESSIVE DISORDERS AND SUICIDE

Major depressive disorder is the one diagnosis most commonly associated with suicidal ideation, intent, and planning. Research has indicated that undiagnosed depression has been the primary factor related to suicide attempts in various populations, including the elderly (aged 65+), college students, and adolescents. Untreated depression can lead to the development of other mental health disorders such as substance use disorders, anxiety disorders, and even eating disorders. Symptoms of major depressive disorder are typically pervasive and chronic and vary from mild to severe. The symptoms of feelings of burdensomeness, worthlessness, hopelessness, helplessness, and intermittent insomnia are highly correlated with attempted and completed suicides.

Depression can cause a constricted world-view and an inability on the part of the client to objectively understand and manage their condition. The symptoms of depression respond well to psychotropic medication management and psychotherapeutic treatment.

When working with depressed clients, it is important to frequently assess for the presence of suicidal ideation. It is also important to monitor your clients' affective and cognitive state upon the introduction of psychotropic medication management. Research has indicated that, as energy and motivation return, your client may continue to experience those key depressive symptoms (hopelessness, helplessness, worthlessness, burdensomeness) that make a suicide attempt more likely.

Disruptive Mood Dysregulation Disorder (DMDD) and Suicide Risk

- A new disorder in the DSM 5 that is specific for children.
- Impulsive behavior increases suicide risk.

- Affectively labile, as moods are unpredictable and fleeting. This sudden fluctuation of mood shifts causes an increased risk for impulsivity and acting out, and possibly an increase in suicide risk.
- These children may be using illicit substances in order to self-medicate and thus the presence of a substance use disorder diagnosis may increase suicide risk.
- Lack of a social support network may increase risk.

When working with children who are experiencing any type of mood disorder diagnosis, suicide risk should be frequently monitored. Disruptive mood dysregulation disorder is a new diagnosis in the DSM-5 and helps to categorize children who display chronic agitation, irritation, and frustration. The chronicity of these disruptive mood states differentiates this diagnosis from the episodic presentation of children diagnosed with bipolar disorder. Children who present with this diagnosis typically have a limited social support network as they have strained relationships with friends, family members, teachers, daycare workers, clergy people, and others with whom they have contact. These children are typically impulsive and irrational and have a limited worldview, which increases their risk for suicide. These children may also use illicit substances (cocaine, alcohol, marijuana, etc.), which will aggravate this condition and impair cognitive functioning and decision making.

The DSM-5 has been very specific as to how we diagnose this disorder. These specifics have been clearly delineated in order to avoid misdiagnosis of this disorder.

Bipolar Disorder versus DMDD

Bipolar Disorder	DMDD
Lifelong episodic illness	Severe, non-episodic irritability: It is persistent and present over the months
Discrete mood episodes of mania and depression	
During a manic episode, the mood must be accompanied by cognitive, behavioral, and physical symptoms that are different from the child's usual baseline	Does not develop bipolar disorder
	Severe outbursts, rage, and tantrums
	Elevated or expansive mood and grandiosity not present
Elevated or expansive mood and grandiosity	Cannot be first diagnosed before age 6 or after age 18
Less irritability than in DMDD (DSM-5)	
Can be diagnosed at any age, but rare in childhood	Not associated with psychosis
Peak onset in the twenties and thirties	
Psychosis may be present	

Oppositional Defiant Disorder versus DMDD

Oppositional Defiant Disorder	DMDD
Disruptive behavior	Depressive disorder
Irritability is a common factor but not required for a diagnosis	Mood expression significantly abnormal
	Impacts the environment and associates with dangerous behavior
Pattern of defiant and resistive behavior toward authority figures	

Conduct Disorder versus DMDD

Conduct Disorder	DMDD
Disruptive behavior disorder	Depressive disorder
Serious violation of the rules	Mood expression significantly abnormal
Lack of empathy and conscience	Irritability is a key feature
No mood or anxiety criteria	Impacts more than one setting (e.g., school, home, church)
Can be co-morbid with oppositional defiant disorder	

Other Characteristics of Disruptive Mood Dysregulation Disorder

- These children may also meet criteria for attention-deficit hyperactivity disorder (ADHD). They may present with symptoms including difficulty focusing and concentrating, disruptiveness, forgetfulness, inattention, difficulty completing tasks, being bored easily, and restlessness.
- Chronic irritability is present even when these children are not experiencing an acute temper tantrum, rage, or outbursts. This irritability remains present in all settings and is not specific to authority figures or parental figures, which differs from oppositional defiant disorder.
- Poor decision making occurs as a result of emotional liability and impulsive cognitions.
- Reality testing is limited and poor as a result of age and world experiences.

Major Depressive Disorder and Suicide Risk

- Major depression is the psychiatric diagnosis most commonly associated with suicide.
- Lifetime risk of suicide among patients with untreated depressive disorder is nearly 20%.
- The suicide risk among treated patients is 141/100,000.
- About two-thirds of people who complete suicide are depressed at the time of their death.
- The risk of suicide in people with major depression is about 20 times that of the general population.
- Individuals who have had recurrent episodes of depression are at greater risk for suicide than those who have had a single depressive episode.

Other Characteristics of Major Depressive Disorder

- MDD is associated with a high mortality rate.
- This disorder is usually present with chronic pain and other debilitating physical health conditions.
- Symptoms are reported to have a lifelong onset.
- Suicide attempts usually occur during a depressive episode.
- There is high co-morbidity with Cluster B personality disorders.

Substance-/Medication-Induced Depressive Disorder and Suicide Risk

- Presence of depressive symptoms increases suicide risk.
- The medical condition that is being treated by the prescribed medication may be terminal or progressive in nature, increasing suicide risk.

- Use of these substances could result in irrational thinking and poor decision making.
- Substances could illicit impulsive and erratic behavior, which may increase suicide risk.

Substance-/medication-induced depressive disorder is caused by the use of either a prescribed or an illicit substance that has been ingested by the client. The onset of symptoms typically occurs within 1 month of use of the substance, as this is the typical time required for certain medications to produce any effect on the body. Suicide risk should be assessed with these clients, as the medication use may be treating a terminal illness or an illness that may be progressively debilitating. Some medications affect various neurotransmitters in the brain, including serotonin and/or dopamine, which may impact mood management. Other drugs affect brain structures that are responsible for mood management and homeostasis.

Common medication types that can lead to secondary symptoms of depression are: anti-convulsants, anti-depressants, anti-migraine medications, anti-psychotics, antivirals, cardio-vascular medications, hormonal medications, immunological medications, retinoic acid derivatives, and smoking cessation medications.

Other Characteristics of Substance-/Medication-Induced Depressive Disorder

- The onset of symptoms usually occurs within 3–4 weeks of substance use.
- Once substance use stops, the symptoms remit.

Depressive Disorder Due to Another Medical Condition and Suicide Risk

- The medical condition may be chronic, debilitating, or terminal, which may increase suicide risk.
- Medication interaction effects may cause impulsivity, confusion, cognitive disruption, psychotic symptoms, and/or compromised decision making.
- Lack of access to medical care may increase suicide risk.
- Development of chronic pain associated with the physical health condition may increase suicide risk.
- A debilitating nature of the physical health condition may lead to feelings of helplessness, hopelessness, shame, and/or guilt. The medical condition may also affect quality of life, as the individual may be unable to engage in activities of daily living or occupational functioning, and may have cognitive deficits.
- The individual may have a limited social support system due to isolating themselves, being withdrawn, and/or having no interest in establishing or maintaining relationships with others.
- The individual may develop a substance use disorder as a result of self-medicating in order to manage either the physical effects of the medical condition or the emotional and/or psychological effects of the medical condition.

It is important to understand the medical condition causing the depressive symptoms when working with your client. The medical condition could be terminal or progressive and this could increase suicide risk. It is also important to understand the medications associated with the medical condition, as interaction effects could influence the presence of suicidal ideation, intent, or planning. As in psychotic disorder due to a medical condition, it is always important to consult with other health professionals to provide optimum care.

Common medical conditions leading to secondary symptoms of depression include Cushing's disease, Huntington's disease, hypothyroidism, Parkinson's disease, stroke, and traumatic brain injury.

ANXIETY DISORDERS AND SUICIDE

As clinicians, most of us have been trained to "automatically" assume or to at least be aware that suicidal ideation may be present when our clients report symptoms of depression. However, clients presenting with an anxiety disorder are also at an increased suicide risk.

Anxiety is simply the body's reaction to stressful, dangerous, or unfamiliar situations. It is the sensation of uneasiness, distress, or dread you feel before a significant event and is normal and even beneficial, as it helps us to prepare for situations that concern us. But, for those experiencing an anxiety disorder, these reactions feel far from normal. Anxiety that may need treatment is often irrational, overwhelming, and disproportionate to the situation. The symptoms of anxiety often leave clients feeling overwhelmed, helpless, hopeless, out of control, fearful, avoidant, guilty, or ashamed. Anxiety can also lead to the development of physiological symptoms, including nausea, gastrointestinal problems, decreased appetite, intermittent insomnia, headaches, and tremors (e.g., shaking, trembling). This condition can be debilitating for some clients and may even lead to them abusing anti-anxiety medication or other substances in an effort to alleviate or eliminate these symptoms. Typically, clients experiencing symptoms of anxiety may also present a co-morbid diagnosis of depression and/or a substance use disorder.

I have worked with clients who have presented with all types of anxiety disorders, from generalized anxiety disorder to social anxiety to panic disorder to phobias to separation anxiety disorder to anxiety related to medical conditions to unspecified anxiety. With all of these disorders, the common thread is a sense of helplessness. Inability to predict or control the anxiety, feelings such as "I am going to die and no one will listen to me!" and feeling as if these symptoms will be never-ending can cause clients to develop learned helplessness or even tunnel vision about their condition. Anxiety is disruptive to one's everyday functioning and causes significant conflict at work and problems in interpersonal relationships, and even aggravates medical conditions.

Stress is another factor that impacts levels of anxiety. Stress can be defined as "a response to a **perceived** threat, demand or change," the operative word being "perceived." Perception is a subjective experience and is dependent upon one's genetic make-up, environmental influences, culture, and daily demands. This means that the way in which we interpret an event will affect our behavior or response to that event. If you are living with anxiety, your threat perception is going to be skewed, thereby causing you to experience even more anxiety. Sounds pretty helpless, right? Now imagine living this way every day of your life with no treatment or feeling as if your treatment will remain unsuccessful. Those battling this disorder daily do report increased frequency of suicidal ideation and/or morbid ideation. This is why it is imperative to remain aware of the severe and devastating effects of this disorder and continually monitor each client's suicidal potential.

Separation Anxiety Disorder and Suicide Risk

- The presence of one or more anxiety disorders has been significantly associated with lifetime suicidal ideation and suicide attempts.
- Research has demonstrated that anxiety disorders are significantly associated with suicidal ideation and suicide attempts.

- Among those with suicidal ideation, 52.4% have reported having at least one anxiety disorder.
- Individuals diagnosed with separation anxiety disorder typically have limited social support networks and can be isolated from others.
- This diagnosis could co-occur with other disorders, including a depressive disorder, bipolar disorder, a substance use disorder, and/or a personality disorder, which could increase suicide risk.
- Individuals diagnosed with anxiety disorder typically demonstrate depressive symptoms, including feelings of helplessness, hopelessness, sadness, guilt, shame, and/or being easily overwhelmed.

Separation anxiety disorder causes major disruption in work, educational, and interpersonal interactions. This can lead to difficulty establishing and/or maintaining relationships with others, in addition to increased isolation and feelings of loneliness. This disorder typically occurs during childhood but has also been deemed appropriate to assign to adults when warranted. Adults can develop this disorder, as they can experience this anxiety in relation to a child, a spouse, or even an elderly or disabled parent. As it is usually diagnosed during childhood, the presence of this disorder has been associated with increased suicide risk. Children present with a limited worldview, limited life experiences and problem-solving abilities, and impulsivity.

It is also difficult for children to maintain objectivity; thus, they are unable to understand that their parents or others in their space are displeased with their behavior, not who they are as people. They may internalize verbal and non-verbal feedback about their behavior and make assumptions that they are undesirable or unlovable. These thoughts can lead to an increase in feelings of guilt, shame, sadness, loneliness, and/or worthlessness. This diagnosis can co-occur with others, including a depressive disorder or a substance use disorder, which may increase suicide risk.

When conducting an SRA with these individuals, it is imperative to note co-occurring symptoms and to assess for social support. This will provide pertinent information when determining the client's level of suicide risk.

Other Characteristics of Separation Anxiety Disorder

- When separated from the focus of their anxiety, children may present as apathetic, withdrawn, or sad and may have difficulty attending, focusing, and/or concentrating.
- Clients may develop other fears (e.g., animals, flying, monsters).
- Symptoms may lead to academic problems due to the disruptive nature of this disorder.
- Clients may exhibit anger or aggression and may be easily agitated, irritated, and/or frustrated.
- Clients may report odd perceptual experiences (e.g., seeing people, feeling touched).
- Clients may present as demanding, intrusive, or inappropriate when experiencing distress.
- Demandingness may contribute to feelings of resentment or frustration by loved ones.

Specific Phobia and Suicide Risk

- Research has indicated that those diagnosed with specific phobia are 60% more likely to make a suicide attempt than those without the diagnosis.
- May have a co-occurring diagnosis such as a depressive disorder, another anxiety disorder, a mood disorder, a personality disorder, and/or a substance use disorder.
- Onset of these symptoms typically occurs between 7 and 11 years of age; thus, these individuals may present with poor reality testing, a limited worldview, limited coping abilities, poor impulse control, and limited resources.
- This diagnosis causes major disruption in social, occupational, and academic functioning and is disruptive to relationships. These individuals may have a limited social support network and may experience feelings of loneliness and sadness, and they may be withdrawn from others.

Although phobias may seem silly to others, they can be devastating to the people who have them, causing problems that affect many aspects of life. These individuals may isolate themselves socially by avoiding places and things they fear, which can cause academic, professional, and relationship problems. Children with these disorders are at an increased risk of academic problems and loneliness, and they may not develop good social skills.

Many people with phobias may develop symptoms of depression as well as other anxiety disorders. Substance abuse may also develop as a result of attempting to manage these symptoms or alleviating the stress associated with this disorder. The combination of these factors increases the risk of suicide for the client and should be consistently assessed.

Other Characteristics of Specific Phobia

- Clients typically experience increased physiological responses, including high blood pressure, increased heart rate, increased perspiration, shallow breathing, and dilated pupils.
- Situational, natural environment, and animal-specific phobias cause sympathetic nervous system arousal.
- Those that suffer from blood-, injection-, or injury-specific phobias experience fainting or near fainting due to acceleration of heart rate and increased blood pressure followed by deceleration and decreased blood pressure.
- Phobias typically develop following a traumatic event, observation of a traumatic event, having an unexpected panic attack in the presence of an object, or informational transmission (watching others be fearful of an object).
- Onset typically occurs during early childhood (7–11 years).

Panic Disorder and Suicide Risk

- Panic attacks and a diagnosis of panic disorder in the past 12 months are related to higher rates of suicide attempts and suicidal ideation.
- Suicide risk is elevated when this diagnosis co-occurs with other diagnoses, including substance use disorder, depressive disorders, bipolar disorders, and other anxiety disorders.
- Suicide risk also increases as a result of depressive symptoms, including feelings of helplessness, hopelessness, being overwhelmed, and trapped. Many feel as if their

> symptoms are minimized by others and they are unable to receive the proper care needed to treat their symptoms.
>
> • Suicide risk is also elevated when psychotropic medications are abused in order to better manage these panic symptoms, as such medications can affect cognitive functioning, impulse control, and decision-making abilities.

Panic disorder, which is found in about 1.5 percent of the population at some time in their lives, includes recurrent episodes of sudden, unpredictable, intense fear accompanied by symptoms such as palpitations, chest pain, and faintness. Panic attacks, which do not meet these diagnostic criteria fully, are two to three times more prevalent, than panic disorder in the population.

Clients may be so afraid of having more panic attacks that they live in a constant state of fear, ruining their quality of life. This disorder can lead to several complications, including the development of specific phobias, such as fear of driving or leaving one's home (agoraphobia); a need for frequent medical care for health concerns and other medical conditions, which could lead to financial difficulties; avoidance of social situations; and/or complications at work or school. These individuals may also develop symptoms of anxiety, depression, substance abuse disorders, or other mental health conditions. Research has also shown that the cognitions related to panic disorder (e.g., fear of dying, going crazy, and losing control) are highly correlated with suicide attempts.

When assessing those who report a history of panic disorder or panic attacks, it is important to remain aware that suicidal ideation may be present. It should also be noted that panic disorder and/or panic attacks should be assessed in those individuals who report suicidal ideation.

The fear of dying during a panic attack is an independent risk factor related to suicide attempts.

Other Characteristics of Panic Disorder

- Clients may experience constant or intermittent feelings of anxiety that are related to their physical health condition (e.g., feeling as if one is "having a" tightness of the chest, other physiological condition).
- The onset of symptoms typically occurs between 20 and 24 years of age.
- The onset of these symptoms after age 45 is rare.

OBSESSIVE–COMPULSIVE AND RELATED DISORDERS AND SUICIDE

Obsessive–compulsive disorder (OCD) is characterized by recurrent distressing thoughts and repetitive behaviors or mental rituals performed to reduce anxiety. Symptoms of this disorder are often accompanied by feelings of shame and secrecy because clients realize that these thoughts and behaviors are excessive or unreasonable. This silence, in addition to the misdiagnosis of OCD symptoms by health care professionals, can lead to an extended delay in diagnosis and treatment, which can cause an increase in suicide risk.

Symptoms of OCD usually begin during adolescence, and more than 50% of individuals report experiencing symptoms prior to their mid-twenties. Recent studies regarding OCD indicate that between 5% and 25% of people with OCD have attempted suicide at some point in their lives. Suicidal ideation is also relatively common among those affected by OCD.

Some factors that are reported to predict the likelihood of a suicide attempt for those clients suffering from this condition include the severity of their OCD symptoms, the co-occurrence of depression (specifically feelings of hopelessness, helplessness, worthlessness, and burdensomeness), the presence of a personality disorder such as obsessive–compulsive personality disorder, and a prior history of self-harm (such as cutting). This risk also increases if the client is actively using drugs or alcohol. Some other factors that may increase this possibility include unemployment and social isolation.

Clients who have been diagnosed with these types of disorders often report feelings of helplessness, loss of control, and worthlessness as well as a desperate desire for the ability to better manage these symptoms. Teenagers have reported feeling "odd or weird," not fitting in with their peers, and feeling fearful that others will "find out" about their difficulty and feelings of shame and guilt. These thoughts and feelings typically exacerbate the OCD symptoms and the functional impairment related to the diagnosis.

Clients are often reluctant to report symptoms of OCD, which they may find embarrassing. They may be hesitant about discussing the details of this disorder and may instead offer clues by mentioning intrusive thoughts or repetitive behaviors. They may also report avoiding particular locations or objects, report excessive concerns about illnesses or injury, and/or (very commonly) display repetitive reassurance-seeking behaviors. You may even note chapped, cracked, or even bleeding hands from excessive handwashing or other physical indicators.

Obsessive–Compulsive Disorder and Suicide Risk

- Suicidal ideation occurs in approximately half of individuals diagnosed with obsessive–Compulsive Disorder.
- Research demonstrates that suicide attempts are reported for one-quarter of those diagnosed with OCD.
- Co-morbidity of MDD increases suicide risk.
- Co-morbid diagnoses of anxiety and substance use disorders also increase suicide risk.
- Recent studies suggest that between 5% and 25% of people with OCD have attempted suicide.
- Suicidal ideation is reported to be relatively common among people affected by OCD.

Other Characteristics of Obsessive–Compulsive Disorder

- Common themes include cleaning, symmetry, forbidden or taboo thought, and harm.
- These individuals may experience feelings of anxiety or disgust.
- While performing compulsions, clients experience incompleteness or uneasiness until things are "just right."
- Clients will often avoid people, places, and things that trigger obsessions or compulsions.
- The onset of symptoms typically occurs around 20 years of age.
- The onset of symptoms after 35 years of age is unusual.

Body Dysmorphic Disorder and Suicide Risk

- The onset of these symptoms typically occurs between 16 and 17 years of age. These individuals typically present with decreased impulse control, a limited worldview, and limited coping abilities.

- Rates of suicidal ideation and attempts are high for children, adolescents, and adults with this disorder.
- Research has attributed suicidal ideation and/or attempts to appearance concerns.

During the past century, clients diagnosed with body dysmorphic disorder (BDD) have been described as being so distressed over their "hideousness" that they have contemplated, attempted, or committed suicide. BDD symptoms are about images of the self; about "looking ugly," defective, or abnormal; and about being inadequate, unlovable, and unacceptable. Studies have found that 24% to 28% of individuals diagnosed with BDD have attempted suicide. Many clients are too embarrassed and ashamed of their appearance concerns to address them with a clinician; thus, these symptoms may go undiagnosed or misdiagnosed for several years, increasing suicide risk.

Individuals with BDD present with many risk factors for suicide. These factors include increased rates of suicidal ideation, suicide attempts, psychiatric hospitalizations, unemployment and disability, being single or divorced, a poor social support network, and a history of physical or sexual abuse. Other risk factors are high co-morbidity with MDD, eating disorders, and substance use disorders.

Other Characteristics of Body Dysmorphic Disorder

- Clients usually have ideas or delusions of reference.
- BDD is associated with high levels of anxiety, social anxiety, social avoidance, depressed mood, neuroticism, and perfectionism.
- Individuals diagnosed with this condition are reluctant to reveal their concern to others.
- The majority of individuals undergo cosmetic treatment to try to improve their looks.
- Clients may perform surgery on themselves, which could ultimately worsen their condition.
- Co-morbidity of MDD, anxiety, and/or substance use disorder increases suicide risk.

TRAUMA-AND STRESSOR-RELATED DISORDERS AND SUICIDE

Research indicates that a relationship exists between trauma and suicidal behaviors. Trauma has been defined by the APA as the emotional response someone has to an extremely negative event. Sources of such trauma can include a history of sexual, emotional, mental, and/or physical abuse; sexual assault; relational trauma; medical trauma (e.g., a near-death experience); the sudden and unexpected loss of a loved one; or even the unexpected loss of employment, financial stability, and well-being (e.g., the stock market crash of 1929). Trauma is a normal reaction to a horrible event. However, the lasting and prolonged effects can be so severe that they disrupt one's ability to live a normal life.

These effects can be both emotional and physical. Emotion is one of the most common ways in which trauma manifests. Some of the more common emotional symptoms of trauma include denial, anger, sadness, and overall emotional volatility. Victims of trauma may project these negative emotions onto other sources, such as friends or family members, thereby causing interpersonal problems with loved ones and family members. These relationship problems can lead to isolation, creating a limited or nonexistent social support system, or even self-confirmation of distorted beliefs of not being worthy, or possibly even being deserving of the traumatic event. Some common physical indicators of trauma include lethargy, fatigue, poor concentration, being easily distracted, decreased levels of energy, poor appetite, insomnia, an elevated heart rate, and even difficulty breathing. Your client may even report symptoms of anxiety or panic attacks and be unable to cope in certain circumstances.

All of these effects will have an impact on your client's worldview and their perceptions about their ability to manage these feelings. Some people are so overwhelmed they may begin to experience symptoms of helplessness, hopelessness, worthlessness, or even burdensomeness. These symptoms will negatively affect their interpersonal life, employment, peace of mind, and ability to experience some type of internal homeostasis. This inner turmoil and inability to cope or manage can often lead to suicidal ideation, intent, or planning.

Traumatic grief is also experienced by those exposed to suicide attempts made by others. Research has examined exposure to suicide as being a traumatic event and has found that being exposed to a suicide or suicide attempt can contribute to symptoms of post-traumatic stress disorder (PTSD). This is more likely to occur if the client witnessed the attempt, was extremely close to the person who attempted or completed suicide, or has a history of mental health concerns. Studies have also indicated that these individuals are more likely to develop traumatic grief, which is independent of depression or other mood disorder symptoms. Traumatic grief has been defined as a syndrome that leads to functional impairment, a decline in physical health, and suicidal ideation.

Post-traumatic Stress Disorder and Suicide Risk

- Anyone with PTSD is at an increased risk for suicide.
- Some studies link suicide risk in those with PTSD to distressing trauma memories, anger, and poor control of impulses.
- Co-morbidity with other diagnoses, including substance use disorder, MDD, and other mood disorders, can increase risk for suicide.

Some research has even indicated that chronically suicidal clients meet the formal criteria for PTSD. Severe and prolonged suicidal pain is not something that most people suffer, and clients in suicidal crises feel that they have no other option and are no longer able to cope with their current situation.

Suicidal clients often report problems with memory and may have insistent, intrusive, and vivid memories related to the traumatic situation. Even engaging in daily-life events may trigger distressing memories related to the trauma. Clients may describe memory lapses for parts of the suicide attempt or even report experiencing vivid images related to their suicide attempt that continue to remain intrusive and incessant. They may avoid reminders or conversations or even deny the seriousness of the attempt (e.g., "I only took eight Xanax and drank a fifth of vodka. I always drink like that. I was just having a bad day and made a mistake taking too much. It's really not a big deal.").

Clients who remain chronically suicidal may also describe ongoing feelings of anxiety and remain fearful that they may choose to make a future attempt. They may experience disturbing and violent impulses, may have thoughts or feelings of helplessness or hopelessness, and may feel "forever changed" by the experience. These clients may describe an inability to experience joy, happiness, or autonomy, and they may question their existence.

Other Characteristics of Post-traumatic Stress Disorder

- Clients may experience difficulty regulating emotions or maintaining stable relationships.
- The onset of symptoms can occur at any age.
- Symptoms usually begin after 3 months of experiencing a stressor.
- PTSD is typically co-morbid with substance use disorders.
- Research has estimated that at least 7.5% of Americans will experience PTSD in their lifetime.
- It has been estimated that 5 million Americans will suffer from PTSD during any year.
- Women are twice as likely to experience PTSD as men.
- War veterans, law enforcement officers, firefighters, and EMT workers are particularly vulnerable to PTSD.

DISSOCIATIVE DISORDERS AND SUICIDE

Dissociative disorders typically develop as a means to cope with trauma. These disorders most often begin in childhood after an individual is subjected to long-term physical, sexual, or emotional abuse; medical trauma (invasive medical procedures); or residing in a home environment that is terrifying and/or highly volatile. Some research has even indicated that these disorders develop following the strain of war or natural disasters (e.g., Hurricane Katrina, the Haitian earthquake, or the Indian Ocean tsunami).

These types of disorders typically take root in childhood while personality traits and characteristics are being developed. During this sensitive period, children are more able step outside themselves (dissociation) and witness the trauma as though it's happening to a different person. Children who learn to master dissociation during these traumatic periods continue to use this coping mechanism in response to stressful situations throughout their lifetime.

Dissociative disorders are linked to significant difficulties in personal relationships and employment. Clients with these conditions are usually unable to cope well with emotional, relational, or professional stress. Their dissociative symptoms (zoning out, dissociating, disappearing) may raise concerns from loved ones and cause their supervisors and colleagues to perceive them as unreliable.

Those diagnosed with these disorders are at increased risk of complications related to self-harm, suicidal and morbid ideation, and the development of mental health concerns. The most common co-occurring mental health disorders include substance use disorders, symptoms of depression, anxiety, PTSD, personality disorders, eating disorders, and sleep disorders (insomnia, parasomnias).

All of the above-mentioned issues create the perfect storm for a possible suicide attempt or chronic suicidal ideation. These clients typically report feelings of hopelessness, helplessness, sadness, isolation, uncertainty, fear, and excessive worry. This disorder is difficult to manage and causes significant disruption to a client's everyday functioning.

Dissociative Identity Disorder and Suicide Risk

- Demographically, suicide is reported to be the highest among older males, and dissociative identity disorder (DID) populations are characteristic of younger women.
- Individuals with this diagnosis typically have a more frequent history of suicide attempts than other psychiatric patients.
- Over 70% of patients diagnosed with DID have attempted suicide.
- Multiple attempts are common, as is engaging in self-injurious behavior.
- SRAs can be difficult if amnesia is present or the current identity doesn't feel suicidal and is unaware of the suicidal behavior of other identities.

DID is associated with increased risk of complications in the following areas: self-mutilation; suicide attempts; sexual dysfunction, including sexual addiction or avoidance; alcoholism and substance abuse; depression; sleep disorders, including nightmares, insomnia, and sleepwalking; anxiety disorders; eating disorders; and severe headaches.

Other Characteristics of Dissociative Identity Disorder

- Individuals typically conceal or are not fully aware of disruptions in consciousness, amnesia, or other symptoms.
- People with this condition typically report various types of maltreatment during childhood or adulthood.
- If maltreatment is not present, symptoms are usually caused by painful, evasive, and traumatizing recurrent (early life) medical procedures.
- The onset of this disorder can occur at any age.
- DID patients are reported to have a high frequency of self-directed aggressive behaviors.

Dissociative Amnesia and Suicide Risk

- Many clients have a history of multiple suicide attempts, self-mutilation, and other high-risk behaviors.
- Suicidal behavior may be a particular risk when the amnesia remits suddenly and overwhelms the client with intolerable memories.
- Co-morbidity with other disorders (including substance use disorder, MDD, anxiety disorder, and other mood disorders) can increase suicide risk.

Clients diagnosed with dissociative amnesia report recurrent episodes in which they forget important personal information or events, usually connected with a trauma or severe stress. The information that is lost is typically too extensive to be attributed to ordinary forgetfulness or memory lapses related to aging. This condition is devastating to clients' interpersonal, academic, and social functioning. They report a sense of helplessness and hopelessness, and feeling "out of control." Some clients with dissociative amnesia can even lose recollection of their own suicide attempts, periods of self-mutilation, or violent behavior.

Other Characteristics of Dissociative Amnesia

- Individuals diagnosed with this disorder are typically chronically impaired in their ability to form and sustain meaningful relationships.
- Individuals typically present with a history of trauma, abuse, or victimization.
- The onset of symptoms is sudden.

FEEDING AND EATING DISORDERS AND SUICIDE

Most anorexia-related deaths are due to completed suicide attempts. Research has demonstrated that those clients who have been diagnosed with an eating disorder already exhibited depressive disorder and anxiety disorder symptoms prior to the onset of the eating disorder. These symptoms typically include feelings of helplessness, hopelessness, burdensomeness, low self-worth, guilt, and shame. The presence of these factors would indicate that suicide attempts made by those with an eating disorder may follow the premise of the interpersonal-psychological theory of suicidal behavior (IPTS).

The IPTS suggests that those who are at an increased suicide risk have three common factors present: (1) they experience strong feelings of perceived burdensomeness; (2) they lack feelings of belongingness; and (3) they have acquired the ability to enact lethal self-injury.

The Interpersonal-Psychological Theory of Suicidal Behavior Model

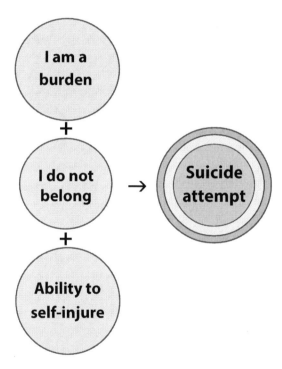

According to the IPTS, individuals choose to die by suicide when they feel that their death would relieve a burden to others. Simply stated, people murder themselves when they believe that their "death is worth more than their life." Perceived burdensomeness may be particularly applicable to those diagnosed with an eating disorder, as they often have a limited social support network and strained relationships with friends and family members. Eating disorders are difficult to manage and often cause dissention and strain in relationships. Parents and loved ones report feelings of hopelessness and helplessness and, at times, may exhibit frustration that is misinterpreted by the client.

Individuals with a feeding or eating disorder (particularly anorexia) often report a lack of connection to others. These clients often choose their disorder over relationships, thereby isolating themselves from others and alienating significant people in their lives. In addition to the above-mentioned issues, those diagnosed with an eating disorder experience other mental health concerns that involve social difficulties. These diagnoses could include symptoms of social phobia, avoidant personality disorder, or an MDD.

Clients diagnosed with eating disorders are frequently exposed to painful and/or injurious events. They typically engage in disordered eating behaviors that are risky and self-injurious (e.g., self-induced vomiting, laxative use, diuretic use). Many will resort to more severe forms of these behaviors (e.g., combining methods, water purging), which can be even more dangerous. Recurrent use of these behaviors results in a habituation to pain, which sets the stage for a more fatal suicide attempt. Research has shown that those diagnosed with certain eating disorders also engage in non-suicidal self-injurious behaviors. This may lead to them developing somewhat of a tolerance to self-harm so that more frequent self-injurious behaviors are required to achieve the same effect. They are also reported to be at a higher risk for suicide as a result of habituating to starvation. The combination of dangerous and injurious disordered eating behaviors, self-harm behaviors, and starvation may create a perfect storm that yields a higher probability of a completed suicide attempt.

Anorexia Nervosa and Suicide Risk

- Research indicates that women with eating disorders (e.g., anorexia, bulimia, or overeating) who attempted suicide usually were suffering from symptoms of depression before the onset of their eating disorder.

- 67% of patients with an eating disorder and a history of suicide attempts suffered from depression before the onset of the eating disorder.

- 3% of patients with an eating disorder and no history of suicide attempts suffered from depression before the onset of the eating disorder.

- Some research has suggested that the extreme nature of the suicide attempts is related to a high tolerance for pain due to prolonged starvation and other physical ailments caused by the syndrome.

- Self-harming behaviors may be exhibited as eating disorder symptoms, such as induced vomiting or exercising excessively with the principal intention of inflicting pain or self-injury (Brown, 2007).

- Suicide is a major cause of death for those with anorexia.

- An analysis of deaths in the female population between the ages of 15 and 24 indicates that the mortality rate among anorexics is 12 times that of all other causes of death combined (non-suicidal deaths).

- Methods of suicide are frequently intended to be lethal with little chance of survival.

- Suicide rates are higher for those with eating disorders or substance abuse issues than for those with a MDD alone.

Anorexia is reported to have the highest mortality rate of any psychological disorder. This is due not only to completed suicide attempts but also to the numerous medical complications that accompany it, such as the early onset of osteoporosis, brain shrinkage, and heart attacks.

This disorder takes over not only clients' behavior but also their physical health and cognitive functioning. One of the biggest frustrations clients with eating disorders report is that they spend the majority of their day thinking about food, planning their activities around food, and essentially focusing on food all day long. This begins to feel intrusive, uncontrollable, and hopeless. They are consumed with this issue.

This condition has been described as "torturous," which is why it is believed that these individuals use more lethal means when they attempt suicide. There is a feeling of desperation wherein they may feel like they can no longer live with this condition but they can't live without it either. The age of onset is also a factor that increases suicide risk, as adolescents and young adults are more impulsive, have a limited worldview, and limited problem-solving abilities.

Other Characteristics of Anorexia Nervosa

- Behaviors related to the diagnosis can result in significant and potentially life-threatening medical conditions.
- Many individuals diagnosed also present with depressive symptoms.
- OCD features, both related and unrelated to food, are typically prominent.
- Most individuals are preoccupied by thoughts of food; some may even collect recipes or hoard food.
- Many clients are concerned about eating in public.
- Individuals typically have a strong desire to control their environment.
- Clients typically present with inflexible thinking, limited social spontaneity, and overly restrained emotional expression.
- The onset typically occurs during early adolescence or young adulthood.
- Onset before puberty or after age 40 is rare but possible.

Bulimia Nervosa and Suicide Risk

- Suicide risk is elevated for this population.
- Co-morbid disorders (including depressive disorder, anxiety disorder, and substance use disorder) may increase suicide risk.
- Individuals typically do not share information about this disorder with others and thus experience feelings of shame, guilt, and loneliness.

Someone diagnosed with bulimia eats a lot of food in a short amount of time (binging) and then tries to prevent weight gain by getting rid of the food (purging). Purging can involve making yourself throw up or taking laxatives (pills or liquids that speed up the movement of food through your body and lead to a bowel movement). Some clients have even reported eating cotton balls soaked with lemon juice as a way to obtain a feeling of satiation to avoid eating food.

Bulimics often feel as if they cannot control the amount of food they eat. They may also exercise a lot, eat very little or not at all, or take pills to pass urine, in an attempt to prevent weight gain.

There is no one primary cause of bulimia and a binge can be triggered by dieting, stress, or uncomfortable emotions, such as anger or sadness. Behaviors such as purging and other actions to prevent weight gain usually occur as a way to feel more in control of one's life and ease stress and anxiety. Bulimia can be related to a variety of factors including culture, family environment, personality changes, biology, and life changes and stressful events.

The risk of suicide is elevated for this diagnosis for several reasons. People with this diagnosis often have co-occurring disorders, including anxiety, depression, BDD, or substance abuse disorders. They may exhibit extreme mood changes and isolate themselves from their support system. This diagnosis also comes with feelings of guilt, shame, and/or a sense of powerlessness, in addition to poor self-image and feelings of worthlessness and self-deprecation. The age of onset is also a factor, as adolescent and young adults are more impulsive and have a limited worldview and problem-solving capabilities.

Other Characteristics of Bulimia Nervosa

- Individuals are typically of normal weight or overweight.
- This disorder is uncommon among obese individuals.
- Menstrual irregularity can occur.
- Onset typically occurs during adolescence or young adulthood.
- Onset is uncommon before puberty and after age 40.

SUBSTANCE-RELATED AND ADDICTIVE DISORDERS AND SUICIDE

Clients who abuse alcohol and/or drugs attempt suicide nearly six times as frequently as people who don't abuse these substances. Women are four times more likely than men to complete suicide using alcohol and/or drugs. In some cases, substance abusers make these attempts through means not directly related to alcohol or drugs. However, in many cases, they complete suicide through an intentional substance overdose. Those who abuse substances typically have a pre-existing problem or mental health issue. Substance use disorders can co-occur with any diagnosis listed in the DSM-5, as many people attempt to self-medicate in order to better manage their symptoms.

When using alcohol and/or other substances, we are unable to make appropriate decisions and our impulse control is compromised. Research has indicated that approximately 33% of all completed suicides involve people who present significant elevated blood alcohol levels. Nearly two-thirds of these alcohol-affected individuals were legally drunk when they died from their suicide attempt. In addition to lowering inhibitions and contributing to a loss of mental or emotional control, which can increase short-term suicide risk, use of alcohol and/or drugs can contribute to the onset of depressive symptoms. Alcohol and drugs can also exacerbate these depressive symptoms.

Research has shown that 70% of people who complete suicide by deliberate overdose use only a single substance to achieve their goal. In nearly 80% of these single-substance suicides, the drug of choice is a type of prescription medication. The most commonly used substances during a suicide attempt include acetaminophen (aspirin) and other over-the-counter medications, or illegal "street drugs." When suicide is completed using two or more substances, alcohol has been reported to be amongst these substances. Clients also use other or unknown substances combined with alcohol when attempting suicide. The most common substance used during a suicide attempt is alcohol.

Other Hallucinogen Intoxication and Suicide Risk

- Use may lead to increased suicidality, even though this can be rare among users of hallucinogens.
- Increased suicide risk is related to psychosis, which may be experienced by user, as they may become paranoid and/or experience auditory, visual, tactile, or olfactory hallucinations.
- Decision-making and reasoning abilities are compromised as a result of the intoxication.

- Impulsivity may be increased while an individual is intoxicated.
- These substances can cause permanent damage to brain functioning.

Even though it is well known that **any** use of an illicit substance or alcohol can increase suicide risk, the DSM-5 specifically delineates Other Hallucinogen Intoxication as having a particularly high risk for suicide. These substances include mescaline, LSD, STP (Serenity, Tranquility and Peace, which is a psychedelic and is substituted for amphetamine) and MDMA (Ecstasy). While intoxicated following use of these substances, the user may be paranoid, delusional, violent toward the self and/or others at times, irrational, and impulsive, and may also be experiencing auditory, visual, tactile, or olfactory hallucinations. All of these symptoms are likely to increase suicide risk.

Other Characteristics of Other Hallucinogen Intoxication

- Perceptual disturbances and impaired judgment occur when individuals are using these substances.
- Continued use can lead to neurotoxic effects.
- Continued use can result in organic damage to various parts of the brain responsible for controlling and managing behavior, impulse control, speech, and reasoning ability.

Opioid Use Disorder and Suicide Risk

- Use of this substance is associated with heightened risk for suicide attempts and suicide deaths.
- Individual could be suffering from another medical condition that causes chronic pain, which could cause an increased suicide risk.
- Disorder could be co-morbid with other disorders, including depressive disorders, trauma disorders, anxiety disorders, and personality disorders.
- Research has demonstrated that opiates are the preferred substance for individuals diagnosed with borderline personality disorder (BPD).
- Withdrawal symptoms from this substance can be severe and may lead to poor decision making and cognitive impairment.

Opioid use disorder is associated with increased suicide risk, for various reasons. Most individuals who begin using opiates are attempting to manage a medical condition. This condition could be progressive or may cause the client to experience chronic pain. Chronic pain sufferers are more likely to experience symptoms of major depression and anxiety and more likely to report immense feelings of helplessness and hopelessness. Chronically ill depressed clients are shown to remain non-compliant with their treatment plan and show poorer outcomes. Any time clients report chronic pain, as clinicians we should be assessing for suicidality and substance abuse.

While opiates are able to help clients better manage pain, their use can lead to tolerance, dependence, and addiction, even when the drugs are used correctly. After dependence develops, the body needs more and more of the drug in order to experience the same effect, which increases the risk for a drug overdose. This can result in an "accidental suicide." The withdrawal symptoms related to this substance are another reason dependence is likely to develop.

Other Characteristics of Opioid Use Disorder

- The individual may have a history of drug-related crimes.
- Opioid use can cause significant problems with relationships and employment.

- Accidental and/or deliberate overdoses can occur.

- Repeated intoxication and withdrawal may be associated with severe depressive symptoms.

PERSONALITY DISORDERS AND SUICIDE

A personality disorder is defined as a type of mental disorder in which a person presents with a rigid and unhealthy pattern of thinking, functioning, and behaving. A person with a personality disorder has difficulty with perception and relating to situations and people. This type of functioning causes significant problems and limitations in relationships, social interactions, and/or interactions with others while at work or school.

In most cases, a person may not even realize that they have a personality disorder because their thinking and behaving are normal to them, and they may blame others for the challenges and problems they deal with on a regular basis. Personality disorders usually begin in the teenage years or early adulthood and there are many types.

Cluster B personality disorders are characterized by dramatic, overly emotional, and/or unpredictable thinking or behavior. These sets of disorders include antisocial personality disorder, borderline personality disorder, histrionic personality disorder, and narcissistic personality disorder. This particular cluster of personality disorders is more highly correlated with suicide risk, than cluster A (typically referred to as the odd or eccentric cluster and includes: Paranoid Personality Disorder, Schizoid Personality Disorder, and Schizotypal Personality Disorders) or C (these disorders are typically characterized by anxious, fearful cognitions or behavior and include Avoidant Personality Disorder, Dependent Personality Disorder and Obsessive-Compulsive Personality Disorder), as these disorders cause major disruption in social relationships, involve high emotional volatility and impulsiveness, and are characterized by the inability to emotionally self-regulate. These deficits can lead to clients making impulsive and irrational decisions, and often the consequences of their actions do not guide their decision making when they experience intense and negative affect.

Borderline Personality Disorder (BPD) and Suicide Risk

- 70% of people diagnosed with BPD will have at least one suicide attempt in their lifetime, and many will make multiple suicide attempts.

- 8 to 10% of those diagnosed with BPD will complete suicide; this rate is more than 50 times the rate of suicide in the general population.

- Increased suicide risk is related to common factors, including unemployment, financial difficulty, family discord, and other interpersonal conflicts or losses.

- Co-morbid diagnoses (often depressive symptoms or substance use disorders) are frequent in people with personality disorders and thus increase the risk for suicide.

- These individuals also engage in self-injurious behaviors such as cutting, burning, and small drug overdoses, cutting being the most common form of self-harm.

Unfortunately, suicidal behaviors and completed suicides are very common in individuals diagnosed with BPD. Research has shown that approximately 70% of people with BPD will make at least one suicide attempt in their lifetime, and many more will make several suicide attempts. Clients diagnosed with BPD are more likely to complete suicide than individuals with any other psychiatric disorder. Between 8 and 10% of people with BPD will complete suicide, which is more than 50 times the rate of suicide in the general population.

Suicide and suicide attempts are very common in those diagnosed with this disorder for several reasons.

First, this disorder is associated with immensely intense negative emotional experiences. These experiences are described as being unbearable and intolerable, and many clients diagnosed with BPD report wanting to escape, wanting to "make it go away," or "just wanting anything to make the pain stop." They may use a variety of strategies in an attempt to lessen the emotional pain, including deliberate self-harm, substance use, and even suicide.

Second, BPD is highly associated with impulsivity, or a tendency to react to a situation without considering the consequences. Thus, individuals may impulsively engage in suicidal behaviors in a moment of intense emotional pain without fully considering the consequences of their actions.

Third, this diagnosis often co-occurs with substance use or a substance use disorder diagnosis. The use of drugs and/or alcohol already increases a person's risk for suicide without the presence of BPD characteristics. Thus, substance use issues combined with BPD may be a lethal combination because the substance use can lead to even more problems with impulse control. This difficulty with impulse control also increases the chance of overdosing on the substance being used.

Fourth, this is a chronic and, for the most part, lifelong diagnosis that requires hard work to be adequately managed. The chronicity and pervasiveness of this diagnosis may also lead to a heightened risk for suicide. Clients may feel as if they are helpless or hopeless and that their lives will forever be ruined, specifically if treatment is not provided. This may leave them feeling that there is no other way out, and they may develop tunnel vision about their life.

Fifth, BPD tends to co-occur with other mental health diagnoses such as anxiety disorders, eating disorders, delusional disorders, mood disorders, and even psychotic disorders. The presence of these co-morbid disorders can increase risk of suicide for these clients.

Other Characteristics of Borderline Personality Disorder

- Clients typically engage in self-sabotaging behaviors.
- Clients can develop psychotic-like symptoms during times of distress and feel more secure with transitional objects.
- Common co-occurring disorders include depressive disorders and bipolar disorders, substances use disorders, eating disorders, PTSD, and ADHD.
- The onset of these symptoms typically occurs during early adulthood.
- Common patterns include chronic instability during early adulthood with episodes of serious affective impulse dyscontrol and high levels of use of both mental health and medical resources.
- During their thirties and forties, these individuals become less emotionally volatile.

Chapter 3 | Suicide Risk Assessment

ASKING THE QUESTIONS

Asking questions about suicidal ideation, intent, planning, and attempts is not easy! Sometimes, the client will provide the opportunity to inquire about suicide, but typically the topic is not one the client will address when presenting with their initial complaint and when providing a history related to the present concern. Regardless, it is essential to ask some sort of screening questions whenever the clinical situation or presentation warrant.

A really good way to broach this topic is to set the stage for these types of questions and then help the client understand that this type of inquiry is a normal part of the overall assessment process. The ability to thoroughly and accurately assess for suicidality is contingent upon the clinician's familiarity with the targeted screening questions, comfort level with the topic of suicidality, and ease with asking these type of questions.

A good point in the clinical interaction to address this issue is typically following the report of any distress (physical or affective). Opening statements that lead into these questions set the tone to ensure an enlightening and smooth interchange, and it helps to reassure the client that you are listening and ready for whatever information they provide.

Here is an example of an opening statement:

I can certainly appreciate how difficult talking about this issue must be for you today. I am asking you some very personal questions and you don't know me from Adam. So it makes perfect sense to me that you would be hesitant to share.

But, you know, some of my clients with similar problems or symptoms have shared with me that they have thoughts about ending their life. I'm just wondering whether you have ever had similar thoughts.

SUICIDE RISK ASSESSMENT

Assessing for suicidality can be intimidating and overwhelming at times. We are typically completing a suicide risk assessment (SRA) under duress, as a complete SRA may not ALWAYS be part of the intake process, and we want to ensure that we are documenting all information accurately. We want to ensure that we incorporate all pertinent information, but sometimes we may not know the **most important information** to include when completing this assessment.

As mental health professionals, we know that suicides can be unpredictable, impulsive, or planned. We also know that we can only be of assistance to our clients if they are open and honest with us. We can only be as helpful as they allow. However, it is our ethical obligation to be as informed, trained, and prepared as possible to appropriately assess for risk of suicide. When we are assessing for suicidality with a client, it is important to understand that there is never just **one** cause of these thoughts, feelings, and (at times) behaviors. Suicide is motivated by a complex combination of biopsychosocial factors of which we need to be aware in order to accurately assess for suicide risk.

A national survey found that 13.5% of Americans report having experienced **suicidal ideation** at some point during the course of their lifetime, 3.9% of individuals report having made a **suicide plan**, and 4.6% report having **attempted suicide**. Among those who report attempting suicide, approximately 50% report having made a "serious" attempt (e.g., hanging, overdose). These numbers are even higher when a psychiatric disorder is present.

It is critical to thoroughly explore suicidal ideation, as research has indicated that, often, there is a transition that occurs along the continuum from ideation to plan to attempts. Of those who experience suicidal ideation, 34% move forward to developing a suicide plan and 72% of suicide planners report eventually making a suicide attempt. Among those who make a suicide attempt, 60% of **planned** attempts occur within the first year of the onset of suicidal ideation and 90% of **unplanned** attempts (which probably represent impulsive self-injurious behaviors) occur within this time period.

Suicidal ideation and behaviors are found at increased rates among individuals diagnosed with psychiatric disorders, specifically major depressive disorder, bipolar disorders, schizophrenia, post-traumatic stress disorder, anxiety, substance use disorders, dependency, and personality disorders (e.g., antisocial and borderline). Having a history of suicide attempts is the strongest predictor of future attempts and even of completed suicides. Intentional self-harm, also called non-suicidal self-injury (NSSI), which has been defined as intentional self-injury without the expressed intent to die, is also associated with long-term risk for repeated attempts and with completed suicide attempts.

There are also many psychosocial factors associated with risk for suicide and suicide attempts. These include recent life events, such as losses (death of a loved one or losses related to employment, careers, finances, housing, marital relationships, physical health, or a sense of a future), and enduring or long-term difficulties, such as relationship problems, prolonged unemployment, and legal problems.

It is imperative to gather all of the above information in addition to information regarding protective factors when assessing for levels of suicide risk (low, moderate or high). I have developed and frequently use an SRA that encompasses all of these areas.

I have used this particular assessment format in various settings for several years, and it has been useful and reliable. It is a comprehensive tool and provides an adequate description of your client's current suicidal status. You would most likely use this assessment during an initial suicide screening and then as needed when following up or having to reassess for suicidality. The sections of this SRA are outlined in the following section.

CRITICAL ASSESSMENT DATA

Reason for Referral

This area should include information about the sources used during the assessment (medical records, other documents), who referred the patient, why the client was referred, where the assessment occurred, and the time and date of the assessment.

This section should also include whether and when the referring person was contacted, if possible, and a quote from this person. If this person cannot be contacted, state the reason why.

Identifying Data

This area should include demographics about the patient, including their age, race, sex, and information about time in facility (if warranted).

Personal History

This area should include a brief summary of the client's personal history, including their placement prior to the current facility, educational information, work information, any military history, their marital status, and brief details of their children.

Mental Health and Suicide History

This section should include information about the following:

- Previous and current diagnoses
- Substance abuse history
- Past mental health treatment (where and when)
- Past suicidal ideation, intent, or planning
- Past suicide attempts (explored in more detail below)
- Head injuries
- Relevant health problems
- Requests for mental health services
- Self-harm and/or violent behaviors
- Hospitalizations for suicidality
- Current or past medication use

Why is it Important to Assess History of Suicide Attempts?

Most people who attempt suicide report that they do not desire to make another attempt. However, research indicates that about 16% repeat a suicide attempt within 1 year and 21% repeat an attempt within 1–4 years. The majority of repeat attempters will typically choose more lethal means on subsequent attempts—increasing the likelihood of mortality.

Approximately 2% of repeat attempters die by suicide within 1 year of their first attempt and 8–10% of attempters will eventually die by completion of suicide. Research has also shown that a history of prior suicide attempts is the best known predictor for future suicidal behaviors.

When assessing for past suicide attempts, there should be specific data requested in order to procure the most useful information. These data are outlined in the following sections.

First and Worst Attempt

If you are working with a client who is reporting 15, 20, or 30 suicide attempts, it is not efficient or helpful to document the details of every single attempt. The most pertinent information will come from the first attempt, as this will provide information about when the client's ability to manage duress began to disintegrate. This will also provide you with other pertinent information, including the client's age at the time of the attempt and the availability of social support. Details of the worst attempt provide information about general level of severity of the client's attempts.

Reaction to Attempt

This type of information provides insight into the client's current thinking and feelings about suicide. For example, a client may state: "I was so glad the gun didn't go off! I wasn't thinking clearly and I could have really died! I can't believe I did this. When I think back on it, it seems surreal. I'm not even the same person today!" Such statements may provide information about protective factors and the client's desire to continue living.

However, a client may say something quite different: "Man! If I would have timed it better, and my mom wouldn't have caught me, I would have been out of here! I wish I would have planned it better" or "I don't know how I feel . . . I'm kind of numb about it all. I don't have any regrets, but I'm not thrilled either. If they would have left me for dead, I think I would have been fine with it." Such statements indicate the possibility of current suicidal ideation, intent, or planning and provide information about the client's affective functioning. These statements should be assessed carefully.

Lessons Learned From Previous Attempts

The kinds of information mentioned in the previous section also provide insight into your client's current cognitive and affective state. Did your client learn that they wanted to live and that they were not thinking clearly when they made their attempt? Or are they grateful to be alive, having learned that, in conjunction with alcohol use, their symptoms of depression impacted their judgment? Or did they learn that they needed to ingest 50 painkillers versus 10 painkillers? Or that using a certain method was ineffective and they should have chosen another? Same question, very different answers—and, again, this provides critical information when assessing for current suicide risk.

Perceived Lethality/Medical Lethality

This question is related to the client's motive and desire to end their life. Did your client really believe that jumping off a 5-foot bridge would end their life, or did they think it would cause enough injury to bring attention to their current concerns? Did your client really believe that cutting themselves with a staple would cause significant injury? Were they hospitalized as a result of this attempt? By asking these questions, you are able to assess intent to die and the seriousness (by way of method) of the attempt. This also provides crucial information about possible future attempts and the client's current level of ideation.

Probability of Rescue

This question allows you to assess, again, for motive, secondary gain, and severity of the attempt. Did your client attempt to cut their wrist at 3:08 p.m. knowing that their spouse would arrive home at 3:10 p.m. or did they make this attempt at 3:08 p.m. knowing that their spouse would arrive home at 8:00 p.m.? Same question, two very different answers. These questions are not designed to minimize the attempt, as we are all aware that even an "accidental suicide" is a suicide. Instead, these questions are designed to allow the person completing the assessment to include information that may or may not influence how they choose to rate the client's level of suicide risk (we discuss levels of suicide risk later in this part) and determine the most effective way to manage each client.

RISK ASSESSMENT FINDINGS

Social–Relational Factors

This area should address significant relationships or lack thereof (including relationships with significant others, family, and friends), recent losses, significant changes in life circumstances, suicide history of family or friends, and the client's reaction to these issues.

It is critical to inquire whether the client has any history of family or friend suicide. Some research (social learning theory) has asserted that suicidal behavior is a learned behavior that is often mimicked by others. This assertion hypothesizes that suicide is a learned response to stress; thus, being exposed to knowledge about others who have committed suicide increases your risk for suicide.

Situational Factors

This area should include any information about current issues, including problems with facility adjustment; any current changes in the client's life situation; any recent death of a loved one; and any changes in financial status, employment, physical health condition, and/or marital status.

Medical Factors

This area should include any major medical concerns or life-threatening conditions, pain level (if applicable), and any symptoms of withdrawal from medications or illicit substances. This area can also include any mental health diagnosis.

Mental Status

This section should include comprehensive information on the client's mental status, including regarding their mood, affect, thought processes, cooperation, and speech, and the presence or absence of auditory, visual, tactile, or olfactory hallucinations or delusions.

Psychological Factors

This section should include information about hopelessness, perception of personal control, perceived emotional discomfort, cognitions about self-image, and coping abilities.

Why is it Important to Ask About Feeling Hopeless?

Hopelessness, about the present and the future, has been found to be a very reliable predictor of suicidal ideation and NSSI behaviors. Research indicates there are five components of hopelessness and has shown that, when hopelessness is present, if these other factors are reported, the risk for suicide is heightened:

- Shame
- Guilt
- Burdensomeness
- Sleep disturbance
- Inability to manage distress

These other components may indicate the existence of a major depressive disorder diagnosis or other diagnosis with major depressive features. Even if your client has not previously been diagnosed with a depressive disorder, it is recommended that these symptoms be further assessed in order to determine whether this diagnosis is warranted. This is critical because, as has been mentioned earlier in this workbook, undiagnosed depression is one of the major factors related to suicide attempts in most of the populations discussed.

Behavioral Factors

This area should include any observable behavioral changes, including a change in habits or interactions and any staff and/or family observations of significant behavioral changes.

Motivation Factors

This section should address the client's reported desire to die, any ambivalence about dying, malingering, secondary gain, help-seeking behaviors, motivation for treatment, desire to participate in treatment, and the therapeutic alliance.

Summary of Chronic Risk Factors

This area should include any chronic factors, which are risk factors that **will not** change or will remain relatively stable. These could include past mental health history, past suicide attempts, past suicide history (family and friends), life-threatening injuries, compliance or non-compliance, chronic life stressors, terminal illness, death of loved one, and so on.

Examples of Chronic Risk Factors

- History of substance use and/or dependence
- Health problems (terminal illness)
- Threatened livelihood due to progressive factors
- Age
- Cognitive decline
- History of self-harm behaviors

Summary of Acute Risk Factors

This section should include acute risk factors such as a current mental health diagnosis, a recent medical diagnosis, loss of a job, divorce, use of alcohol and/or drugs (current intoxication), psychotic episodes, homelessness, imminent suicidal intent or planning, near-term risk in the next few hours, day, or weeks, and any other factors that may be contributing to an immediate risk of suicide.

Examples of Acute Risk Factors

- Health problems
- Current affective state
- Sleep disturbance
- Current life stressors
- Access to weapons
- Recent use of illicit substances
- Recent preparation and/or rehearsal

Summary of Protective Factors

This area should include any information about protective factors, such as social and/or familial support system, spirituality, treatment compliance, insight, help-seeking behaviors, and denial of suicidal ideation, intent, or planning.

Examples of Protective Factors

- Marriage
- Children
- Participation in treatment

- Resiliency
- Treatment compliance
- No reported intent
- No presence of characterological deficits
- No previous mental health treatment
- Cultural aspects

Current Suicidality

This area should include information about current suicidal ideation, intent, and/or planning. It should also include information about preparation or rehearsal, risk for self-harm behaviors, level of agitation, and sleep deprivation. Risk (low, moderate, or high) should also be addressed in this section.

Why is it Important to Ask About Ideation?

Suicidal ideation is predicted to precede the onset of suicidal intent, planning, and action. Suicidal ideation can be linked with a desire or wish to die (**intent**) and a reason or rationale for wanting to die (**motivation**). Thus, it is vital to explore the presence or absence of current, past, or fleeting suicidal ideation when the client has been faced with any major life stressor (e.g., death, loss, unemployment, or diagnosed medical condition).

Many clients will initially deny the presence of suicidal ideation for many reasons, including:

- Fear of being hospitalized or another consequence that may have a negative impact on their academic, educational, or occupational functioning.
- Fear of being mocked, criticized, and/or judged.
- Desire to avoid the stigma of being labeled "crazy" or as having a mental health diagnosis.
- Fear of losing autonomy or control of the situation.
- Fear of no one believing their claims or of nobody taking their claims seriously.

Even if your client denies the presence of suicidal ideation, there may still be other observable indicators (affective and behavioral) that will prompt you to remain alert regarding possible suicidal ideation.

Some of these signs and symptoms include social withdrawal or having no interest in establishing and/or maintaining relationships with others; irrational thinking; insomnia; and being easily agitated, irritated, or frustrated, or being easily provoked to anger, despair, shame, guilt, humiliation, paranoia, or flat affect. If your client continues to deny the presence of suicidal ideation, it may be helpful to highlight your client's incongruent behaviors and reports.

Asking about suicidal ideation and intent does not increase the likelihood of someone thinking about suicide for the first time or engaging in such behaviors. In fact, most patients report a sense of relief and support when a caring, concerned clinician non-judgmentally expresses interest in exploring and understanding the patient's current psychological pain and distress that lead them to consider suicide or other self-injurious behaviors.

> *All Suicidal Ideation And Suicidal Threats Need To Be Taken Seriously*

When Assessing Current Suicidality

Always always, always **obtain a quote** from the client! It is beneficial to document the client's own words when discussing their current reports of suicidal ideation, intent, or planning. Such statements should not be paraphrased or interpreted by the writer.

Ensure that you gather information about the **frequency and duration** of ideation (how often these suicidal thoughts occur) so as to assess whether these ideas are fleeting or chronic in nature.

Why is it Important to Ask About Timing of Suicidal Ideation?

Most people become suicidal in response to negative life events or psychosocial stressors that compromise their ability to cope and/or maintain control of their life. If your client's coping abilities have deteriorated, it is possible for them to experience chronic suicidal ideation, especially if a mental health disorder is present. Thus, it is imperative to understand what provokes suicidal thoughts and the context in which these thoughts occur.

Knowing how much time has been spent contemplating suicide helps to alert you to its role and influence in the daily life of your client. Treatment planning is also guided by this information. Being aware of factors that make things better or worse for your client regarding the onset, intensity, duration, and frequency of suicidal thoughts and feelings helps to determine what areas should be of particular interest when you are developing the treatment plan. Exploring and understanding this information can also be beneficial when attempting to develop a safety plan. In order to develop an effective and useful safety plan, the clinician and the client need to have a good idea of which situations the client should avoid and triggers that elicit suicidal ideation. Having this type of insight also empowers the client in their ability to better manage these situations.

Why is it Important to Ask About the Presence of a Plan?

The presence of a suicide plan indicates that your client has some intent to die and has begun preparing to take their own life. It is important to be aware of the possibilities and potential for implementation of the plan, the likelihood of the client being rescued if the plan is executed, and the lethality of the plan.

Intent: When assessing for suicidal intent, I have found that "scaling" is helpful for clients who are unable to articulate this information. For example, you can ask the client, "On a scale from 1 to 10 (1 being not at all and 10 being certain), how likely are you to attempt suicide in the next minutes, hours, days, or weeks?" This information assists with assessing for acute suicidal risk.

Suicidal planning should **not** be dismissed or minimized if the risk of lethality is determined to be minimal by the clinician, as the important aspect is the perceived lethality for the client.

Methods: It is also imperative to know whether your client has begun to enact the plan, by engaging in such behaviors as writing notes, preparing to give objects away, writing a will recently, rehearsal, hoarding of medications, or gaining access to firearms or other lethal means. When discussing the method, attempt to have the client be as descriptive as possible. If the client discusses multiple methods, document this information.

Subjective information: This information includes any indication of the presence of ambivalence or resolve about suicide. Is the client expressing any strong affect when discussing their suicidal ideation? Is affect incongruent? What are they reporting they feel when discussing this issue with you? Fear? Excitement? Sadness? Relief?

When you are assessing for suicidality, your client may not express blatant suicidal ideation or specificity. Sometimes, these statements can be vague or passive. It is important to distinguish suicidal ideation from morbid ideation when exploring these thoughts with your client. Morbid ideation should never be ignored, but it should not be the **sole** reason for your choice to hospitalize a client or break confidentiality.

Suicidal Ideation Versus Morbid Ideation

Suicidal ideation is the explicit expression of the desire to die or to take one's own life in the absence of making plans to commit suicide. Examples:

- "I think about killing myself every day. Sometimes I just want to put a gun to my head and pull the trigger."
- "I had the chance . . . if I would have just taken six more pills."
- "I mean . . . it's easy, I could just cut my wrist from here to here and then that's it."

Morbid ideation is the vague expression of thoughts of death, or not wanting to be in the "here and now." This communication is more passive. Examples:

- "If I could just go to sleep and never wake."
- "Would people care if I left and never came back?"
- "I would rather die than live with this sickness."
- "What's the point of living if I never know when the end is coming?"

Imminent Versus Chronic Suicide Risk

Imminent suicide risk means that the client is at an acute level of distress. This level of risk could indicate an attempt occurring in the near future. It can include the following:

- Serious suicidal planning or intent (preparation, rehearsal, method, capability).
- Current disruption of cognitive processes (sleep disturbance; auditory, visual, tactile, olfactory hallucinations; delusions; negative affect).
- Recent suicidal behavior.
- No protective factors present.
- May be in danger of a suicide attempt within minutes, hours, or days from the time of the assessment.
- Requirement for crisis management.

Chronic suicide risk is typically seen in clients being treated for a major depressive disorder, bipolar disorder, or a Cluster B personality disorder. These individuals may always experience suicidal ideation and tend to report a baseline of fleeting ideation without any current intent or plan. You may not choose to conduct a full SRA with these clients during each session; however, you will still need to assess their baseline behavior to ensure that no changes have occurred and that no significant triggering events have transpired. This type of risk may include:

- Consistent fleeting suicidal ideation
- History of attempts
- History of self-harm behaviors
- Presence of pathology (personality or depressive)
- Substance dependence history

- No current suicidal intent or planning
- Protective factors present

ASSESSING FOR LEVEL OF SUICIDE RISK

Level of suicide risk is determined by **your** clinical judgment and the incorporation of all the data gathered during this SRA, to include acute and chronic risk factors as well as protective factors.

Risk level is determined by personal circumstances, vulnerabilities, current stressors, history, and risk factors.

Risk Levels

- **Low risk:** No history of previous suicide attempts, protective factors are present, no current suicidal ideation, some chronic risk factors may be present, some acute risk factors may be present, the client may demonstrate resiliency, adequate adjustment, there is the presence of hope, and cultural implications are positive (e.g., religion, spirituality).
- **Moderate risk:** Elevated risk as a result of the presence of suicidal ideation, chronic stressors, compromised coping ability, limited social support network, presence of pathology (e.g., depression, adjustment disorder), chronic drug and/or alcohol use, presence of capability (resolve vs. ambivalence), more frequent and enduring periods of suicidal ideation, and the presence of positive cultural implications.
- **High risk:** Elevated risk due to previous history of multiple attempts, triggering event, limited or no social support network, current suicidal ideation and planning, activities including preparation and rehearsal, limited distress tolerance, presence of pathology (personality disorder or depressive disorder), sleep disturbance, increased agitation, irritation, history of self-harm behavior, and negative of cultural implications.

Conclusions and Follow-Up Recommendations

This section should include any information about your recommendations for the client. It should be comprehensive and specific. **Do not** include any follow-up statements that you will not be able to execute. For example, if one of your recommendations is that you will follow up with the client within 1 week but you are out of town or have a full case load, **don't make this statement**. Or, if you do, you will need to make alternative arrangements to have the client seen by a colleague or even via phone consultation. This is a vital detail, because, if your client completes a suicide attempt and you did not complete your documented follow-up, it is possible to be accused of negligence.

Make sure that all follow-up recommendations are performed. Be careful when using document templates, as you will need to ensure that all information is accurate and referencing the targeted client (e.g., don't forget to change names, dates of birth, and specific recommendations).

Also note that the following list of recommendations includes examples in which the clinician notes consideration of a following intervention and reasoning as to why this intervention would be appropriate or inappropriate for the client. Including such a consideration demonstrates that you were thoughtful in your choice and exercised discernment in selecting your treatment strategies.

Examples of Recommendations

- Hospitalization is/is not warranted at this time.
- Placement on observation/hospitalization was considered and determined to be inappropriate at this time based on the patient's ability to establish rapport and his ability to list safe coping strategies while adjusting to the institution.
- Referral to psychiatry was considered and was completed/not completed for review of medication appropriateness.
- In order to facilitate adjustment to the (facility, program, group, etc.) client will participate in a check-in process for the first two weeks of treatment.
- Client will be seen for a follow-up appointment within 2 weeks.
- Placement in a support group was considered and determined to be appropriate/ inappropriate as a result of . . .

CONDUCTING A POST-SUICIDE RISK ASSESSMENT

A Post-SRA occurs after an acute period. This typically occurs following the stabilization of the client and after they have returned to treatment. A post-SRA is not as comprehensive as the initial SRA and contains fewer sections, to which most of the information will be transferred from the original SRA.

Risk Factors Assessed

In this section, you are reiterating the rationale for your conclusions or recommendations previously provided in the SRA. For example: "Client was hospitalized due to the presence of several salient risk factors, specifically . . ." (list from previous SRA).

Reason for Hospital Discharge

This section should include the clinical rationale for discharging the client (list the clinical risk factors that have changed, stabilized, or been addressed and how). If the client was released for reasons out of the clinician's control, then this should be documented as well.

Risk Factors That Remain

This section should include any information about residual risks for suicide. These risks would include chronic factors. For example: "Client continues to display the following factors indicative of suicide risk: terminal illness, past history of suicide attempts, and NSSI behavior."

Follow-Up Recommendations

End with a list of specific recommendations with regard to the client's care upon discharge.

Examples of Recommendations

- Initiation of a treatment plan to address
- Incorporation of family therapy
- Referral to
- Psychotropic medication to be continued

Completed Sample

Suicide Risk Assessment (SRA) for Mental Health Professionals

SOURCES OF INFORMATION: This area should include information about the sources used during the assessment (medical records, other documents), who referred the patient, why the patient was referred, where the assessment occurred and time and date the assessment was conducted. This should also include if and when the referring person was contacted and a quote from this person if possible. If this person cannot be contacted, state reason why.

Mr. Franklin Brown was referred to this author by his case manager, Ms. S. Worker on April 4, 2016, at approximately 3:30 pm. She stated, "I am not exactly sure what's happening with him today, but he isn't himself. He was non-responsive to my questions, and he seems more depressed than usual. He hasn't mentioned suicide, but when I asked him about it, he didn't say no. I am a little worried and really need you to check him out for suicidality. Something isn't quite right . . ." Mr. Brown's medical records were available and reviewed prior to conducting this SRA. Mr. Brown was assessed by this author in the case manager's office on April 4, 2016, at approximately 4:08 pm.

IDENTIFYING DATA: This area should include demographics about the patient including, but not limited to age, race, sex, information about time in facility, history of violence or self-harm.

Mr. Brown is a 65-year-old, multiracial male (he self-identifies as Asian and African American), who appears younger than his stated age. He has been a client at this facility for approximately four years. Staff members identify him as "feisty and mean" at times and his records indicated a history of becoming verbally abusive when he is angry with staff members. He has been issued six verbal warnings and two written reprimands, of which he signed, in acknowledgement of refraining from this behavior in order to avoid termination from treatment.

PERSONAL HISTORY: This area should include brief summary of patient personal history, including placement prior to the facility, educational info, work info, military history, marital status, and children.

Mr. Brown is recently widowed and stated that he was married to his partner for 20 years. He stated that his partner died approximately six months ago and that he remains close with his in-laws. He also reported that he has three children, ages 23, 32, and 36, of whom reside in the area and have frequent contact with him. He has been retired for five years and was employed as a Registered Nurse (RN) for 30 years. He stated, "I miss my job very much. I had meaning when I was working. My life had meaning, I had a purpose every day and even when I quit to take care of David, I was still serving a purpose. I felt needed, so it wasn't giving anything up. But now, he's gone and I don't know what I am supposed to do with myself." He stated that he is not currently involved in any volunteer activities and remains isolated, unless he is visited by family and "a few friends." He stated that he receives most of his social interaction when attending church on Wednesdays and Sundays, but he is not an active member of his church (only attending church services). He stated that he has been a member of the First United Methodist Church since 1989. He reported that he has attended church "on and off" with his family since this period. He denied any mental health treatment until approximately four years ago wherein he began treatment for depressive symptoms.

MENTAL HEALTH/SUICIDE HISTORY: This area should include any previous or current mental health history, including previous/current diagnosis, substance abuse history, any past mental health treatment (where and when), any past suicidal ideation, intent, or plan, head injuries, any relevant health problems, requests for mental health services, self-harm behaviors, hospitalizations for suicidality, or any current or past medication use.

Mr. Brown's medical records indicated a diagnosis of Major Depressive Disorder, Recurrent, Moderate and Uncomplicated Bereavement. He denied any prior mental health treatment. He has attended treatment at this facility for approximately four years and has remained compliant with his treatment plan. He was prescribed Zoloft six months ago and described this medication as being somewhat effective in better managing his symptoms, as he continues to report depressive symptoms. These symptoms include feelings of sadness, hopelessness, helplessness, loneliness, intermittent insomnia, rumination, racing thoughts (at times), anhedonia and isolating himself from others. He described these symptoms as mild to moderate in severity. He denied any substance abuse history, however; he reported an increase in his drinking activities in the last four months. He stated, "Typically, I am more of a social drinker, having a drink with a friend when I am having dinner. But, lately, I have been drinking alone, at home, as I have not felt like being social. Usually, it's just a glass of wine or maybe two before I go to bed. It helps me to sleep." He denied any past suicidal ideation, intent or plan.

RISK ASSESSMENT FINDINGS:

A. Social-Relational: This area should address significant relationships or lack of (including relationships with significant others, family, friends), recent losses, significant changes in life circumstances, suicide history of family or friends, reaction to this issue.

Mr. Brown stated that his partner recently died from a terminal illness approximately six months ago. He stated that he remains in close contact with his in-laws and speaks with them on a weekly basis. He also reported having a close relationship with his children. His eldest children, ages 32 and 36, reside approximately 15-20 miles from his home and his youngest child "lives within driving distance from me, but she chose a different path. I am not as close to her as I am my other two." He stated that he continues to have difficulty adjusting to his widower status and that his family members (siblings) have not been supportive during this time period. He indicated, "I am not that close to my own family. My brother and sister never agreed with my lifestyle and have always remained in judgment of me. They showed up to the funeral, but I haven't heard much from them since then. My parents are deceased. My mother died 10 years ago and my father died 8 months after my mother. I was close to my father. Not my mother though." Upon query about other losses in his life, Mr. Brown denied having any relatives die as a result of suicide.

B. Situational: This area should include any current issues: problems with facility adjustment, any current changes in life situation, current death of a loved one, change in financial status, employment, physical health condition, marital status, etc.

Mr. Brown reported that his partner is recently deceased. Mr. Brown stated, "I knew that David was sick, we all knew, but it still didn't prepare me for his death. I thought I was ready. We made all of the funeral arrangements together, and we even completed our Living Wills together, but this loss is still devastating for our family. He was the rock and I feel lost without him. I feel like I have this empty hole in my heart . . . am I making sense to you? Have you ever lost someone you loved? He was my soulmate."

C. Medical: This area should include any major medical concerns or life threatening conditions, pain level (if applicable), any symptoms of withdrawal from medications or illicit substances.

He did not report any impressive medical problems and/or concerns during this interview.

<u>D. Mental Status:</u> This area should include comprehensive mental status information, including, but not limited to affect, thought processes, cooperation, speech, AVH, etc.

Mr. Brown presented as well-groomed and clean. He appeared to attend to his personal hygiene and appearance. He made good eye contact with this author, and appeared to have no difficulty understanding this author's instructions or questions. His psychomotor activity was normal and his speech was normal in rate and volume and was coherent, rational, and goal-directed. Thought content appeared to be normal and he denied any delusional ideation and he denied any suicidal ideation, intent or harm. He did not appear to be responding to internal stimuli during this interview. His affect was congruent to content and mood at times during this interview. His mood appeared dysphoric throughout the interview.

<u>E. Psychological Factors:</u> Include information about hopelessness, perception of personal control, active diagnostic symptoms, perceived emotional discomfort, cognitions about self-image and coping abilities.

Mr. Brown stated that although he is currently experiencing depressive symptoms, he has been able to cope with his loss and his symptoms via support from his family members, seeking therapy and psychotropic medication management and utilizing coping skills learned since attending treatment. He described experiencing current symptoms of depression to include hopelessness, helplessness, sadness, guilt, loneliness and anhedonia at times. He also reported experiencing intermittent insomnia, rumination, racing thoughts, isolating himself from others and remaining withdrawn.

<u>F. Behavioral:</u> This area should include behavioral changes, including a change in habits or interactions, any staff and/or family observations of significant behavioral changes.

No significant behavioral changes were noted during this interview. He denied any notable changes in habit or moods. His case manager indicated a behavioral change during their meeting, which prompted her request for this SRA. She noted that Mr. Brown was "non-responsive and seemed more depressed than usual" during their meeting.

<u>G. Motivation:</u> This area should address desire to die, any ambivalence about dying, malingering, or secondary gain information, help seeking behaviors, motivation for treatment, and desire to participate in treatment, therapeutic alliance.

Mr. Brown stated that he has remained compliant with treatment while in therapy. He has attended most of his sessions and has remained compliant with his psychotropic medication regimen. He reports getting along well and trusting his primary therapist and following the directives of his case manager. His primary therapist, psychiatrist and case manager concurred with these statements.

<u>H. Current Suicidality:</u> This area should include information about current ideation, intent, or plan. Information about preparation or rehearsal, risk for self-harm behaviors, level of agitation and sleep deprivation.

Mr. Brown denied any current suicidal ideation, intent or plan. Upon query about suicidal ideation, he stated, "No, no, no . . . I would never do anything to harm myself. I don't want to kill myself. I am just having a bad day. Today is my wedding anniversary and I am just missing David. He always enjoyed our anniversaries. He was the planner, you know. Sometimes I would forget, especially if I had a crazy shift at work or had to work really late. But not David, he was always on it. It's funny that I had no problem remembering this year. I miss him so much. I do think about seeing him again, and I think about not waking up some days, but I would never kill myself. David would have none of that! And I know I will see him again. My faith is strong Doc, it's part of the reason I have made it this far!"

SUMMARY OF CHRONIC RISK FACTORS: This area should include any chronic factors including past mental health history, past suicide attempts, past suicide history, resiliency, life threatening injuries, compliance/non-compliance, chronic life stressors, etc.

Client is a 65-year-old male

SUMMARY OF ACUTE RISK FACTORS: This area should include acute factors such as current mental health diagnosis, imminent suicidal intent or plan, near-term risk in the next few hours, day, weeks, and any factor that may be immediately contributing to immediate risk of suicide.

- *Current diagnosis of major depressive disorder, recurrent, moderate and uncomplicated bereavement*
- *Client reports intermittent insomnia*
- *Client reports active depressive symptoms*
- *Client experienced recent death of spouse approximately 6 months*
- *Wedding anniversary is today*
- *Affect was dysphoric during this interview*
- *Client resides alone and his profession was a registered nurse, thus he may have access to means although he denies any current ideation, intent or plan*
- *Client recently began using anti-depressant medication 6 months ago*

SUMMARY OF PROTECTIVE FACTORS: This area should include any info about protective factors, such as support system, spirituality, treatment compliance, insight, and denial of suicidal ideation, intent, or plan, help-seeking behaviors.

- *Client reports close relationship with children and close physical proximity*
- *Client denied any current suicidal ideation, intent or plan*
- *Client has remained compliant in treatment*
- *Client reports good rapport and positive therapeutic alliance with current therapist and case manager*
- *Client reports utilizing coping skills learned in treatment*
- *Client appears to have good insight into his current affective state and relates his feelings to mourning and the anniversary of his wedding*
- *Client remains communicative with therapist and children when experiencing depressive symptoms*
- *Client does not report a history of mental health concerns or self-harm behaviors*
- *Client does not present with personality disorder traits*
- *Client reports that he remains rooted in his spiritual beliefs and attends church twice weekly, even though he is not an "active member"*

DIAGNOSIS:

Major Depressive Disorder, Recurrent, Moderate and Generalized Anxiety Disorder

CONCLUSIONS/FOLLOW-UP RECOMENDATIONS: Risk should also be addressed in this section (Low, Moderate, and High) and document if you used a suicide screening tool and the results of this tool.

- *As a result of the findings, Mr. Brown appears to be at **Low Risk** for suicide and does not appear to be at imminent risk for suicide.*
- *Hospitalization is not warranted at this time. Placement on observation/hospitalization was considered and determined to be inappropriate at this time based on patient's ability to establish rapport and his ability to list safe coping strategies while adjusting to the institution.*
- *Referral to Psychiatry was considered and was completed for review of medication appropriateness, as Mr. Brown reported being prescribed Zoloft approximately 6 months ago.*
- *A copy of this SRA will be provided to the client's primary therapist, psychiatrist and case manager.*
- *This author will follow-up with the above-mentioned treatment providers within the next 2 weeks regarding the client's progress.*

Suicide Risk Assessment

Sources of Information:

_____

_____

_____

_____

_____

Identifying Data:

_____

_____

_____

_____

_____

Personal History:

_____

_____

_____

_____

_____

Mental Health/Suicide History:

_____

_____

_____

_____

_____

Risk Assessment Findings:

_____

_____

_____

_____

_____

A. Social–Relational Factors:

_____

_____

_____

_____

B. Situational Factors:

_____

_____

_____

_____

C. Medical Factors:

_____

_____

_____

_____

D. Mental Status:

_____

_____

E. Psychological Factors:

_____

_____

_____

_____

F. Behavioral Factors:

_____

_____

_____

_____

G. Motivation Factors:

_____

_____

_____

_____

H. Current Suicidality:

_____

_____

_____

_____

Summary of Chronic Risk Factors:

_____

_____

_____

_____

_____

Summary of Acute Risk Factors:

_____

_____

_____

_____

_____

Summary of Protective Factors:

_____

_____

_____

_____

_____

Diagnosis:

_____

_____

_____

_____

_____

Conclusions/Follow-Up Recommendations:

_____

_____

_____

Clinician Worksheet

Post-Suicide Risk Assessment

Client is no longer at imminent risk for suicide. The clinical decision was determined consulting with other medical staff, consultation with psychologists, records review, etc.—as appropriate.

Risk factors assessed: Client was hospitalized due to the presence of several salient risk factors, specifically:

_____

_____

_____

_____

Reasons for hospital discharge: The clinical decision to discharge the client was made based on the following:

_____

_____

_____

_____

Risk factors that remain: The client continues to display the following factors indicative of suicide risk:

_____

_____

_____

_____

Follow-up recommendations: The following specific recommendations are made with regard to the patient's care upon discharge:

_____

_____

_____

_____

SUICIDE ASSESSMENT VERSUS SUICIDE SCREENING

Suicide assessment usually refers to a more comprehensive evaluation completed by a trained clinician to confirm assumed suicide risk, estimate the imminent danger to the patient, and then determine a course of treatment. Although most assessments involve structured questionnaires, they also can include a more open-ended discussion with the client and/or their friends and family to help gain insight into the client's thoughts and behavior, risk factors (e.g., access to lethal means or a history of suicide attempts), protective factors (e.g., immediate family support), and medical and mental health history.

Research has shown that suicide prevention experts usually use the term **suicide screening** to refer to a process in which a standardized tool or protocol is used to recognize clients who may be at risk for suicide.

Suicide screenings can occur independently or as a piece (section) of a more comprehensive health or behavioral health screen. These screenings can occur verbally (by just asking questions) or may be done in written format, using pencil and paper, or even a computer.

These screening tools can help to inform a SRA and provide additional information when attempting to determine your client's level of suicide risk.

SUICIDE SCREENING TOOLS

The Columbia Suicide Severity Rating Scale (C-SSRS)

This is a questionnaire that is used for suicide assessment in a variety of settings and is reported to be specifically useful during an initial screening. It is available in 14 languages. Mental health training is not required to administer the C-SSRS. Various professionals can administer this scale, including physicians, nurses, psychologists, social workers, peer counselors, coordinators, research assistants, high school students, teachers, and clergy.

I have provided an example of this assessment in this section; however, it is available to download for free at http://www.cssrs.columbia.edu/scales_practice_cssrs.html. This site provides free training on how to use this instrument.

Suicide Behaviors Questionnaire (SBQ-R)

This instrument has been used to assess suicide-related thoughts and behavior. The original SBQ was developed by Marsha Linehan in 1981 and was a 34-item self-report survey designed to measure the frequency and severity of suicidal behaviors and past history of suicide attempts. Since this period, Linehan has developed 4-item and 14-item versions. This instrument has been revised and adapted by several researchers for use in various settings. It has been reported to be useful with clinical and non-clinical populations.

Suicide Assessment Five-Step Evaluation and Triage (SAF-T)

This tool was developed in collaboration with the Suicide Prevention Resource Center and the organization Screening for Mental Health. This measure is used to identify risk factors and protective factors, conduct a suicide inquiry, determine risk level and potential interventions, and document a treatment plan. You can purchase the SAF-T pocket cards for clinicians at http://store.samhsa.gov/product/Suicide-Assessment-Five-Step-Evaluation-and-Triage-SAFE-T-Pocket-Card-for-Clinicians/SMA09-4432.

The Kessler Psychological Distress Scale (K10) and the Patient Health Questionnaire (PHQ-9)

These are supplemental assessments that have been reported to be helpful when conducting a SRA with terminally ill clients or clients who report chronic health problems. These two instruments can be used in conjunction with a thorough clinical interview and provide additional information about your client's affective and cognitive state. These screening tools are available to you later in this chapter.

Columbia Suicide Severity Rating Scale

SUICIDAL IDEATION				
Ask questions 1 and 2. If both are negative, proceed to "Suicidal Behavior" section. If the answer to question 2 is "yes", ask questions 3, 4 and 5. If the answer to question 1 and/or 2 is "yes", complete "Intensity of Ideation" section.	**Lifetime: Time He/She Felt Most Suicidal**		**Past 1 month**	
1. Wish to be Dead Subject endorses thoughts about a wish to be dead or not alive anymore, or wish to fall asleep and not wake up. Have you wished you were dead or wished you could go to sleep and not wake up? If yes, describe:	Yes ☐	No ☐	Yes ☐	No ☐
2. Non-Specific Active Suicidal Thoughts General non-specific thoughts of wanting to end one's life/commit suicide (e.g., "I've thought about killing myself ") without thoughts of ways to kill oneself/associated methods, intent, or plan during the assessment period. Have you actually had any thoughts of killing yourself? If yes, describe:	Yes ☐	No ☐	Yes ☐	No ☐
3. Active Suicidal Ideation with Any Methods (Not Plan) without Intent to Act Subject endorses thoughts of suicide and has thought of at least one method during the assessment period. This is different than a specific plan with time, place or method details worked out (e.g., thought of method to kill self but not a specific plan). Includes person who would say, "*I thought about taking an overdose but I never made a specific plan as to when, where or how I would actually do it . . . and I would never go through with it.*" **Have you been thinking about how you might do this?** If yes, describe:	Yes ☐	No ☐	Yes ☐	No ☐
4. Active Suicidal Ideation with Some Intent to Act, without Specific Plan Active suicidal thoughts of killing oneself and subject reports having <u>some intent to act on such thoughts</u>, as opposed to "*I have the thoughts but I definitely will not do anything about them.*" **Have you had these thoughts and had some intention of acting on them?** If yes, describe:	Yes ☐	No ☐	Yes ☐	No ☐

5. Active Suicidal Ideation with Specific Plan and Intent Thoughts of killing oneself with details of plan fully or partially worked out and subject has some intent to carry it out. ***Have you started to work out or worked out the details of how to kill yourself? Do you intend to carry out this plan?*** If yes, describe:	Yes ☐	No ☐	Yes ☐	No ☐
INTENSITY OF IDEATION				

The following features should be rated with respect to the most severe type of ideation (e.g., 1-5 from above, with 1 being the least severe and 5 being the most severe). Ask about time he/she was feeling the most suicidal.
<u>Lifetime</u> - **Most Severe Ideation:** _____ _____
           Type # (1-5) Description of Ideation
<u>Recent</u> - **Most Severe Ideation:** _____ _____
           Type # (1-5) Description of Ideation
	Most Severe		Most Severe	

Frequency ***How many times have you had these thoughts?*** (1) Less than once a week (2) Once a week (3) 2-5 times in week (4) Daily or almost daily (5) Many times each day	_____		_____	
Duration ***When you have the thoughts how long do they last?*** (1) Fleeting - few seconds or minutes (2) Less than 1 hour/some of the time (3) 1-4 hours/a lot of time (4) 4-8 hours/most of day (5) More than 8 hours/persistent or continuous	_____		_____	
Controllability ***Could/can you stop thinking about killing yourself or wanting to die if you want to?*** (1) Easily able to control thoughts (2) Can control thoughts with little difficulty (3) Can control thoughts with some difficulty (4) Can control thoughts with a lot of difficulty (5) Unable to control thoughts (0) Does not attempt to control thoughts	_____		_____	

Deterrents		

Deterrents
Are there things - anyone or anything (e.g., family, religion, pain of death) - that stopped you from wanting to die or acting on thoughts of committing suicide?
    (1) Deterrents definitely stopped you from attempting suicide
    (2) Deterrents probably stopped you
    (3) Uncertain that deterrents stopped you
    (4) Deterrents most likely did not stop you
    (5) Deterrents definitely did not stop you
    (0) Does not apply
	_____	_____

Reasons for Ideation *What sort of reasons did you have for thinking about wanting to die or killing yourself? Was it to end the pain or stop the way you were feeling (in other words you couldn't go on living with this pain or how you were feeling) or was it to get attention, revenge or a reaction from others? Or both?* (1) Completely to get attention, revenge or a reaction from others (2) Mostly to get attention, revenge or a reaction from others (3) Equally to get attention, revenge or a reaction from others and to end/stop the pain (4) Mostly to end or stop the pain (you couldn't go on living with the pain or how you were feeling) (5) Completely to end or stop the pain (you couldn't go on living with the pain or how you were feeling) (0) Does not apply	_____	_____

SUICIDAL BEHAVIOR *(Check all that apply, so long as these are separate events; must ask about all types)*	**Lifetime**	**Past 3 months**
Actual Attempt: A potentially self-injurious act committed with at least some wish to die, *as a result of act.* Behavior was in part thought of as method to kill oneself. Intent does not have to be 100%. If there is **any** intent/ desire to die associated with the act, then it can be considered an actual suicide attempt. **There does not have to be any injury or harm**, just the potential for injury or harm. If person pulls trigger while gun is in mouth but gun is broken so no injury results, this is considered an attempt. Inferring Intent: Even if an individual denies intent/wish to die, it may be inferred clinically from the behavior or circumstances. For example, a highly lethal act that is clearly not an accident so no other intent but suicide can be inferred (e.g., gunshot to head, jumping from window of a high floor/story). Also, if someone denies intent to die, but they thought that what they did could be lethal, intent may be inferred. *Have you made a suicide attempt?* *Have you done anything to harm yourself?* *Have you done anything dangerous where you could have died?*	Yes ☐ No ☐ Total # of attempts _____	Yes ☐ No ☐ Total # of attempts _____

	Yes	No	Yes	No
What did you do? ***Did you_____ as a way to end your life?*** ***Did you want to die (even a little) when you_____?*** ***Were you trying to end your life when you _____?*** ***Or Did you think it was possible you could have died from_____?*** ***Or did you do it purely for other reasons / without ANY intention of killing yourself (like to relieve stress, feel better, get sympathy, or get something else to happen)?*** (Self-Injurious Behavior without suicidal intent) If yes, describe: **Has subject engaged in Non-Suicidal Self-Injurious Behavior?**	☐	☐	☐	☐
Interrupted Attempt: When the person is interrupted (by an outside circumstance) from starting the potentially self-injurious act *(if not for that, actual attempt would have occurred).* Overdose: Person has pills in hand but is stopped from ingesting. Once they ingest any pills, this becomes an attempt rather than an interrupted attempt. Shooting: Person has gun pointed toward self, gun is taken away by someone else, or is somehow prevented from pulling trigger. Once they pull the trigger, even if the gun fails to fire, it is an attempt. Jumping: Person is poised to jump, is grabbed and taken down from ledge. Hanging: Person has noose around neck but has not yet started to hang - is stopped from doing so. ***Has there been a time when you started to do something to end your life but someone or something stopped you before you actually did anything?*** If yes, describe:	Yes ☐ Total # of interrupted _____	No ☐	Yes ☐ Total # of interrupted _____	No ☐
Aborted or Self-Interrupted Attempt: When person begins to take steps toward making a suicide attempt, but stops themselves before they actually have engaged in any self-destructive behavior. Examples are similar to interrupted attempts, except that the individual stops him/herself, instead of being stopped by something else. ***Has there been a time when you started to do something to try to end your life but you stopped yourself before you actually did anything?*** If yes, describe:	Yes ☐ Total # of aborted or self-interrupted _____	No ☐	Yes ☐ Total # of aborted or self-interrupted _____	No ☐
Preparatory Acts or Behavior: Acts or preparation towards imminently making a suicide attempt. This can include anything beyond a verbalization or thought, such as assembling a specific method (e.g., buying pills, purchasing a gun) or preparing for one's death by suicide (e.g., giving things away, writing a suicide note). ***Have you taken any steps towards making a suicide attempt or preparing to kill yourself (such as collecting pills, getting a gun, giving valuables away or writing a suicide note)?*** If yes, describe:	Yes ☐ Total # of preparatory acts _____	No ☐	Yes ☐ Total # of preparatory acts _____	No ☐

	Most Recent Attempt Date:	Most Lethal Attempt Date:	Initial/First Attempt Date:
Actual Lethality/Medical Damage: 0. No physical damage or very minor physical damage (e.g., surface scratches). 1. Minor physical damage (e.g., lethargic speech; first-degree burns; mild bleeding; sprains). 2. Moderate physical damage; medical attention needed (e.g., conscious but sleepy, somewhat responsive; second-degree burns; bleeding of major vessel). 3. Moderately severe physical damage; *medical* hospitalization and likely intensive care required (e.g., comatose with reflexes intact; third-degree burns less than 20% of body; extensive blood loss but can recover; major fractures). 4. Severe physical damage; *medical* hospitalization with intensive care required (e.g., comatose without reflexes; third-degree burns over 20% of body; extensive blood loss with unstable vital signs; major damage to a vital area). 5. Death	*Enter Code* _____	*Enter Code* _____	*Enter Code* _____
Potential Lethality: Only Answer if Actual Lethality=0 Likely lethality of actual attempt if no medical damage (the following examples, while having no actual medical damage, had potential for very serious lethality: put gun in mouth and pulled the trigger but gun fails to fire so no medical damage; laying on train tracks with oncoming train but pulled away before run over). 0 = Behavior not likely to result in injury 1 = Behavior likely to result in injury but not likely to cause death 2 = Behavior likely to result in death despite available medical care	*Enter Code* _____	*Enter Code* _____	*Enter Code* _____

Disclaimer: This scale is intended to be used by individuals who have received training in its administration. The questions contained in the Columbia Suicide Severity Rating Scale are suggested probes. Ultimately, the determination of the presence of suicidal ideation or behavior depends on the judgment of the individual administering the scale.

For reprints of the C-SSRS contact Kelly Posner, PhD, New York State Psychiatric Institute, 1051 Riverside Drive, New York, New York, 10032; inquiries and training requirements contact posnerk@nyspi.columbia.edu.

KESSLER PSYCHOLOGICAL DISTRESS SCALE

The Kessler Psychological Distress Scale is a 10-item questionnaire intended to yield a global measure of distress based on questions about anxiety and depressive symptoms that a person has experienced in the most recent 4-week period.

The use of a consumer self-report measure is a desirable method of assessment because it is a genuine attempt on the part of the clinician to collect information on the patient's current condition and to establish a productive dialogue.

As a general rule, patients who rate most commonly "Some of the time" or "All of the time" categories are in need of a more detailed assessment. Referral information should be provided to these individuals. Patients who rate most commonly "A little of the time" or "None of the time" may also benefit from early intervention and promotional information to assist raising awareness of the conditions of depression and anxiety as well as strategies to prevent future mental health issues. (Information sourced from the *NSW Mental Health Outcomes and Assessment Training (MH-OAT) Facilitator's Manual*, NSW Health Department 2001.)

The following questionnaire is for patients to complete. It is a measure of psychological distress. The numbers attached to the patient's responses are added up and the total score is the score on the Kessler Psychological Distress Scale (K10). Scores will range from 10 to 50. People seen in primary care who:

- score under 20 are likely to be well
- score 20–24 are likely to have a mild mental disorder
- score 25–29 are likely to have moderate mental disorder
- score 30 and over are likely to have a severe mental disorder

13% of the adult population will score 20 and over and about 1 in 4 patients seen in primary care will score 20 and over. This is a screening instrument and practitioners should make a clinical judgment as to whether a person needs treatment.

Scores usually decline with effective treatment. Patients whose scores remain above 24 after treatment should be reviewed and specialist referral considered.

Kessler Psychological Distress Scale (K10)

These questions concern how you have been feeling over the past 30 days. Circle an answer for each question that best represents how you have been.

1. During the last 30 days, about how often did you feel tired out for no good reason?				
1. None of the time	2. A little of the time	3. Some of the time	4. Most of the time	5. All of the time

2. During the last 30 days, about how often did you feel nervous?				
1. None of the time	2. A little of the time	3. Some of the time	4. Most of the time	5. All of the time

3. During the last 30 days, about how often did you feel so nervous that nothing could calm you down?				
1. None of the time	2. A little of the time	3. Some of the time	4. Most of the time	5. All of the time

4. During the last 30 days, about how often did you feel hopeless?				
1. None of the time	2. A little of the time	3. Some of the time	4. Most of the time	5. All of the time

5. During the last 30 days, about how often did you feel restless or fidgety?				
1. None of the time	2. A little of the time	3. Some of the time	4. Most of the time	5. All of the time

6. During the last 30 days, about how often did you feel so restless you could not sit still?				
1. None of the time	2. A little of the time	3. Some of the time	4. Most of the time	5. All of the time

7. During the last 30 days, about how often did you feel depressed?				
1. None of the time	2. A little of the time	3. Some of the time	4. Most of the time	5. All of the time

8. During the last 30 days, about how often did you feel that everything was an effort?				
1. None of the time	2. A little of the time	3. Some of the time	4. Most of the time	5. All of the time

9. During the last 30 days, about how often did you feel so sad that nothing could cheer you up?				
1. None of the time	2. A little of the time	3. Some of the time	4. Most of the time	5. All of the time
10. During the last 30 days, about how often did you feel worthless?				
1. None of the time	2. A little of the time	3. Some of the time	4. Most of the time	5. All of the time

Kessler R. Professor of Health Care Policy, Harvard Medical School, Boston, USA, printed with permission.

PATIENT DEPRESSION QUESTIONNAIRE (PHQ-9) - OVERVIEW

The PHQ-9 is a multipurpose instrument for screening, diagnosing, monitoring and measuring the severity of depression:

- The PHQ-9 incorporates DSM-5 depression diagnostic criteria with other leading major depressive symptoms into a brief self-report tool.
- The tool rates the frequency of the symptoms which factors into the scoring severity index.
- Question 9 on the PHQ-9 screens for the presence and duration of suicide ideation.
- A follow up, non-scored question on the PHQ-9 screens and assigns weight to the degree to which depressive problems have affected the patient's level of function.

CLINICAL UTILITY

The PHQ-9 is brief and useful in clinical practice. The PHQ-9 is completed by the patient in minutes and is rapidly scored by the clinician. The PHQ-9 can also be administered repeatedly, which can reflect improvement or worsening of depression in response to treatment.

SCORING

See PHQ-9 Scoring on next page.

PSYCHOMETRIC PROPERTIES

- The diagnostic validity of the PHQ-9 was established in studies involving 8 primary care and 7 obstetrical clinics.
- PHQ scores $\geq$ 10 had a sensitivity of 88% and a specificity of 88% for major depression.
- PHQ-9 scores of 5, 10, 15, and 20 represents mild, moderate, moderately severe and severe depression.[1]

---

1. Kroenke k, Spitzer R, Wiliams W. The PHQ-9: Validity of a brief depression severity measure. JGIM, 2001, 16:606-616

THE PATIENT HEALTH QUESTIONNAIRE (PHQ-9) - SCORING

Use the PHQ-9 to Make a Tentative Depression Diagnosis:

The clinician should rule out physical causes of depression, normal bereavement and a history of a manic/hypomanic episodes.

Step 1: Questions 1 and 2

Need one or both of the first two questions endorsed as a "2" or "3" (2 = "More than half the days" or 3+ "Nearly every day").

Step 2: Questions 1 through 9

Need a total of five or more boxes endorsed within the shaded area of the form to arrive at the total symptom count. (Questions 1-8 must be endorsed as a "2" or a "3"; Question 9 must be endorsed as "1" a "2" or a "3").

Step 3: Question 10

This question must be endorsed as "Somewhat difficult" or "Very difficult" or "Extremely difficult."

Use the PHQ-9 for Treatment Selection and Monitoring

Step 1

A depression diagnosis that warrants treatment or a treatment change, needs at least one of the first two questions endorsed as positive ("more that half the days;" or "nearly every day") in the past two weeks. In addition, the tenth question, about difficulty at work or home or getting along with others should be answered at least "somewhat difficult."

Step 2

Add the total points for each of the columns 2-4 separately

(Column 1=Several days; Column 2= More that half the days' Column 3= Nearly every day. Add the totals for each of the three columns together. This is the Total Score.

The Total Score = the Severity Score

Step 3

Review the Severity Score using the following table.

PHQ-9 Score	Provisional Diagnosis	Treatment Recommendation Patient Preferences should be considered
5-9	Minimal symptoms*	Support, educate to call if worse, return in one month
10-14	Minor Depression++ Persistent Depressive Disorder* Major Depression, mild	Support, watchful waiting Antidepressant or psychotherapy Antidepressant or psychotherapy
15-19	Major Depression, Moderately severe	Antidepressant or psychotherapy
<20	Major Depression, severe	Antidepressant and Psychotherapy (Especially if not improved on monotherapy)

* If symptoms present > two years, then probable chronic depression which warrants antidepressants or psychotherapy (ask "In the past 2 years have you felt depressed or sad most days, even if you felt ok sometimes?")

++If symptoms present≥ one month or severe functional impairment, consider active treatment

The Patient Health Questionnaire (PHQ-9)

Name: _____ Date of Visit _____

Over the last 2 weeks, how often have you been bothered by any of the following problems?	Not at all	Several days	More than half the days	Nearly every day
1. Little interest or pleasure in doing things	0	1	2	3
2. Feeling down, depressed, or hopeless	0	1	2	3
3. Trouble falling or staying asleep, or sleeping too much	0	1	2	3
4. Feeling tired or having little energy	0	1	2	3
5. Poor appetite or overeating	0	1	2	3
6. Feeling bad about yourself — or that you're a failure or have let yourself or your family down	0	1	2	3
7. Trouble concentrating on things, such as reading the newspaper or watching television	0	1	2	3
8. Moving or speaking so slowly that other people could have noticed. Or, the opposite — being so fidgety or restless that you have been moving around a lot more than usual	0	1	2	3
9. Thoughts that you would be better off dead or of hurting yourself in some way	0	1	2	3

Column Totals _____ + _____ + _____

Add Totals Together _____

10. If you checked off any problems, how difficult have those problems made it for you to do your work, take care of things at home, or get along with other people?

Not difficult at all	Somewhat difficult	Very difficult	Extremely difficult
☐	☐	☐	☐

Developed by Drs. Robert L. Spitzer, Janet B.W. Williams, Kurt Kroenke and colleagues, with an educational grant from Pfizer Inc. No permission required to reproduce, translate, display or distribute.
Copyright © Pfizer Inc. All rights reserved.

HOSPITALIZATION

When to Hospitalize a Client

Choosing to hospitalize a client can be an anxiety-provoking experience for some clinicians. This is why it is important to be proactive and know the hospitalization procedures in the city, state, or agency in which you are employed.

Whether you are a licensed clinical psychologist, a licensed clinical social worker, a psychiatrist, a licensed professional counselor or a licensed marriage and family therapist, there is an obligation on your part to intervene under certain types of circumstances. Intervening means that you must report that someone is in imminent danger of harming him/herself. This obligation overrides laws of confidentiality when it is clear that a client is in danger of attempting and/or completing suicide or homicide.

How Does "Reporting" Really Work?

If a clinician is absolutely convinced a client is in danger of suicide, a call can be made to 911 to report the suicide risk and have paramedics go to the client's home. Depending on your agency, county, city, or state, you may be able to contact a mobile crisis unit instead of contacting 911.

Other options may include contacting family, friends, or neighbors and having them take the client to the emergency room. One last possibility is to get the client to go voluntarily. The problem therein lies that, if someone is really suicidal and they are left to their own devices, there is a chance that they will make a suicide attempt.

I have been fortunate to have most clients voluntarily report to the hospital, sometimes with a family member present to escort them. When this occurs, I have the responsible family member sign a release form stating which hospital I advised, that they agreed to escort the client, that they assume responsibility for ensuring the client's arrival at the hospital, and that they are aware of the risk of suicide should they choose not to comply with my directives. I have provided an example of this form at the end of this chapter.

Being prepared for these occurrences lessens the angst associated with the event. I have provided a few guidelines concerning hospitalization below.

Guidelines for Hospitalization

- When clients have a plan, access to lethal means, recent social stressors, and active symptoms of mental health disorder, hospitalization may be warranted.
- When imminent danger is present, confidentiality can be breached. The limits of confidentiality should be discussed with your client upon the onset of the initial session or assessment. They should also should be delineated in your informed consent form, which the client must sign to acknowledge understanding.
- Clinicians should have a clear strategy for dealing with suicidal patients in the office, hospital, and emergency room.

Be Aware of the Available Resources

The last thing you want is to have a suicidal client in your office and be scrambling to locate resources! You need to be aware of all of the options available for helping a client who is in crisis or who presents as acutely suicidal. Again, every state, county, agency, and city has various resources and it is imperative to have a list of these resources easily accessible. I would even advise having these resources divided into sections to include which facilities admit or treat adults, adolescents, and children; which accept private insurance only; and which accept clients with no insurance and indigent clients. Having this kind of information updated and ready helps to alleviate the clinician's anxiety when helping a suicidal client.

Examples of Resources to Compile

- Mobile crisis
- Availability and accessibility of hospitals (insurance/no insurance)
- Network of clinicians for referrals
- How to use law enforcement
- Locations and options for long-term treatment facilities
- Locations and options for intensive outpatient programs (IOP)
- Crisis and outreach options

Voluntary Versus Involuntary Hospitalization

A client may be admitted to hospital voluntarily or involuntarily.

Voluntary Hospitalization

- Voluntary hospitalization takes place when a person willingly signs forms agreeing to be treated in the hospital.
- A person who signs in voluntarily may also ask to leave. This request should be made in writing.
- The hospital must release people who make requests within a period of time (2 to 7 days, depending on state laws), unless they are a danger to themselves or others.

Involuntary Hospitalization

- Involuntary hospitalization occurs when someone's symptoms have become so severe that they will not listen to others or accept help.
- This may involve the use of other doctors, the police, or lawyers.
- Involuntary hospitalization is an option of last resort only.
- Every state differs on laws about involuntary hospitalization.

Using Law Enforcement

When electing to use law enforcement to assist in a hospitalization procedure, it is critical to understand the bounds of confidentiality. While it is necessary to reveal certain pieces of information including the client's name, birthdate, address, and age and to report that the client has suicidal intentions, it is **not** warranted to report specific details.

For example, the client reports to you that she is suicidal due to discovering she is pregnant as a result of being sexually abused by her uncle. The only information law enforcement officers need to know is that "the client is suicidal due to a distressing concern in her life." Unless the client is a minor or other child abuse laws are relevant, the information about the pregnancy and the uncle is irrelevant in having the client hospitalized.

Guidelines for Using Law Enforcement

- The client should not be allowed to leave the office until the clinician can thoroughly assess their condition.

- If the client is hostile or demands to leave, law enforcement should be called. However, if a client is intimidating or aggressive toward the clinician or office staff, gallant actions should not be used to avert the client from leaving the office or facility.
- Providing law enforcement with a description of the client's vehicle and direction of travel may be helpful.
- Document details of this incident in client's file for treatment and legal purposes.
- Be sure to request a police report and/or case number when warranted.

DUTY TO WARN AND DUTY TO PROTECT

History of This Precedent

Prosenjit Poddar and Tatiana Tarasoff were students at the University of California, Berkeley. Poddar stated to the university health science psychologist that he intended to kill an unnamed woman, who was identified as Tatiana Tarasoff. Although the psychotherapist did not directly warn Tarasoff or the family, the psychologist notified the police, who interviewed Poddar for commitment. The police only warned Poddar to stay away from Tarasoff. After Tarasoff returned from a summer in Brazil, Poddar murdered her with a knife. Tarasoff's family sued the campus police and the university health service for negligence.

The *Tarasoff* case imposed a liability on all mental health professionals to protect a victim from violent acts. The first *Tarasoff* case (1974) imposed a **duty to warn** the victim, whereas the second *Tarasoff* case (1976) implies a **duty to protect**. There continue to be many concerns about the implications of the *Tarasoff* case, specifically concerning confidentiality and dangerous or violent clients.

Statute

When a therapist determines, or pursuant to the standards of his profession should determine, that his client presents a serious danger of violence to another, he incurs an obligation to use reasonable care to protect the intended victim against such danger.

The discharge of the duty may require the therapist to take one or more various steps, depending on the nature of the case. Thus, it may call for the therapist to warn the intended victim or others likely to appraise the victims of that danger, to notify the police or take whatever steps are reasonably necessary under the circumstances.

This statute can at times cause conundrums for mental health professionals who work with various kinds of issues, where HIPPA laws and other guidelines prevent the clinician from ability to warn clients who may be exposed to life-threatening situations. These areas include working with clients who are being treated for anger and domestic violence, dealing with HIV/AIDS cases wherein the infected person continues to intentionally expose others to the transmission of the virus, even following this issue being discussed in treatment and even working in a medical setting where revealing certain information may have a life-or-death result.

There has been significant research and there have been multiple advisements for these types of issues since the Tarasoff ruling in 1976; however, the ethical dilemmas associated with many of these situations remain very much a concern for many mental health professionals.

This is why it is imperative to **always** remain aware of the most current literature on this topic, not only within your mental health discipline but also regarding your state licensure board. **Not all states are the same** with respect to mandatory reporting laws and duty to protect and duty to warn mandates. This becomes an issue when engaging in interjurisdictional practice by providing teletherapy services to clients. Most state laws require the clinician to abide by the rules of the state in which the client resides, not the state in which the practicing clinician is located.

For example, the state of Texas, in which I reside, does not have a duty to protect or duty to warn mandate. On June 24, 1999, the Supreme Court of Texas held that a physician does not have a duty to warn a third party when a client makes specific threats of harm toward a readily identifiable person.

The 77th Texas legislative session, which ended in the spring of 2001, did not address the *Tarasoff* duty to warn or protect a third party. Thus, the current holding in Texas allows that there is no *Tarasoff* duty to warn or protect a third party. Although the *Tarasoff* decision has been adopted by many jurisdictions across the nation, the decision has never been formally adopted in Texas because the Texas Supreme Court has not been willing to create a new common law cause of action based on negligence.

Under existing Texas law, if I report confidential information directly to a third party who is the subject of a specific threat, I do so in violation of state law. If I report confidential information to local law enforcement, I do so at my own risk because there is no protection for good-faith reporting under the present statute. However, I do have two other options available to me in dealing with this issue: (1) If the client poses a substantial risk of serious harm to him/herself or others, I may contact the county mental health deputies or local law enforcement to have the client admitted to a mental health facility through emergency detention or (2) I may initiate an emergency admission and detention under a certain mandate.

This is a perfect illustration of how important it is to be aware of your state's laws and the options available to you when addressing and enforcing various ethical concerns.

Homicidal Ideation
- Homicidal urges are not as clearly related to specific psychiatric conditions as are suicidal urges.
- The victims of violence perpetrated by psychiatric patients are most often family members or others in a care-taking role for the client.
- In many instances, it is necessary to warn potential victims and/or legal authorities of the homicidal urges of the client.

Not all states have Tarasoff laws. Know the law in your state!

Chapter 4 | Short-Term Treatment:
Crisis Intervention

Acutely suicidal clients require crisis intervention skills. A **crisis** is any situation in which the individual perceives a sudden loss of their ability to use effective problem-solving and coping skills (Ellis, 1990). Numerous events and circumstances can be considered crises, including real or perceived life-threatening situations, medical illness, and mental illness.

Crises are time-limited, and **crisis intervention** refers to the methods used to offer immediate, short-term help to individuals who experience an event that produces emotional, mental, physical, and/or behavioral distress or problems.

Crisis intervention is conducted in a supportive manner and may range from one session to several weeks, with the average time being 4 weeks. Crisis interventions assist in developing ways for clients to cope and solve problems, and they aim to assist the client in recovering from the crisis and to prevent serious long-term problems from developing.

CLINICIAN RESPONSES TO CRISES

First Manage *Your* Own Anxiety!

This is the first step in managing any crisis situation. When our clients are in crisis, they may present as agitated, irritable, excitable, or overwhelmed. They may also present with loud and unintelligible speech, confusion, shock, anger, or a combination of these emotions. This can be anxiety-provoking for some clinicians, and it is important to remain aware of your own countertransference and responsiveness in these situations. If you find yourself becoming uneasy or anxious while intervening in a crisis, you should take a moment to assess your reactions, process with a colleague if possible, and then resume your work with the client. A primary component of crisis intervention is the clinician's ability to instill hope and help the client develop options and a better ability to problem solve and regulate distress.

Calm the Situation

It is important you keep your affective reactivity in check in order to defuse the situation and help the client to return to a more stable and calm state.

Communicate Effectively

When managing a crisis, it is important to clearly communicate with your client and listen. In addition, at times our individual filters, assumptions, judgments, and beliefs can garble what we hear. As a listener, your role is to **understand** what the client is conveying. This may involve reflecting on what is being said by the client and asking questions.

Active listening is a model of communication developed for demonstrating respect and understanding. Through using this model, you are able to gather information about the client's perspective. Active listening is key when communicating effectively and involves several skills.

Pay Close Attention to Your Client

- Give the client your undivided attention and acknowledge the message.
- Recognize that non-verbal communication also "speaks" loudly.
- Look at the client directly.
- Put aside distracting thoughts.
- Don't mentally prepare a response.
- Avoid being distracted by environmental factors (e.g., noises).
- "Listen" to the client's body language (e.g., crossed arms, using their hands when speaking, poor eye contact, psychomotor agitation).

Show That You're Listening

- Use your own body language and gestures to convey your attention.
- Nod occasionally.
- Smile and use other facial expressions.
- Attend to your posture and ensure it is open and inviting.
- Encourage the speaker to continue with small verbal comments such as "yes" and "uh-huh."

Provide Feedback

- Paraphrasing can be used. Some examples are, "What I'm hearing you say is that . . ." and "Sounds like you said . . ."
- Ask questions to clarify specific points: "What did you mean when you said?" and "Is this what you mean?"
- Periodically, it is helpful to summarize the client's statements.

Defer Judgment

- Interrupting the client is not effective. It only frustrates the client and limits complete understanding of their message.
- Allow the client to finish each point before asking questions.
- Don't interject with counter-arguments.

Respond Appropriately

- Be frank, open, and honest in your responses.
- Courteously state your views.

Cognitive Therapy

This type of therapy is the most effective for managing a crisis situation. Cognitive therapy is a general term for a classification of therapies that emphasizes the role of **thinking** in how we feel and what we do. It is aimed at reducing or suppressing a client's symptoms as quickly and as economically as possible.

Most of these therapies are based on the assumption that our thoughts cause our feelings and behaviors, not external things such as people, situations, and events. Cognitive therapy aims to help clients uncover and alter distortions of thought or perception in order to change their behavior and emotional state.

FOUR KEY ELEMENTS OF CRISIS INTERVENTIONS

1. Assess for the client's strengths, coping skills, and social support networks.
2. Explore coping strategies with the client (previous strategies may be enhanced or bolstered).
3. Help the client to develop problem-solving strategies.
4. Help the client to reinforce previously learned strategies. Encourage the use of these skills, help the client to recognize red flags, and help with preventive efforts by assisting the client in developing a plan to better manage future crises.

Crisis Intervention Work-Up

Directions: Use the following as an outline to guide your assessment of your client's current ability to cope with a crisis situation, skills they have previously used to cope with similar crises, their ability to think critically and identify areas that warrant attention, and their skill development.

What other areas of your life do you feel more secure about or feel as if you have more under control?

_____

_____

_____

_____

Why do you feel secure in these areas?

_____

_____

_____

_____

What talents and abilities help you to feel more secure these areas?

_____

_____

_____

_____

When things don't go well in these other areas, what have you typically done to fix it or feel better about it?

_____

_____

_____

_____

What do you do when you get stressed or worried about something? How do you manage your worry? If you can, describe your process step by step.

_____

_____

_____

_____

What strategies have worked best for you in the past? What is happening now to make these skills less effective?

_____

_____

_____

_____

What happened in the current situation that makes it different from other situations?

_____

_____

_____

_____

What physical sensations do you notice right before you begin to feel overwhelmed (e.g., headache, tightness of chest, increase in body temperature, dizzy)? (This question can assist in helping to recognize red flags for future crises.)

_____

_____

_____

_____

PROBLEM SOLVING AND CRISIS MANAGEMENT

Problem solving during a crisis situation requires the clinician to thoroughly understand the client's problem and the desired changes. When attempting to problem solve in these situations, there are a few steps that will make the process more effective.

Consider Alternatives for Solving the Problem

It always important to help your clients develop plans A, B, C, D, and even E if warranted! Having options helps clients to feel empowered and it helps them to understand that plans don't always work the way they are intended. Having alternatives will help to better manage their anxiety related to implementing newly developed skills and increases the likelihood that they will attempt to apply these new skills.

Discuss the Pros and Cons of Alternative Solutions

Discussing the benefits and costs of these alternative solutions helps your client to anticipate the possibilities of each course of action. This anticipation allows for adequate preparation for an upcoming event and hopefully alleviates the client's fear.

Select the Solution That Is the Most Effective

Help your client choose a solution that is the most feasible for their current situation. While your client may develop a plan that is amazing, if it requires financial support that is not possible or is otherwise based in fantasy, it will not be helpful in any upcoming crisis. Help the client stay realistic when developing plans and ensure that their plans will be useful for their current situation or similar situations.

Develop a Plan to Execute the Solution

While the client may develop a solution to a potential situation, they may not have actually thought about how they would put this plan into action. Help the client develop a step-by-step plan to execute their solution. Don't be afraid to play devil's advocate and challenge parts of the plan that may become problematic or potentially cause the client to experience more distress.

Evaluate the Outcome

Following the development and execution of the solutions, be sure to follow up with the client in order to assess the solutions' success or failure. Discuss these in depth with the client and develop more solutions if warranted, following the same process.

DEVELOPMENT OF NEW COPING SKILLS

The development and implementation of new coping skills can be intimidating for some clients. Any time we are tasked to incorporate a new behavior into our everyday lives, it requires repetition and successful outcomes to become useful or, rather, "dependable."

When clients do not use newly provided skills, this is typically because the client feels inadequate using the skill, is not receiving positive reinforcement for the behavioral change, or does not have opportunities to apply these skills. When we are helping clients to develop coping skills to assist in the management of crises, it is important to ensure their comfort with and understanding of the exercise. These coping skills may include:

- Relaxation techniques (e.g., progressive muscle relaxation techniques, deep breathing).
- Exercises to reduce body tension and stress.
- Putting thoughts and feelings on paper through journal writing instead of keeping them inside.
- Options for social support or spending time with people who provide a feeling of comfort and caring.

FINAL PHASE OF CRISIS INTERVENTION

During this final phase of treatment, when managing a crisis, we want to take this opportunity to highlight the client's progress, the improvements in their symptoms, and their ability to manage crisis situations. We encourage insight and self-reflection and assist the client in remaining proactive in the prevention of future emergencies. The final phase involves the following steps:

- Review changes the client has made to reinforce their ability to cope with difficult life events.
- Encourage the continued use of newly learned coping skills.
- Make plans for dealing with crises in the future.
- Discuss "red flags" and triggers to help your client be more proactive in preventing future crises.

When clients experience a crisis, they sometimes forget basic information about themselves. They may forget about important phone numbers, people, health needs, service provider information, and even directions to their own homes! Clients experience a sensory overload during a crisis that affects basic functioning. The following worksheet should be used to gather some of this basic information about your client. It can then assist in the development of a more thorough crisis plan or be provided to the client for them to keep handy in case they experience memory lapses associated with a crisis.

Crisis Planning:
Client Information

Clinician Directions: Use this worksheet to document information about your client that will be helpful when memory lapses occur during a crisis.

Client Directions: Keep this information in a handy place (e.g. bedroom, car, backpack, purse, wallet, night stand, refrigerator) and use when experiencing a crisis. The information will help you when need to immediately locate helpful resources when you are feeling overwhelmed.

Name:

_____

Address:

_____

_____

Phone Number:

_____

Birthdate:

_____

Gender:

_____

Emergency Contact:

_____

_____

_____

_____

Health Needs:

_____

_____

_____

_____

_____

Directions to Home:

_____

_____

_____

_____

Service Providers:

_____

_____

_____

_____

_____

Pets:

_____

_____

_____

_____

_____

Children:

_____

_____

_____

_____

_____

Cultural Heritage and/or Spirituality:

_____

_____

_____

_____

_____

Example adapted from Maine.gov Sample Crisis Plan.

Crisis Planning

Directions: Use this worksheet to help you better understand your responses, feelings, behaviors, and coping skills when dealing with a crisis. We will use this worksheet to examine your use of your support network during a crisis.

Describe what crisis looks and feels like to you. What is different in times of crisis in comparison to other times in your life? (For example, think about having "bad days" versus "good days.")

Crisis:	Other times in my life:

When you have been in a crisis situation, what kinds of support did you seek? What things (e.g., people, places, services) were the most helpful? Why?

Source of Support	Why was it helpful?

What are the most difficult feelings for you to experience? Please circle the *most* difficult feelings, and you can also add any you don't see listed here:		Think about what happens when these feelings get overwhelming. Consider the following: What does it feel like inside your body? What do you need when this happens? What can you do for yourself? What has been helpful?
Happiness	**Boredom**	
Joy	**Loneliness**	
Sadness	**Emptiness**	
Grief		
Fear		
Anger		
Rage		
Anxiety		
Overwhelmed		

How do you decide to seek or reach out to others for support? How do you identify when you need someone to respond to you in a more empathic manner? Document this here.

_____

_____

_____

Think about the people around you when you experience crisis. Are there behaviors or actions you take that might alarm others? Please describe.

_____

_____

_____

How do you feel about these behaviors? What would you like the people around you to understand about them? How would you like them to react? What do you need to hear? Also identify what can make the crisis worse: what you *don't* want people to do. What do you need to do personally? Write about that.

_____

_____

_____

Are there people in your life who are important to you (e.g., children, partner, spouse, friends, relatives, clergy, staff)? Think about who they are, who you may want to be in touch with if you're experiencing crisis, and where you might end up getting support other than in your home. List their information here.

Name	Relationship	Phone Number

Can you identify things that you're not likely to talk about when you're in crisis, or "code words" you may use?

_____

_____

Are there people from this list who you would want consulted if there were any question of "next steps" when you are in crisis? Name those people. Make sure their contact information is included in the list above.

_____

_____

Is there any additional information that you would like people to know or consider when you're in crisis? Is there anything else you need to remind yourself about when you're in crisis?

_____

_____

_____

Crisis Management

Directions: This worksheet should be used to help learn the steps involved in de-escalating when in crisis mode. You cannot be anxious in a relaxed state and you cannot make good choices and decisions when enduring a crisis.

Pause

Don't act immediately. Pause and wait.

Take a Breath

Breathe in through your nose and out through your mouth slowly. The more oxygen, the better. This allows your fight-or-flight mode to disengage.

Observation

What am I focusing on? What am I reacting to? Am I reacting to the **actual** event or am I reacting to how I **feel** about the event? What am I feeling physically (e.g., tightness of the chest, perspiration, increased heart rate)?

Be Objective

See the bigger picture. Am I catastrophizing? Is this fact or fiction? What would (fill in the blank) say? How does this affect other people? How urgent is this matter?

What Works for Me

Consider other options. How have I coped in the past? What are my resources? How have I managed similar situations?

Chapter 5 | Long-Term Treatment of Suicidal Clients

COGNITIVE–BEHAVIORAL THERAPY

Several approaches have been researched in the management of suicidal clients. The treatment that has been determined as having the most positive outcome is cognitive–behavioral therapy (CBT).

CBT is a general term for a group of therapies that have similar characteristics. There are several approaches to CBT, including rational emotive behavior therapy, rational behavior therapy, rational living therapy, cognitive therapy, and dialectic behavior therapy (DBT).

CBT is based on the idea that it is our **thoughts** that cause our **feelings** and **behaviors**, not external things like people, situations, and events. The benefit of this fact is that we have the power and ability to change the way we think, feel, and act even if the situation remains the same.

CBT is **brief** and **time-limited**. This type of therapy is considered to be very rapid with respect to obtained results. The average number of sessions needed to address an issue (across all types of problems and approaches to CBT) is approximately 16. The brevity of CBT is related to its highly educational aspect and the fact that it incorporates homework assignments. CBT is time-limited in that, even during the initial session, clients are informed that there will be a point when the formal therapy will end. The point at which the treatment will terminate is a decision made by the therapist and client.

CBT is very structured and directive. CBT-oriented therapists have a specific agenda for each session, though the agenda will always be based around the client's specific goals. Specific techniques and concepts are taught during each session, and therapists do not direct the client's goals. We are not to instruct clients what their goals "should" be or what they "should" tolerate. This therapy is directive in the sense that you show your clients how to think and behave in ways to obtain what they want.

Homework is a central feature of CBT. The skills and techniques you teach are only useful when clients practice and apply these skills. Goal achievement could be delayed if a client only ponders these ideas and never applies the concepts to their everyday functioning. This is why CBT therapists assign bibliotherapy techniques and encourage their clients to practice the techniques learned.

COGNITIVE–BEHAVIORAL THERAPY WITH SUICIDAL CLIENTS

Research has demonstrated that, over the course of our development, we acquire beliefs about ourselves, others, our environment, and our future. Aaron Beck hypothesized that, from these beliefs, we develop **core beliefs** about ourselves that are determined by our sense of lovability, worth, and control. These core beliefs can turn out to be either adaptive or maladaptive, contingent on our long-term experiences with significant people and situations. Maladaptive core beliefs are associated with views and beliefs of unlovability, worthlessness, and helplessness.

Clients who have been reared in a primarily adverse environment will be more likely to develop maladaptive than adaptive core beliefs. When these maladaptive beliefs are activated by events that occur in the present but that we associate with events that happened in the past, this influences our objectivity and we then interpret these events based on these negative and maladaptive beliefs. This typically occurs when we are under duress, in a crisis, or affected by either an acute onset or chronic recurrence of a mental health disorder (e.g., depression, anxiety). These beliefs begin to surface and negatively impact how we scan the environment and process new information.

According to Beck, depressed suicidal clients view themselves as defective, inadequate, diseased, or deprived and thus worthless and undesirable; they view others as rejecting and unsupportive by making too many demands; and they view their future as hopeless since they do not believe that they have the internal and external resources to solve their problems.

Their sense of defectiveness contributes to a more passive approach to solving the problems that are generating their distress. They may avoid making attempts to solve their problem(s) and may even hope for a spontaneous solution. They will often just give up, because they feel helpless about their situation and they feel as if others do not care.

Suicidal clients also begin to develop very rigid and dichotomous thinking. They are unable to see options or alternative courses of action in problematic situations, and they tend not to anticipate the consequences of problematic issues. Dichotomous thinking is the "black or white," "all or nothing," good/bad, love/hate type of thinking. This type of cognitive processing negatively affects problem-solving ability and can lead to "tunnel vision," wherein the client becomes overwhelmed and unable to access any higher-order processing or solution-focused skills and is therefore unable to broaden their perspective about their current situation.

The emphases of CBT when working with a depressed suicidal client is to:

1. Identify the perceived unsolvable problem.
2. Reduce cognitive distortions and errors in logic with regards to the patient's views of self, others, and the future.
3. Improve problem-solving skills.
4. Increase motivation to problem solve.
5. Reduce perceived emotional pain.
6. Encourage acceptance of emotional pain as part of everyday life.

Treatment Goals of CBT With Suicidal Clients
- Address specific cognitive biases and distortions
- Develop behavior skills (problem solving)
- Develop acceptance and tolerance of emotional pain
- Improve communication skills (social skills, assertiveness training, conflict-resolution skills)
- Reduce environmental stress
- Develop supports

Hopelessness

When treating the cognitions and feelings of a suicidal client, hopelessness has to be addressed at the onset of treatment. The immediate goal in therapy in terms of addressing hopelessness is to challenge the belief that the patient's situation cannot get better. It is important to create an imbalance in the client's distorted beliefs by presenting evidence that opposes the beliefs. Other ways to achieve this goal include incorporating problem-solving skills and identifying available family and community resources so as to provide internal and external resources that can be used to solve the client's problem, thus enhancing self-efficacy.

Cognitive Rigidity

When addressing rigid thinking, it is imperative to first define beliefs as testable theories and not fixed rules. It is also important to generate alternative explanations and test them behaviorally. This type of work will require your client to actively engage in treatment, and role plays and visual imagery have been reported to be effective strategies. These techniques also help to develop and improve problem-solving skills.

Client Exercise

Role Playing

This exercise can be used when working to address your client's rigid "black or white" thinking. This exercise will help to improve your client's cognitive flexibility in recognizing alternative explanations and testing these explanations.

Directions: Have your client play the role of their critical voice. You will then rationally respond to this critical voice, providing alternative explanations. Then reverse the role play so that the client is played by you and the client responds to the critical voice. Make sure that your client is detailed in responding to what the voice is saying and sounding, and in how they are feeling in response to this critical voice. Document the interchange. Remember to highlight themes, the client's responses, and the client's reactions to this exercise.

Client Exercise

Visual Imagery Exercise

Visual imagery provides your client with an opportunity to imagine various solutions and potential outcomes to situations.

Directions: Discuss and document various solutions and potential outcomes to current situations that are causing your client to experience significant duress. Remember to be detailed when conducting this exercise and to assist the client in developing alternatives.

Acceptance of Pain

One of the essential goals of therapy with suicidal clients is to assist them in being able to live and enjoy their life regardless of their emotional pain. When clients are suicidal, they are functioning according to the belief that there is no reason to live if suffering exists. This results in the client putting all their focus on avoiding or resisting their pain, pondering "How could this have happened to me?" and ruminating about future suffering. If your clients are hyper-focused on this aspect, then there is no time or space for experiencing a purposeful and meaningful life. In most cases, the problems that create our clients' suffering have no immediate solution. Therefore, the task becomes to learn how to accept that suffering will occur but that you can still carry on with your daily responsibilities and work on solutions to the problem that's causing this suffering.

This is achieved by what research refers to as **recontextualization**, wherein your client learns that negative thoughts and feelings do not block adaptive behavior. Clients learn that both things can occur simultaneously. **Comprehensive distancing** is another technique and refers to the willingness of the suicidal client to detach from their suicidal thoughts and emotional distress.

Challenging the Belief That Suicide Is a Better Option

Most suicidal clients believe that suicide will be the catalyst for the change they want to see in their relationships or in their situations. Characteristic motives include revenge or to offer relief for family and friends (feelings of burdensomeness). CBT allows this assumption to be challenged, which in turn allows the client to achieve a more realistic perspective. This also provides the client with the opportunity to contemplate the short- and long-term consequences of attempting and completing suicide.

By exploring this issue, you gain good information about the positive and negative reinforcers related to your client's suicidal beliefs. Detecting the positive reinforcers helps to guide treatment toward identifying alternatives to suicide in order lessen the client's desire for suicide. It also allows the opportunity to correct any cognitive distortions the client has about the benefits of dying. Having knowledge about the negative reinforcers provides information about the client's motivation to not commit suicide. Both inform the therapy and provide a way to move your client away from ruminating about the possibility of suicide.

Clinician Worksheet

Why Suicide?

Directions: Use this worksheet to challenge your client's views about suicide being beneficial in attaining their goals. This will help to identify the positive and negative reinforcers of suicide for your client.

Advantages	Disadvantages

Why Live?

Directions: Use this worksheet to challenge your client's views about suicide being beneficial in attaining their goals. This will help to identify the positive and negative reinforcers of suicide for the client.

Advantages	Disadvantages

Other Factors Affecting Treatment With CBT

CBT with this population involves multiple steps, collaborative efforts, and more integrative approaches. Engaging in CBT with clients requires more than just a knowledge and understanding of the basic premises of CBT. It requires the ability to combine and integrate various approaches to meet the needs of your clients. Treatment plans for your suicidal clients should be updated at least once every 6 months. For chronically suicidal patients, ongoing assessment of suicidality may be warranted.

Following are some additional factors that will affect the outcome when using CBT with suicidal clients.

Establish a Therapeutic Alliance

- The alliance is an excellent protective factor when working with suicidal clients. The client has to believe that you have their best interest at heart and that you are being genuine and collaborative. The working relationship is pivotal in continuing to remain effective in working with these issues.

- Allow the client to tell their story.

- The alliance can also involve the use of and communication with relevant others, including family members, friends, and anyone in the client's social support network.

- When working with the client, it is imperative to ensure emotional safety and a supportive working environment.

- While establishing this therapeutic alliance, you can help patients define suicide risks and red flags.

- Communicate a collaborative approach by incorporating "we" language when working with your client.

- Establishing this relationship helps to convey permanence in your client's ability to successfully manage a temporary crisis.

- Clinicians should aim to model hopefulness, and this can be established when the therapeutic alliance is strong.

Psychoeducation

- Help clients and relevant others better understand suicide risks as well as protective factors that insulate the client from suicidal urges.

- Educate your clients about their mental health diagnosis (if warranted), the course of the mental health diagnosis, the cognitive triad (thoughts, feelings, and behaviors), the role of suicidal ideation, and the importance of treatment planning.

- Help your client to recognize the role of warning signs and precipitating factors leading to suicidal behavior.

- Help to develop a safety plan.

- Use bibliotherapy, which is an expressive therapy that involves the reading of specific texts with the purpose of healing. It uses the client's relationship to the content of books and/or poetry and other written words as therapy. This type of therapy is often combined with journaling.

Nurture Hope

- Collaborate when goal setting with the client. Being involved in their own treatment planning encourages clients to remain compliant with and invested in treatment.

- Recognize progress. The clinician should always provide feedback about the client's minor and major accomplishments while in therapy. Any positive behavioral change should be highlighted and any decrease in negative or self-destructive behaviors should be celebrated.

- Teaching coping techniques to your clients will assist in their self-efficacy in managing difficult situations while they are continuing treatment.

- Involve relevant and significant others when warranted.

- Build on the client's assets and strengths.

- Encourage the client to seek social support systems (e.g., groups, online blogs, forums).

Teach Coping Skills

- Help your client to develop internal and external compensatory strategies.

- Address impulsiveness issues. Impulsive behaviors are those that occur quickly without control, planning, or consideration of the consequences of the behavior. Impulsive behaviors tend to be connected with immediate positive consequences (e.g., relief from emotional pain).

- Assist the client in problem solving and communication training in interpersonal effectiveness, or transactional analysis (TA). TA is a psychoanalytic theory, developed by Eric Berne, and method of treatment in which social transactions are analyzed to determine the ego state of the client (parent-like, child-like, or adult-like) as an origin for understanding behavior and communication.

- Help the client to increase adaptive use of their social support system.

- Provide skills training (e.g., stress inoculation training).

- Incorporate mindfulness and acceptance techniques.

- Increase compliance with other modalities of therapy (e.g., medication management, group therapy, family therapy).

Address Co-morbid Disorders

- Provide integrative treatments that address other mental health conditions (e.g., substance use disorders, anxiety disorders, eating disorders).

- Discuss how suicidal ideation manifests as a symptom of the relevant disorder (depressive symptoms).

- Use the interventions that best treat the disorder that is most prevalent.

Relapse Prevention Procedures

- Educate the client on how to handle future problems, recurrences, lapses, mood fluctuations, and set-backs.

- Decrease cognitive constriction and rigidity. Help your client to broaden their perspectives and become more flexible in their problem-solving abilities.

- Acknowledge the gains and your client's abilities.

- Help the client to develop reasons for living.
- Help your client to imagine obstacles and develop solutions.
- Involve family—assist in enhancing communication and problem-solving skills.
- Taper treatment with your client.

OTHER INTERVENTIONS

Safety Plan

Safety planning interventions provide clients with an explicit set of tangible tactics to use in order to minimize the risk of suicidal behavior.

A safety plan can include coping strategies which can be implemented during a crisis. Significant others or agencies can also be listed to contact during a crisis. Safety planning is described as a collaborative effort between a treatment provider and the client. It involves a limited time frame and can typically be completed within 25-30 minutes.

The basic steps of a safety plan include:

1. Recognizing the warning signs of an impending suicidal crisis.
2. Using your own coping strategies.
3. Contacting others in order to distract from suicidal thoughts.
4. Contacting family members or friends who may help to resolve the crisis.
5. Contacting mental health professionals or agencies.
6. Reducing the availability of means to complete suicide.

Safety Plan

Directions: This form is to be used when you are contemplating suicide or NSSI behaviors. This plan should be developed with the help of your clinician and should be followed in a step-by-step format. This plan is to be used when you are unable to manage negative emotions and experience suicidal ideation, or urges to engage in NSSI.

Keep this plan in a convenient place, you can take a picture of this plan using your smart phone or upload it if able.

What do I need to help decrease the risk of acting on my current feelings?

_____

_____

_____

What have been some things in the past that have helped me? What have I previously used to cope with problems?

_____

_____

_____

What are my warning signs and triggers?

_____

_____

_____

What do I typically do when I am overwhelmed? What coping methods work for me?

_____

_____

_____

A safe place (with no weapons, other objects used to self-harm):

_____

_____

_____

What are some positive things happening in my life? What are some positive thoughts that make me smile?

_____

_____

_____

What would I say to my best friend/spouse/significant other/close friend if they were feeling this way?

_____

_____

_____

What do I need from other people in my space to be helpful?

_____

_____

_____

What will I do if I continue to feel overwhelmed and continue to experience urges?

_____

_____

_____

What smartphone apps do I have to use? Or what websites have I used to seek comfort? (Should include recovery sites or websites used in therapy sessions.)

_____

_____

_____

Who do I trust to contact to talk with me through crises if my therapist is unavailable?

_____

_____

_____

Friend	
Spouse	
Relative	
Crisis hotline phone number	
Additional person	

Safety Plan Cards

Directions: These cards can be laminated, uploaded, or placed on your smartphone and should be kept with you at all times. They will provide you with a visual representation when you are unable to locate your entire safety plan.

I will tell myself: I will call: I will seek comfort from: I will use my coping skills, including:	I will tell myself: I will call: I will seek comfort from: I will use my coping skills, including:
I will tell myself: I will call: I will seek comfort from: I will use my coping skills, including:	I will tell myself: I will call: I will seek comfort from: I will use my coping skills, including:

Anti-suicide Kit / Hope Box

When a hope box is created, it is important that you, as the clinician, be involved in this intervention with the client. The client should share the meaning of each item placed into this box. You want to ensure that your client is not placing any dangerous items into the hope box or items that will trigger negative thoughts and/or emotions. This intervention can be used in an array of settings, including inpatient, outpatient, group therapy, individual therapy, prison, and school.

Any receptacle can be used as a hope box: a Kleenex box, a cardboard box, or you can even build a box. This box can be decorated and personalized by the client. It can be used as an exploratory intervention while in session and used outside the therapy room in order to provide your client with tangible items to remind them of the positive things in their life when they are experiencing suicidal and/or NSSI urges. The box can contain the following:

- Items that remind the client of reasons to live
- Pictures
- Letters
- Transitional objects
- Personal items
- Poems
- Anything that promotes resilience, strength, and ability

Address the Client's Impulsiveness

Clients can be taught that, typically, during the outset of recovery, urges can be intense, but each one will subside if they can wait it out and have a plan for relapse prevention. Cravings and urges will decrease in strength and frequency over time. Urges typically last 10–15 minutes and, if they persist, there must be something triggering in the environment.

Educate your client to look for any such triggering stimuli and remove them from their environment. This would include any items used to engage in NSSI behaviors or prior suicide attempts.

Clients can also be taught to delay acting on impulses to self-harm. This can be taught to your client by way of teaching emotion regulation skills, using the hope box, or engaging in other interventions imparted upon your client.

Practice delay techniques. There are many delay techniques that can be used with your client. Most of these techniques involve the basic steps of acceptance, delaying, and distracting.

Acceptance

Although we have no control over urges, we do have full control over how we react to them. Instead of attempting to control these urges, it is more effective to accept their presence and let them run their course. Remind the client that an urge is only a feeling and that it is not dangerous and does not need to be resisted. Allow the urge to rise and fall again. Acceptance should feel like a "softening" or a feeling that it's okay to experience these feelings. Two statements that may help your clients reinforce their acceptance are "It's okay to be uneasy right now" and "I can handle these urges."

Delay

Challenge your client to resist their urges for only 10 minutes at a time. By doing this, they are able to keep their goals realistic and cannot "fortune-tell" and predict their failure at completing this task long-term. This makes it more likely that they will be successful at the task. Inform your client that, if they still experience the urge after 10 minutes have passed, then that's okay, normal, and to be expected. Encourage your client to use a watch or their phone to document the time and attempt to wait the entire 10-minute period before making any decisions as to whether or not they will act on the urge.

Distract

This can involve teaching your clients to engage in various activities, including activities that involve physical movement and activities that remove the client from the trigger. This could involve going for a short jog, taking a bath, talking to a friend, using an online support forum, or listening to their favorite music.

Psychotropic Medication Management

Even if we have not received formal training in psychopharmacology, it is still imperative that we remain aware and educated about any psychotropic medications our clients may be administered by their primary care physician or psychiatrist.

It is very possible that your client may be prescribed one or more medications to assist in the management of their symptoms. When managing symptoms of depression, antidepressants are more effective than no medications. Selective serotonin reuptake inhibitors (e.g., citalopram and fluoxetine) have a rapid effect on these symptoms, and research has shown that tricyclics (e.g., doxepin and amitriptyline) should be avoided due to their potential for overdose and abuse.

Patients and families should be educated on what they can expect in terms of symptom improvement. They should also remain aware that the client may, initially, be at an increased suicide risk due to their energy level improving but their symptoms of hopelessness and depressed mood remaining. The client should remain under constant supervision upon initial administration of medication.

Chapter 6 | Special Populations

THE IMPORTANCE OF RECOGNIZING CULTURAL DIFFERENCES

Ethnicity refers to racial kinships of an individual. It is related to country of origin or the place in which one's ancestors were born (e.g., nationality, religious faith or tribe). Race involves self-identification and externally assigned physical characteristics. The scientific community does not consider race a valid biological classification (e.g., skin color). Culture is non-biological and is defined as a common heritage or set of beliefs, norms, values. Those within a culture learn and share common practices and values which provide a sense of belonging and identity. These practices or customs are passed on generationally.

Ethnicity and race inform culture and when working with clients, we must take culture into consideration when forming hypotheses or developing treatment strategies. Culture affects the presentation or description of problems/mental illness symptoms. The presentation of distress, anxiety or depression may vary amongst cultures. For example, there are generational differences in how those in the "millennial" generation (17-35) discuss and approach mental concerns when compared to the "baby boomer" generation (ages 53-71) as a result of the better understanding and information provided about these issues. Cultures even vary in the very meaning of "mental health problems." This refers to attitudes and beliefs about the origins of mental health symptoms, the perception of stigma, the causes of the mental health disorder and who the disorder may affect. Culture and social factors can also play a role in the **causation** of mental health symptoms. For example, chronic exposure to poverty, racism, discrimination, and violence, can lead to the development of post-traumatic stress disorder or a mood disorder.

As culturally-aware clinicians, we have to ensure that we recognize and understand that within-group differences and individual differences exist and should be considered when we are working with clients. It is never advised to assume that an individual identifies with a particular cultural group based on observed characteristics and the client's perception about their identity and culture should be thoroughly explored.

GERIATRIC CLIENTS AND SUICIDE

Those individuals, aged 65 and up, form what is referred to as the elderly or geriatric population. In the United States, this group makes up about 12.6% of the total population but accounts for 15.7% of completed suicides. Research has indicated that one elderly suicide occurs every 97 minutes, totaling 14.9 completed suicides per day. These statistics are striking and alarming, as the elderly are the fastest-growing segment of the population. Similarly to the general population, males complete suicide more often than females, constituting 84.4% of completed suicides, as men use more lethal means (firearms). Also similarly to the general population, Caucasian males are reported to be at the highest risk for completed suicides, with a rate of 31.2 suicides per 100,000 people each year.

A major impediment faced by mental health specialists and other caregivers in reaching this group is that older adults do not typically seek services for mental health concerns. Discussing mental health concerns is stereotypically viewed as taboo by this population, as there is a negative stigma associated with mental health concerns. Another problem is that many of the elderly are unaware of the symptoms of mental health problems and may not recognize the symptoms of anxiety, depression, psychosis, or other disorders. Undiagnosed depression has been related to the increased suicide rate among the elderly. The increased presence of health problems in this population is also an issue that impacts the underdiagnosis of mental health problems, as many physical health conditions mimic symptoms of mental health disorders and vice versa. This makes the notion of "rule-outs" imperative for this age group.

Other factors that place these individuals at increased risk for mental illness include the recent death of a spouse, a family member, or a close friend; fear of prolonged illness; major life changes (e.g., retirement, rapid decline of health); and social isolation. Some individuals may even be home bound and have no access to medical care.

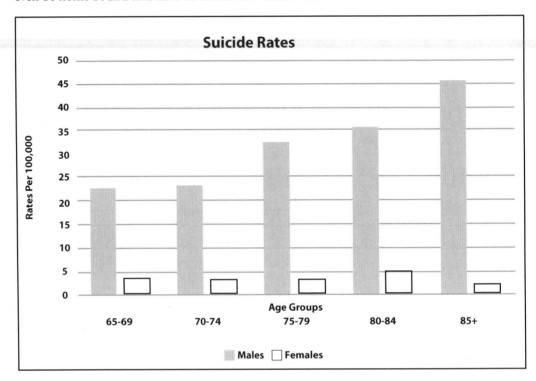

According to research, as males become older, their rate of completed suicides increases; however, in women, the rate of completed suicides decreases (see chart above). This significant variation is attributed to various reasons:

Males	Females
Worsening of chronic health problems	More intact social support network
Limited social support	May reside in residential care
Underreporting of mental health concerns	Better management of chronic illnesses
Loss of identity and role in the family	More vocal about mental and physical health
Access to more lethal means	

Presentation of Masked Depression in the Elderly

Depressive symptoms are often undiagnosed in this population for several reasons. Misdiagnoses typically occur due to the presence of other medical conditions that may mimic mental health symptoms. Ageism is also a major factor in the misdiagnosis of mental health concerns, as many people misattribute depressive symptoms to age and stereotypes are associated with age (e.g., easily agitated, irritated, and frustrated; lack of desire to establish and/or maintain relationships with others; withdrawn; fatigue; no interest in daily activities). Due to minimal understanding of or exposure to mental health issues, some people lack the ability to communicate depressive symptoms, and there is a generational ideology and stigma associated with mental health problems.

Limited access to medical care may occur as a result of lack of insurance or physical health conditions that keep the client homebound. The individual may also be residing in a rural area and may be unable to procure advantageous healthcare.

As a result of the above-mentioned issues, the presentation of depression or other mental health concerns may be masked as somatic complaints or be evident in more observable behavior, including:

- Weight loss
- Unexplained somatic complaints
- Weakness
- Hopelessness
- Anxiety, worry and rumination
- Loss of feelings of pleasure (anhedonia)
- Irritability
- Focus on multiple somatic complaints
- Minimizing or denying presence of mood-related symptoms
- Lethargy
- Helplessness
- Memory complaints with or without objective signs of cognitive impairment
- Slowed movement
- Lack of interest in personal care

Ruling Out Chronic Illness

There are several medical disorders that mimic mental health conditions, and conducting medical rule-outs is always important when providing mental health treatment. Ruling out medical conditions when treating this population is **mandatory** in order to provide adequate care and to incorporate holistic treatment options in the management of clients.

A few of the more common medical conditions diagnosed in this population will be highlighted in this section in order to provide a brief overview of co-morbidity and the presentation of parallel symptomology among these illnesses.

Thyroid disorders

Hyperthyroidism is caused by an overactive thyroid and thus increased levels of thyroxin. It can sometimes be misdiagnosed as Graves' disease and the symptoms can include:

- Overactive metabolism
- Increased heart rate
- Excessive perspiration
- Moodiness and feelings of nervousness
- Tremors
- Intermittent insomnia

Hypothyroidism is caused by an underactive thyroid and thus decreased levels of thyroxin. The symptoms of this disorder can include:

- Fatigue
- Underactive metabolism
- Depressive symptoms in some cases
- Decreased concentration
- Vague aches and pains

Diabetes

Diabetes is a disease in which the body's ability to produce or respond to the hormone insulin is impaired, resulting in abnormal metabolism of carbohydrates and elevated levels of glucose in the blood and urine. Type 1 diabetes usually affects children, adolescents, and young adults and was previously known a juvenile diabetes.

Type 2 diabetes is the most common form of diabetes. With type 2 diabetes, the body does not use insulin properly. This is called insulin resistance. Type 2 diabetes can be treated with lifestyle changes, oral medications (pills), and insulin. This condition can affect the way that a person metabolizes medications, which can impact the effectiveness of certain medications, including psychotropic medications. Some of the long-term effects of this condition include:

- Heart and blood-vessel disease
- Neuropathy
- Kidney damage
- Eye damage
- Osteoporosis
- Increased risk of Alzheimer's disease

Extremes in blood-sugar levels can cause significant mood changes. Depression has long been linked to diabetes, especially type 2. It's still not clear, however, whether depression somehow triggers diabetes or whether having diabetes leads to a person being depressed. Also, someone who experiences low blood sugar may suddenly become irritable, even combative, and may act as if they are drunk, slurring their words.

Parkinson's disease

This condition is a progressive and chronic disorder of the nervous system that affects movement. Nerve cells, or neurons, in an area of the brain known as the *substantia nigra* die or become impaired and neurons in the brain produce less dopamine and norepinephrine. During early stages of Parkinson's disease, the face may show little or no expression, or the arms may not swing while the person is walking. Speech may become soft or slurred. Those suffering from this condition can present with mood disorder symptoms (due to lowered dopamine levels) and present with cognitive deficits that can mimic dementia and other neurocognitive problems.

Symptoms can include:

- Tremors
- Bradykinesia
- Rigid muscles
- Impaired posture or balance
- Akathisia
- Slurred speech
- Decreased levels of dopamine, which may increase depressive symptoms
- Dementia (among 50–80% of individuals)
- Decline in concentration, memory, and judgment
- Difficulty interpreting visual information
- Visual hallucinations
- Delusions (paranoid ideation)
- Irritability
- Sleep disturbance

Multiple sclerosis

This is a progressive disease that affects the brain and spinal cord. The early symptoms of multiple sclerosis include weakness, tingling, numbness, and blurred vision. Other possible warning signs are muscle stiffness, thinking problems, and urinary problems. Personality changes (moodiness) can occur with this diagnosis in addition to memory problems. The presence of chronic pain also complicates this condition, as chronic pain is often associated with depressive symptoms. The use of opiates is also an issue that needs to be assessed when working with clients who present with this disease.

Post-stroke

Strokes occur when blood supply to a part of the brain is interrupted or severely reduced, depriving brain tissue of oxygen. Within minutes following a stroke, brain cells begin to die. Around two-thirds of individuals require rehabilitation following a stroke.

Strokes can cause:

- Paralysis or problems controlling movement
- Sensory disturbances, including pain
- Problems using or understanding language
- Problems with thinking and memory
- Emotional disturbances
- Impairment contingent on which part of the brain is affected
- Fear, anxiety, frustration, anger, sadness, and a sense of grief for the individual's physical and mental losses
- Some emotional disturbances and personality changes, caused by the physical effects of brain damage
- Clinical depression appears to be most commonly experienced by stroke survivors

Tumors

Tumors can cause personality and behavioral changes. Mental, emotional, and/or physical impairment is contingent on the location and size of the tumor. Tumors can cause impulse control problems, and a change of inhibitions can occur. Inhibitions may become more restricted (e.g., conservative, paranoid, fear of offending) or more relaxed (e.g., lack of impulse control, poor problem-solving skills, reduction of decorum).

Viral and bacterial infections

Viral and bacterial infections can include herpes zoster, influenza, respiratory syncytial virus, tuberculosis, and urinary tract infection (UTI). These conditions make one more susceptible to other illnesses and environmental factors as they weaken the immune system. These conditions can create infection in the bloodstream and can result in confusion and in increased agitation and irritation.

Research has demonstrated that UTIs temporarily affect mood and symptoms of dementia. If a person has a sudden and unexplained change in their behavior, such as increased confusion, agitation, or withdrawal, this may be because of a UTI. These infections can lead to a person experiencing a delirium, which is a change in mental state that usually develops over 1 or 2 days. There are various types of delirium, and symptoms may include agitation or restlessness, increased difficulty concentrating, hallucinations or delusions, or becoming unusually sleepy or withdrawn. Symptoms of delirium vary in severity (fluctuate) over the course of the day.

This condition alone speaks to the importance of understanding medical conditions and performing rule-outs when working with this population. If it were unknown that a client had a UTI, the above-mentioned symptoms could look like a psychotic episode, a mood disorder with psychotic features, or even a neurocognitive disorder.

Dementia-related disorders

There are various types of diseases that cause dementia to occur, as well as various types of dementia. Some of the more common disorders:

- **Vascular dementia** is the second most common cause of dementia. It is caused by blood-vessel blockage and leads to impaired judgment or the inability to execute planning and other executive functioning.
- **Alzheimer's disease** is the most common cognitive disorder among this population (80%). This condition is progressive and results from plaques and tangles occurring in the brain, leading to nerve cell damage and dying tissue in the brain. A few of the complications associated with this condition include difficulty recalling names and recent events, and symptoms of depression.
- **Frontotemporal dementia** is a primary progressive aphasia. Pick's disease is a form of this dementia. Changes in personality and behavior occur as well as difficulty with expressive and receptive language.
- **Huntington's disease** is caused by a dominant gene and is a progressive illness. Clients may experience abnormal motor activity; a severe decline in thinking and reasoning; and/or irritability, depression, and other mood changes.

Suicide Prevention and Geriatric Clients

Suicide prevention for this population involves educating the public, the client, family members, and other service providers. Information should be provided about depression, symptoms of depression, suicide risk, and the importance of ruling out medical conditions. Education of clients could include:

- Awareness of contextual triggers in their environment.
- Coping strategies once they are aware of these triggers.
- Medication interactions and side effects.
- Interactions between medical conditions and mental health conditions.
- Occupational therapy, if warranted.

Screening for symptoms of depression is also helpful. There are several instruments that can be used to quickly screen for symptoms of depression, including the Beck Depression Inventory and the Patient Health Questionnaire (PHQ-9). The PHQ-9 is a multipurpose instrument used to assist in screening for, monitoring, and assessing the severity of depression. It is a brief self-report tool. It can be used repeatedly and to determine symptom improvement or worsening of symptoms in response to treatment (see chapter 3).

Providing elderly clients with activities is also critical in assisting in the management of various mood disorders. Activities could include:

- Visits with friends and family members.
- Weekly walks, or other physical activity out of the home.
- Age-appropriate exercise regimens.
- Socialization.
- Cognitive- and memory-enhancing activities.
- Spiritual and/or religious activities.

It is effective to use integrative approaches with this population to achieve symptom reduction and increase quality of life. Suitable therapies are those that consist of reclaiming self-identity, bringing a sense of meaning and purpose, and assisting with adaptation to physical and cognitive impairments.

Conducting a thorough clinical interview is also recommended in gathering detailed information from these clients. A clinical interview allows you to establish rapport with the client and gather enough data to assist in treatment planning. An interview also allows dialogue to occur with the client and gives you an opportunity to assess the "masked" symptoms of depression discussed in this section.

Clinical Interview
with an Elderly Client

Referral

Who made the referral? _____

What is the problem being assessed (what was the referral for)? _____

_____

Assessment

Screening tools and other assessment measures that were used: _____

_____

Case History Information

Identifying data: _____

Reason for admittance or treatment and expectations from the client for service: _____

_____

Current concerns: _____

Case History Outline

Family history: _____

Health problems: _____

Education and training: _____

Employment history: _____

Recreation and interests: _____

Marital and family data: _____

Self-description: _____

Future orientation: _____

Additional information: _____

Mental Status Examination *(Includes areas of: Appearance, Behavior, Movements, Suicidal Behavior, Speech and Articulation, Mood, Affect, Thought, Perception, Cognition/Intelligence, Memory, and Orientation.)*

Client's General presentation: _____

Client's (subjective) experiences of current mental and physical health condition(s):
_____

Appearance

Attention to neatness: _____

Attention to dress/clothing: _____

    Bizarre appearance (not common for this population): _____

    Eccentric clothing? Muted clothing? _____

Is there any neglect of personal hygiene? (If so, is it due to dementia? Is psychomotor retardation present?) _____

Behavior

Client's attention to behavior: _____

Is there obvious agitation, irritability or anxiety? _____

Decreased activity? _____

Repetitive movements? _____

Movements

Is echopraxia present (imitation of the movements of others – e.g., crossing legs, touching face, etc.)? _____

Presence of fatigue, sedation, medication, intoxication? _____

Is there evidence of drug intoxication? _____

Is there a presence of catatonic symptoms? _____

Suicidal Behavior

Self-cutting or other NSSI? _____

Other suicidal behaviors or gestures? _____

Speech and Articulation

Dysarthria or mumbling? _____

Volume of speech: _____

Speed (rapid vs. retarded speech): _____

Pressure of speech? _____

Pitch (high vs. constant low-pitched): _____

Any language deficits? _____

Mood

    Is the client's mood:

        Elevated? Special notes: _____

        Expansive? Special notes: _____

        Depressed? Special notes: _____

        Apathetic? Special notes: _____

        Euthymic? Special notes: _____

Affect *(Assessed during the entire examination)*

    Incongruence (e.g., affective vs. mood): _____

    Internal feeling state: _____

    Observation of feeling: _____

    Are there any subtle changes in these observable feelings? _____

    Is there a lack of affect? _____

    Appropriate vs. inappropriate affect: _____

    Restricted vs. blunted affect: _____

Thought *(Can be observed through speech and reflected in the client's behavior)*

    What is the client's baseline of thought processes? (This can be assessed by allowing the client to speak openly and assessing whether there are periods when structured thoughts are interrupted.) _____

    How is the client's form of thought (arrangement of ideas and thoughts; observable disturbances in the rational link between ideas)? _____

    Could there be formal thought disorder? (Attempt to document quotes or examples in the client's life.) _____

    Thought content: Are there any preoccupations, obsessions or delusions? _____

    What is the client's ability to think abstractly? (Tips: pose abstract questions or use proverbs – e.g., "People in glass houses should not throw stones." What do you think that saying means?) _____

    How does the client use silence? _____

What is the client's tangentially (the ability to present with goal-directed associations of thought)? _____

Does client present with any: _____

    Flight of ideas? _____

    Incoherence? _____

    Illogicality (erroneous conclusions or internal contradictions in thinking)? _____

    Hypochondriasis? _____

    Preservation (repetitive expressions of a particular word or phrase) or echolalia (pathological repeating of words or phrases)? _____

    Neologisms (words that are invented by the speaker or distorted)? _____

Is there a presence of delusions (false beliefs that are sustained despite evidence to the contrary, often involving somatic, persecutory, or guilt aspects)? _____

    Any suicidal thoughts? _____

    Homicidal thoughts? _____

Perception (*Transferring physical stimulation into psychological information*)

    Is there any depersonalization and/or de-realization? _____

    Delusional mood? _____

    Presence of hallucinations? _____

    Heightened perception? _____

    Change in perception? _____

Cognition/Intelligence

    Client's ability to think and act rationally and logically: _____

    Intellectual functioning: _____

    Insight and judgment: _____

    Thinking and mental processes of knowing and becoming aware: _____

    Attention and concentration: _____

    State of consciousness: _____

    Clarity of language: _____

Any evidence of neurological disorders? _____

Evidence of chronic psychosis? _____

Memory

Can the client give a concise account of their life from the remote to the recent past?

_____

How is the client's immediate, recent/short-term, and remote memory? _____

_____

Any loss of memory? If so, specify cause: (1) Organic origin? (2) Dementia? (3) Head injury? (4) Amnestic disorder? _____

Orientation

Is the client aware of the current time (today's date, month, day of week, year), the person they are speaking to (examiner's name; ability to identify familiar people), the current place (city, state, place of evaluation, and situation (ability to recognize that they are being assessed evaluated, or interviewed)? _____

_____

_____

_____

_____

_____

_____

_____

Elderly Suicide Risk

Directions: If the client answers yes to three or more concerns on this checklist, a suicide inquiry (presence of any current ideation, intent, or plan) and/or suicide risk assessment is advised.

_____ Has there been any history of depression (diagnosed or undiagnosed), adjustment disorder, anxiety, or any other mental health diagnosis?

_____ Are there any other medical problems occurring (e.g., hypothyroidism, hyperthyroidism, Huntington's disease) that may mimic other mental health disorders?

_____ Has the client previously or recently been admitted to any type of skilled nursing facility for any reason (physical health or mental health)?

_____ Is the client lacking a strong social support system (children, family, friends, life partner, spouse)?

_____ Has there been any significant recent loss of a loved one?

_____ Is the client withdrawn from their facility, home or treatment community (participating in social activities)?

_____ Is the client currently being treated for any medical conditions? If so, how are these symptoms being managed (prescription medication, alternative medicines, over-the-counter medications)?

_____ Is there any history of prior suicide attempts or NSSI behavior?

_____ Is there any history of drug and/or alcohol abuse? Is there any current drug and/or alcohol use?

_____ Are there any current significant life events (loss of income, loss of home, identity concerns)?

_____ Does the client have access to medical care (insurance, service providers, mobile service providers)?

Assessing Depressive Symptoms in the Elderly

Directions: Use the guide below to inquire about depressive symptoms with your clients. If more than 10 of these symptoms are present, your client may be at risk for a major depressive disorder.

It's important to note that everyone exhibits some of these symptoms from time to time and it may not necessarily mean a person is depressed. Equally, not every person who is experiencing depression will have all of these symptoms. Additional information should always be gathered about any of these responses.

Behavior

- ☐ Not going out anymore
- ☐ Not getting things done at work/school
- ☐ Withdrawing from close family and friends
- ☐ Relying on alcohol and sedatives
- ☐ Not doing usual enjoyable activities
- ☐ Unable to concentrate

Feelings

- ☐ Overwhelmed
- ☐ Guilty
- ☐ Irritable
- ☐ Frustrated
- ☐ Lacking in confidence
- ☐ Unhappy
- ☐ Indecisive
- ☐ Disappointed
- ☐ Miserable
- ☐ Sad

Thoughts

- ☐ "I'm a failure"
- ☐ "It's my fault"
- ☐ "Nothing good ever happens to me"
- ☐ "I'm worthless"
- ☐ "Life's not worth living"
- ☐ "People would be better off without me"

Physical

- ☐ Tired all the time
- ☐ Sick and run down
- ☐ Headaches and muscle pains
- ☐ Churning gut
- ☐ Sleep problems
- ☐ Loss or change of appetite
- ☐ Significant weight loss or gain

VETERANS AND MILITARY PERSONNEL AND SUICIDE

Rates of completed suicide for military personnel have increased in the past decade and it has become a very serious concern for active duty military personnel as well as military veterans. Historically, suicide rates in the military have been lower than those found in the general population. However, with the wars in Iraq and Afghanistan, military suicide rates have been rising and surpassing the rates for the general/civilian population. Research has indicated that veterans account for 20% of deaths from suicide in United States. Veterans returning from Operation Iraqi Freedom, Operation Enduring Freedom, and Operation New Dawn are completing suicide at higher rates than previous cohorts of veterans.

In 2014, the Department of Defense reported 259 active-duty completed suicides and 1,034 active-duty attempts. Of these completed suicide attempts, 87 were personnel in the reserve components of the military and 133 were personnel in the National Guard. From 2009 to 2013, the number of completed suicides per year in the Army National Guard increased, rising from 48 completed suicides to 133 completed suicides.

Similar to the general population, firearms were reported to be the most common method (due to accessibility and availability) used in completed suicides, with the second most common being hanging. With respect to suicide attempts, drugs and/or alcohol were the most common method reported.

According to more recent research, women are, currently, the fastest-growing subgroup of U.S. veterans, and their numbers are expected to increase through to the late 2020s. This has resulted in an increase in the request for Veterans Administration Medical Center (VAMC) health care services by the women veterans of Operation Enduring Freedom and Operation Iraqi Freedom. Depression has been reported to be one of the three most common mental health diagnoses for women veterans receiving mental health services at the Department of Veterans Affairs (VA), with the other diagnoses being posttraumatic stress disorder (PTSD) and other anxiety-related disorders.

Research has indicated that suicide rates for male veterans are 1.4 times greater than the rates for males in the general population. Recent research has also shown that female military veterans complete suicide at nearly six times the rate of women in the general population. This rate is almost comparable to that of male military veterans. According to recent news articles and statistics released by Veterans Administration, more than 2,500 women who served in the military have completed suicide over the last 11 years. Women veterans aged 18 to 29 kill themselves at nearly 12 times the rate of civilians, and women veterans aged 18 to 34 are three times more likely than civilians to commit suicide. Research conducted in 2010 by the VA has reported that 40% of the female veterans completed suicide using firearms compared with 34% of women (civilian) in the general population.

Suicide Risk Factors for Veterans and Military Personnel

Veterans who have attempted suicide report acute or chronic stressors associated with deployment, the military environment, and combat intensity. They may report shame and/or guilt associated with the perception of failure and/or weakness. These stressors increase the risk of them developing various mental health conditions, including mood disorders, anxiety disorders, PTSD, and substance-related disorders.

Following interviews with the 1,034 military personnel who attempted suicide mentioned in the previous statistics, specific factors were identified as being related to their suicide efforts. These factors have been delineated in order of importance.

Relationship problems

Relationship problems can include interpersonal difficulties with fellow military personnel, marital problems, divorce, loss of a spouse or partner, infidelity, and a limited social support network.

Legal problems: Article 15 and/or court martial

Disciplinary procedures under Article 15 can lead to various consequences, including loss of pay, loss of rank, loss of position, loss of mobility, and the inability to be promoted. Members of the military may also face court martial.

Work-related and financial stress

These include stressors occurring in a combat zone or while stationed on a military base. Work stressors may include fear of failure, the inability to promote, compromised physical and/or mental ability, interpersonal difficulties, concern about work performance, and stress surrounding evaluations. Financial stress can be associated with loss of pay or rank, if being disciplined, or developing debt as a result of gambling problems or poor money management.

Loss of social support

This loss can include lack of social support, the loss of fallen comrades, loss of family support, death of loved ones not located in a combat zone, loss of camaraderie upon being discharged from service, and loss associated with being involuntarily discharged from service.

Stigma and help-seeking behaviors

Many military personnel under-report their mental health symptoms for fear of loss of promotion, removal from various job positions, loss of security clearances, and "being labeled" or even discharged from military service. Although mental health services are available to personnel, these services may not be widely used. As a result, many mental health disorders are untreated, thereby becoming more chronic and debilitating.

Perception of mental illness

Many military personnel are unaware of symptoms associated with various mental health conditions. Many report stereotypes associated with these perceptions and minimize their symptoms or misattribute their symptoms to other issues.

Ranks E1–E4 (junior enlisted service members)

Most individuals within these ranks are aged 18–24. They may present with limited coping abilities, a limited worldview, and limited problem-solving abilities. Research indicates that many military personnel experience distress during their formative years in service as they feel pressure to be promoted, experience performance anxiety, and are managing the stressors of combat, relationships, and adjusting to the military lifestyle.

Mental health diagnosis

During examination of the 1,034 military personnel who attempted suicide, many of the personnel received mental health diagnoses, including of mood disorders, anxiety disorders, PTSD, and substance-related disorders. Many of these disorders were previously undiagnosed and untreated.

Physical health condition

Military personnel reported concerns about revealing physical health problems, and bodily injuries were under-reported. Some of these service members also reported sustaining injuries that involved the loss of limbs or digits or other debilitating health conditions that could warrant medical discharge from military service.

Suicide and Female Veterans

There are several factors that are related to the increase of suicide rates among female veterans. One of these influences is related to the military and family identity. Research has demonstrated that, typically, men and women who join the military are more likely to have endured difficult childhoods, including emotional and sexual abuse. This history of abuse is believed to leave some military personnel predisposed to certain variables while in service, as it has been hypothesized that these wounds are either triggered or aggravated by the conditions of the military environment.

Interpersonal relationships may not be healthy, specifically in dual military marriages and relationships. This certainly holds true if both people have been deployed and are experiencing difficulty reintegrating into a non-combat zone, if both are experiencing symptoms of PTSD or any other mental health concern that has not yet received attention or treatment, or if both are under job-related stress. If children are involved, this may further complicate relationships. Divorce rates are higher for women in the military than women in the general population.

Another, significant, concern for women veterans involves camaraderie, belongingness, and a sense of purpose. Historically, these relationships have been nurtured and encouraged for men in the military but not for women. Some women report that they face discrimination while in service and are not treated equally to their male counterparts. They may not attain this sense of purpose or "brotherhood," which may lead to feelings of helplessness, feelings of isolation, and/or other serious mental health issues.

Family reintegration has been a reported feature for those women who have attempted suicide. These veterans reported experiencing major difficulties when attempting to acclimate into the "civilian world" or even upon return from prolonged deployments. They reported a lack of social support and understanding from friends and relatives and feeling misunderstood and at times minimized when discussing their concerns. This leads to hesitation in sharing concerns such as symptoms of PTSD or depression, meaning these issues continue to worsen due to remaining untreated. Family functioning and adjustment have been described as stressful, particularly if the veteran is a parent or spouse. When a member of the military is deployed for 1–2 years, their spouses and families must continue managing their lives. Certain household roles are developed and the home is functioning on a "schedule" that has been working for a prolonged period without the veteran. The veteran returns home and may have expectations about how things "will be" or "should be" and discovers that they no longer know their role in the family. It may be difficult to join this family system that has learned to survive and thrive in their absence. This could also lead to feelings of isolation, abandonment, and withdrawal and to feeling minimized and dismissed. The veteran may feel detached from their family, which may cause other communication and interpersonal problems within the family unit. A veteran may also have various roles in relation to various family members and feel as if they are being "pulled in 50 directions at once." This can be overwhelming and, if coping mechanisms have been compromised as a result of prior deployments or work stressors, decompensation is more likely to occur.

Domestic violence is another factor that has been highly correlated with female veterans and suicide attempts. Research has indicated that women veterans and service members are three times more likely than non-veterans to experience domestic violence. It has been found that 39% of women veterans and 30–44% of active-duty women report experiencing domestic violence in their relationships, and married service member and civilian men with active duty-wives lodge more than 2,500 reports each year, which is an average of seven complaints per day.

Military sexual trauma (MST) has also been linked to the increased rate of suicide among female veterans. MST is the term that the VA uses to refer to sexual assault or repeated threatening sexual harassment that occurs while the veteran is in the military. It is defined as "psychological trauma, which in the judgment of a VA mental health professional, resulted from a physical assault of a sexual nature, battery of a sexual nature, or sexual harassment which occurred while the veteran was serving on active duty or active duty for training." MST can occur on and/ or off base, and while a service member is on or off duty. Perpetrators can be men or women, military personnel or civilians, or superiors or subordinates in the chain of command. Even though MST can happen to both males and females, women report MST more often than men, and most inpatient client treatment facilities within the VA that address this concern are for women only.

Examples of Military Sexual Trauma

- Being threatened for refusing to cooperate
- Promotions for sexual favors
- Sexual activity without the ability to consent
- Sexual assault
- Unwanted sexual advances
- Sexual coercion
- Verbal harassment

Problems may not surface until months or years after the MST occurred, and sometimes not until after a veteran has left military service. Some symptoms of MST include reactive emotions, feelings of numbness, sleeping problems (intermittent insomnia or hypersomnia, initial insomnia), difficulty with focus and attention, alcohol and/or drug abuse, hypervigilance and paranoia, relationship difficulties, and physical health problems.

These symptoms can be exacerbated due to unique factors associated with MST and typically lead to the development of PTSD. Some of these factors include continuing to live or work with the perpetrator, and even relying on them for essential things such as food, health care, or safety. The veteran may harbor concerns about damaging cohesion in the unit if the perpetrator is in the same unit or concerns about appearing weak or vulnerable, and they may ruminate about keeping the respect of others. A victim may remain fearful that the discovery of the event will negatively affect their career or chances for promotion.

Other psychosocial factors that have been correlated with female veterans and suicide include homelessness, poverty, and unemployment. Poor veterans are more likely to become homeless and, although women veterans are generally more educated than male veterans, women veterans generally earn less than male veterans and are often paid less than the pay they received in the military. Research has indicated that, between 2010 and 2014, the number of homeless women veterans increased by 50% (3,328 in 2010 to 4,993 in 2014). Veteran women are also reported to be three to four times at greater risk of homelessness than non-veteran women. A high number of homeless women veterans also have a history of MST or other untreated mental health concerns, including PTSD, depression, anxiety, and substance abuse.

MENTAL HEALTH DISORDERS AND MILITARY PERSONNEL

The risks for suicide and mental health disorders for military personnel are similar to those in the general population. Suicide risk is increased if one has been diagnosed with any of the following mental health diagnoses: major depression, dysthymia, and bipolar disorder. Although adjustment disorders are not typically associated with increased suicide risk, this diagnosis presents with more significance when assigned to military personnel and veterans. Adjustment difficulties can be associated with various stressors, including the risk factors identified above; thus, this diagnosis should be closely monitored and suicidal ideation, intent, and planning should be assessed.

Research indicates that PTSD has been diagnosed in 5%–25% of returning veterans who served in Operation Iraqi Freedom, Operation Enduring Freedom, and Operation New Dawn. There is a significant relationship between PTSD and completed suicides. The severity of PTSD symptoms is also a significant predictor of completed suicides. Research has also indicated that the DSM-5 criterion B of PTSD (re-experiencing, flashbacks, and nightmares) is highly correlated with suicidal ideation, intent, planning, and suicide attempts. Women who have been physically injured during active duty are more likely to report PTSD symptoms.

There is also a high co-morbidity of mental health issues and substance abuse among Iraq and Afghanistan veterans, and men are twice as likely as women to report substance use disorders. Most veterans reported substance abuse as a result of attempting to manage their symptoms of PTSD and other mental health symptoms. They described self-medicating in order to "make the dreams stop" or "make the thoughts go away," or to attain sleep. They also reported that using substances helped to better manage their re-experiencing symptoms of PTSD. Abusing substances exacerbates any other mental health symptoms and significantly affects decision making and impulse control.

Another factor that has led to the increase in suicide attempts among this population is an unwillingness to seek mental health services. This resistance is typically related to mistrust of the VA and mental health care providers and is a result of the stigma associated with mental health concerns. Women victims of MST have reported avoiding the mostly "male-dominated" VAMC clinics. Women veterans are also less likely to identify themselves as veterans, as they may choose to distance themselves from their service period as a result of the experienced trauma.

TRAUMATIC BRAIN INJURY AND SUICIDE RISK

Traumatic brain injury (TBI) has been found to be related to increased risk of suicidal ideation, attempts, and completed suicides in the general population and military personnel. Individuals in the general population and military personnel who have been diagnosed with a TBI are three to four times more likely to commit suicide when compared to those who have not been diagnosed with TBI. Around 80% of military-related TBIs are considered of mild severity, and symptoms of this type of TBI are difficult to distinguish from symptoms of PTSD. Research indicates that 15%–23% of veterans returning from Operation Iraqi Freedom and Operation Enduring Freedom have reported incurring a mild TBI.

Suicide Prevention in Veterans and Military Personnel

Clay Hunt Suicide Prevention Act

This act was imparted as a consequence of a veteran suicide, that could have possibly been prevented if he were able to receive his VA benefits and mental health treatment in a more timely manner. He was provided a diagnosis of posttraumatic stress disorder, but remained unable to procure the necessary benefits and treatment. He subsequently completed suicide in 2011.

The Clay Hunt Act was passed in February 2015. It is intended to aid veterans suffering from mental health problems such as PTSD, anxiety disorders, mood disorders, and/or substance use disorders. It has been developed to help advance the VA's mental health care programs and suicide prevention programs. This law was intended to expand suicide prevention programs at the VA in the following ways:

- Accessibility to mental health services by generating peer support programs and community outreach experimental programs to aid transitioning service members.
- Creating a one-stop, collaborative website of accessible resources.
- Meeting the demand for mental health care by enhancing recruitment of psychiatry services staff by way of implementing a pilot program to repay the loan debt services.
- Mandating collaboration on suicide prevention efforts amongst the VA and other non-profit mental health organizations.
- Enhancing the accountability of mental health care by necessitating an annual assessment of VA mental health and suicide prevention programs.

Education

This involves educating returning veterans, military service personnel, family members, employers, and the general public about veteran concerns and mental health issues. Employers should be provided with training and understanding of various diagnoses including PTSD, depression, and anxiety in order to better manage these individuals and to have insight into various mannerisms and behaviors they may present. Family members are often unaware of the changes their loved ones may present and they do not understand why the family member may be distant or aloof, and they may not understand the suicide risk associated with certain mental health disorders or symptoms.

Acknowledging and recognizing subtle signs

Some symptoms of PTSD may not be as blatant as others and many times veterans minimize the severity of their symptoms. It is important to conduct a thorough clinical interview and establish rapport with the veteran in order to better assess these symptoms. Subtle symptoms of PTSD can be found in the checklist provided at the end of this section.

Availability/Accessibility of services

Accessibility is a key component to providing services to this population. Veterans at times, have difficulty procuring services, for a variety of reasons including lack of health care services, lack of service coordination, discharge status and lack of family support. Telehealth has been successfully implemented with this population, allowing hospitals and other mental health treatment agencies to reach veterans located in rural areas or who are physically unable to attend in-person appointments.

Attempting to provide holistic care

Aiming to provide holistic care to this population allows for many needs to be addressed including employment needs, financial needs, and mental, physical and spiritual health needs. This can be incorporated into treatment by way of consulting with various agencies in your community that provide these services. Awareness of resources in your area is a **MUST** when working with this population.

PTSD Symptom Checklist

Directions: Please choose the statement(s) that best describe your state of mind.

_____ Feeling upset by things that remind you of what happened

_____ Having nightmares, vivid memories, or flashbacks of the event that make you feel like it's happening all over again

_____ Feeling emotionally cut off from others

_____ Feeling numb or losing interest in things you used to care about

_____ Becoming depressed

_____ Thinking that you are always in danger

_____ Feeling anxious, jittery, or irritated

_____ Experiencing a sense of panic that something bad is about to happen

_____ Having difficulty sleeping

_____ Having trouble keeping your mind on one thing

_____ Having a hard time relating to and getting along with your spouse, family, or friends

_____ Frequently avoiding places or things that remind you of what happened

_____ Consistent drinking or use of drugs to numb your feelings

_____ Considering harming yourself or others

_____ Working all the time to occupy your mind

_____ Pulling away from other people and becoming isolated

Clinician Worksheet
___

Subtle Symptoms of PTSD

Directions: Remember, your clients may not report DIRECT symptoms of PTSD during an initial interview. The following list includes more subtle indicators that PTSD MAY be present. Please use the list below to guide your clinical interview when gathering information about a potential PTSD diagnosis.

_____ Remaining withdrawn from family and friends

_____ Avoidance of conversations about the event/avoidance of discussing reactions to the event

_____ Emotional numbness

_____ Lack of empathy

_____ Difficulty focusing and/or concentrating

_____ Short-term memory deficits

_____ Being easily distracted

_____ Avoidance of conflict at home and/or at work

_____ Decrease or increase in libido

_____ Emotional detachment

_____ Denial of any problems

_____ Difficulty establishing and/or maintaining relationships with others

_____ Interpersonal difficulty

Veteran Suicide Risk Checklist

If your client answers yes to three or more concerns on this checklist (excluding the social support question), a suicide inquiry (presence of any current ideation, intent or plan) and/or possible suicide risk assessment is advised.

_____ Has there been any prior diagnosis of PTSD, depression, anxiety or other mental health condition? Are these symptoms currently active?

_____ Is the veteran reporting flashback, nightmares, and intrusive ideation as being primary if symptoms are active?

_____ Has the veteran been recently discharged from service? Was this discharge honorable, other than honorable, etc.? Was the discharge voluntary or involuntary? Is the veteran service member connected with the VA or receiving mental health services?

_____ Does the veteran have a strong social support network? Married? Children? Other family members?

_____ Has the veteran experienced any traumatic bodily injuries? Loss of Limbs? TBI?

_____ Is the veteran currently employed? Actively seeking employment? Any current educational pursuits?

_____ Is there any history of MST? Any treatment? Has this issue been reported?

_____ Any history of prior suicide attempts or NSSI behavior?

_____ Any history of drug and alcohol abuse? Any current drug or alcohol use?

_____ Is the veteran experiencing any current legal problems or other psychosocial issues (e.g., homelessness)?

LGBTQI POPULATION AND SUICIDE

There are specific concerns for the LGBTQI community when discussing suicide prevention. While acceptance and tolerance have improved over the last few decades, discrimination still exists and can cause feelings of isolation and hopelessness, which are all major contributors to feelings of suicide. Recent studies have shown higher rates of suicide completions and attempts within the LGBTQI community, hypothesized to be linked to the history of oppression and discrimination experienced by LGBTQI individuals.

Research has indicated that there is a lack of knowledge or information about suicide **DEATHS** among the LGBTQI population, and that there is more data available about suicide **ATTEMPTS.** The majority of information and research available about suicide attempts and this population describe individuals between the ages of 15–24, as suicide rates are higher for LGBTQI youth and young adults.

Statistics show a four-times higher rate of suicide attempts among gay and bisexual adolescents and adult males compared to heterosexual males. Suicide attempts occur twice as often among lesbian and bisexual adolescents and adult females than heterosexual females. Transgendered individuals report markedly higher rates of suicide attempts when compared to lesbian, gay, bisexual, questioning and intersex groups.

Suicide Risk Factors for LGBTQI Individuals

Being LGBTQI **DOES NOT** automatically increase your suicide risk. There are several factors related to sexual orientation that affect suicidality. Stigma, prejudice and discrimination have been associated with elevated risk of suicide attempts and completed suicides, and completed suicides have been highly correlated with rejection, harassment and discrimination. High rates of suicide attempts have also been positively correlated with severe family rejection, peer rejection, and victimization, as 1 in 7 individuals reported experiencing physical attacks and bullying and three-quarters of individuals who attempted suicide reported experiencing verbal abuse.

Abuse

Bullying is a form of verbal, physical or even sexual abuse. When abuse is present it always invokes feelings of depression, helplessness, guilt, shame and hopelessness that can cause suicidal ideation. Coming out or "being outed" may create an actual fear of being "gay-bashed," physically and sexually assaulted, and becoming victims of hate crimes.

Bullying

Research shows that LGBTQI youth report higher rates of anti-LGBTQI harassment and bullying than straight youth. But not every person who is the target of anti-LGBTQI bullying is LGBTQI. Many of these tweens and teens who are bullied are targeted because of their perceived sexual orientation or because they do not conform to someone's expectations about gender.

The relationship between bullying and suicide is very complex. Research has shown that persistent bullying can cause or enhance feelings of isolation, despair, rejection, and exclusion, as well as symptoms of depression and anxiety, which can contribute to suicidal behavior. However, we must note that the large majority of people who experience bullying DO NOT become suicidal.

This idea that people, who are bullied attempt suicide, suggest that suicide is a natural response to bullying. This misconception can lead the media to highlight details that could increase contagion risk. If at-risk individuals see their own experiences of bullying, isolation or exclusion reflected in stories of those who have died, they may be more likely to think of suicide as a solution to their current problems.

Anxiety of coming-out

Many adolescents and even adults fear expressing their true sexual orientation or gender identity, mainly because of their concerns and fears about how family, friends and religious communities will react. Hiding, avoiding or ignoring these true feelings and identity can cause feelings of isolation, helplessness, sadness, guilt, shame and hopelessness. Even for those who are mostly "out," they continue to feel the need to remain hidden in other aspects of their lives, such as work or with particular friends or family members. There is an ever present fear of losing familial support, especially in cultures where the familial unit is collective or cultures wherein same-sex relationships are less accepted. Specifically, teenagers have additional challenges when it comes to exploring and articulating their sexual identity. Many LGBTQI youths remain concerned about others knowing their sexual preference. They may also be concerned about ridicule, threats, and being hassled by their peers, whether this occurs face to face or using a social media platform.

Fear of rejection

Some members of this community may experience sudden rejection when they come out to friends or loved ones. Friends and family may, initially, reject them, and some even experience a complete loss of a social support network. For some, this experience has been described as traumatic and can cause lasting and significant psychological and affective injury.

Domestic violence

Research has indicated that same-sex domestic violence often goes largely ignored by the justice system, and health care providers. Historically, this issue has been minimized. Without adequate resources and education, the survivors of LGBTQI domestic violence continue to live in isolation where they continue to endure emotional, mental, sexual and physical abuse in silence. This issue may be further complicated if the victim is "closeted." This issue may lead to feelings of sadness, helplessness, hopelessness, shame, guilt, worthlessness and developing a sense of learned helplessness about their situation. If the person feels trapped in this situation, then suicide may appear to be a viable option.

Mental health

LGBTQI individuals also report a higher prevalence of developing mental health disorders including depression, anxiety and substance use disorders. These disorders are reported to be 1.5 times more common among this population. Depressive and anxiety symptoms are reported to be more prevalent among gay and bisexual males and completed suicide rates are highest among males in the gay, bisexual, transgender, and questioning and intersex population. Substance abuse symptoms have been reported more frequently among lesbian and bisexual females.

Suicide Prevention in the LGBTQI Population

Systemic approach

A systemic approach is a must when working with this community, as most of the stressors experienced are extraneous and involve interactions with family, friends, and loved ones. Identity development research has indicated that after the age of 24, suicide rates for this population significantly decline and the highest risk involves adolescents. Family systems theory explains that in order to best assist the referred client, the system in which they function must also be addressed and treated.

Education of cultural competence

Cultural competence is ethically and clinically warranted when working with any group. However, if you are unfamiliar with the culture of this population it is critical to educate yourself and request assistance from your client in teaching you about how "they" navigate this culture. You cannot make broad speculations about the individual needs of your client based on general information about a specific group. When attempting to understand your client and when developing treatment plans, you must take several factors into consideration to include: individual differences, worldview, life experiences and current life factors.

Referrals to programs to promote inclusiveness

Group therapy is an extremely effective modality of treatment to utilize with this population. Individuals participating in the group can observe and interact with others who are experiencing similar challenges, which can help them feel less alone. By observing someone successfully coping with a similar issue, other members of the group can see that there is hope. As each person progresses in treatment and their situation improves they may possibly serve as a role model or support figure for others, which can help promote feelings of success and accomplishment. A group setting also permits members to freely express themselves and practice healthier and more adaptive behaviors within the safety and security of the group.

Support groups can be found online as well as in vivo. If you reside in a more rural area, online support groups may be a great way to help your clients progress in treatment. Prior to recommending a group format to any client, the mental health professional should be familiar with the group or assist their clients in researching an appropriate group to join.

Training and education

Training and education are significant factors in becoming more knowledgeable and skillful clinicians. Education can take place in various venues, including the therapy room. Clients appreciate you asking questions, instead of pretending to "get it," and they appreciate genuine interest in understanding more about who they are and their worldview. You also need to be aware of any specific standards of care to follow when treating certain clients. For instance, the Harry Benjamin Standards of Care are intended to provide flexible directions for the treatment of gender dysphoric disorder. Details of these standards can be found on the World Professional Association for Transgender Health website (http://www.wpath.org/).

LGBTQI Suicide Risk Checklist

Directions: If your client answers yes to three or more concerns on this checklist (excluding drug or alcohol use question), a suicide inquiry (presence of any current ideation, intent or plan) and/or possible suicide risk assessment is advised.

_____ Has there been any prior diagnosis of, depression, anxiety or other mental health condition? Are these symptoms currently active? Are these symptoms being currently treated with medication or therapy?

_____ Has the client reported any current bullying behaviors or being ostracized by others? Family rejection? Peer rejection?

_____ Has the client revealed their sexual orientation to friends or family? What were their reactions? Supportive? Non-supportive?

_____ Is there any guilt or shame being experienced that is associated with religious practices?

_____ Any history of prior suicide attempts or NSSI behavior?

_____ Any history of drug or alcohol use?

_____ Does the client have a strong social support network?

COLLEGE STUDENT POPULATION AND SUICIDE

Suicide is the second leading cause of death for college students. The primary cause for suicide attempts and completed suicides has been attributed to **untreated and undiagnosed depression.** College can be a difficult transition period for many students. Research has indicated that 1 in 5 college students believe that their depression level is increased, yet only 6% would seek assistance. Male students (ages 18 to 24) are more than twice as likely as female students to have died by suicide. 18% of undergraduates reported having suicidal ideation at some point, while 6% reported suicidal ideation in the past 12 months. 1 in 12 U.S. college students has made a suicide plan. The National College Health Risk Behavior Study found that 11.4% of students seriously consider attempting suicide. About 12 young people aged 15–24 will commit suicide today and one person under the age of 25 commits suicide within every 2 ½ hours. Non-traditional (25 and older) are at higher risk for suicide. This statistic has been attributed to other stressors to include financial pressures, pre-existing mental health disorder, lack of family support, and difficulty adjusting.

Suicide Risk Factors for College Students

There are certain variables that increase a college student's risk for suicide and when these factors are present, a suicide risk assessment is advised in order to be proactive in the prevention of suicide. Some of these risk factors include, having a history of past suicide attempts and/or non-suicidal self-injury (NSSI) behaviors. Risk is also elevated when there is a history of mental health diagnosis or a current mental health diagnosis. The most common mental health diagnoses among college students are depression and anxiety. Impulsivity is also a risk factor. Impulsivity can affect decision making and judgment and is further exacerbated when there is use of alcohol and drugs. Binge drinking has been reported to be highly correlated with suicide attempts on college campuses. Students who are solitary binge drinkers are more than four times as likely to have made previous suicide attempts. These individuals also present with a limited worldview and experience with problem-solving skills, which makes tunnel vision more likely to occur when assessing their current situation and thus increases the risk for suicide.

Depression

College is a stressful environment for most young people, therefore it's especially important for parents, friends, faculty, and counselors to get involved if they suspect a student is suffering from depression. Students themselves are often reluctant to seek help due to social stigmas related to depression and may not be aware that they are experiencing symptoms of depression. They may attribute these symptoms to "homesickness" or difficulty adjusting to a new environment. A mental health evaluation that encompasses a student's developmental and family history, school performance, and any self-injurious behaviors should be performed to evaluate at-risk students before a treatment plan is made.

Research has indicated that the best treatments for college-aged students suffering from depression are usually a combination of antidepressant medications and talk therapies such as cognitive-behavioral therapy and interpersonal psychotherapy. Depressed students are also more likely to benefit from exercise, eating a healthy diet, and getting enough rest than many other groups.

Other risk factors

Stressful life events can increase risk for suicide in this population. This event can include receiving failing grades, a break-up with a significant other, death of a loved one, date rape, pledging a sorority or fraternity, or financial troubles. Some research has shown that some college students are even dealing with homelessness while attempting to manage their classes and workload.

Natural disasters are another type of stressful event. While I was attending graduate school in Knoxville, Tennessee, I was privileged to be the treating therapist of a young woman, who was a Hurricane Katrina evacuee. She was attending a public university in New Orleans and had been provided the opportunity to attend another public university to complete her educational pursuits until her school was able to reopen. Her presenting complaint was adjustment difficulties and academic concerns. She was residing in the area alone and her other family members were dispersed across various states. She was reporting difficulty acclimating to the culture (Appalachian mountain culture vs. New Orleans culture), being away from home, relationship problems, and a variety of other concerns. The sudden nature of this disaster changed her entire life situation and she was "forced" to adapt and adjust and perform well academically under these conditions.

Suicide Prevention in College Students

Resources

Knowing your local community resources is of benefit when treating this population. Some college students may not seek mental health services on their college campuses and may prefer to seek off-campus mental health professionals. College students also have varying needs and concerns including financial, family concerns, health concerns, spirituality concerns and sexuality concerns. It is important to know resources that can assist with these various areas when warranted.

College counseling centers

College or university counseling centers provide mental health and other services within a university or college environment. The need for these services is critical given the current climate on college campuses. Research has indicated that counseling center directors and other student affairs personnel have reported increases in the mental health needs of college students, as issues like eating disorders, alcohol and drug abuse/dependence, depression/anxiety, suicidality, and sexual assault have become more prevalent in this environment.

College counseling centers generally offer an array of services including individual and group counseling, psycho-educational assessments, alcohol and other drug counseling/evaluation, crisis assistance, campus outreach programs, consultative services, and graduate student training. Although services typically target mental health problems (e.g., eating disorders, adjustment, anxiety, depression), students also use these services to enrich other areas of their life, including relationships, career/vocational choices, academic and athletic performance, and exploring psychological strengths (positive psychology).

By incorporating campus outreach programs, mental health services can be destigmatized by allowing staff at a counseling center to mingle among the students on their turf and in their comfort zone. For example, when I interned at the University of Houston Counseling and Psychological Services Center, we celebrated "National Anxiety Awareness Day." We set up a booth in the court of the University Center "quad area" during high traffic hours (noon until around 2 o'clock or so) and we provided pizza (college students love FREE food!) and all kinds of FREE gear that advertised our services (stress balls, cups, pens, sticky pads, pencils). We also invited students to take a Beck Anxiety Inventory and encouraged them to procure their results at our center. This event allowed us to share information about anxiety and its impact on academic performance, relationships, friendships and daily functioning as well as the opportunity to normalize some of these problems for the students. It was very well received by the students and, did in fact, contribute to more students being aware of the counseling center and utilizing its services.

Education

The primary cause of suicide among this population is **UNDIAGNOSED** depression. This is due to several factors, primarily lack of education or knowledge about depression and other mental health issues. Symptoms of depression can occur during an adjustment period; it could present as homesickness or "just feeling blah." Most people believe that these symptoms are "normal and will pass once they get used to things." What they do not understand is that *severity* and *chronicity* are very important factors to consider when experiencing these types of symptoms. This kind of understanding can only occur by way of educating college students about these issues. This information giving could be providing educational pamphlets, town hall meetings in the dormitories, outreach programs, or educating and encouraging resident assistants (or any personnel) about the "red flags" of suicide and other mental health symptoms.

The QPR (Question, Persuade and Refer) program has been effectively implemented on college campuses for several years. It is a program that has been developed to be utilized by lay people as well as mental health professionals. This program is an emergency mental health intervention for suicidal persons created in 1995 by Paul Quinnett. The intent is also to identify and interrupt the crisis and direct that person to the proper care. This training is available for individuals, groups, and mental health professionals.

Clinician Worksheet

College Students
Suicide Risk Checklist

Directions: If your client answers yes to three or more concerns on this checklist (excluding social support question), a suicide inquiry (presence of any current ideation, intent or plan) and/or possible suicide risk assessment is advised.

_____ Has there been any prior diagnosis of depression, anxiety or other mental health condition? Are these symptoms currently active? Are these symptoms currently being treated with medication or therapy?

_____ Has the client reported a precipitating event (recent break-up, failing grades, financial concerns, loss of a loved one)?

_____ What is their affective responsiveness to this event? Are they coping? Is affect incongruent? Dysthymic?

_____ Have there been any significant changes in behavior (isolating themselves, withdrawn, acting out behaviors, increased drug or alcohol use)?

_____ Any history of prior suicide attempts or NSSI behavior?

_____ Any history of drug and alcohol abuse? Any current drug or alcohol use?

_____ Does the client have a strong social support network?

_____ Does the client report familial pressures?

_____ Does the client report adjustment difficulties?

_____ Has the client reported any prior or current incidences of date rape, or being involved in hazing practices with various organizations on campus? Have these issues been reported to the appropriate authorities?

ADOLESCENT POPULATION AND SUICIDE

Suicide among adolescents continues to be a major concern in the United States. Each year, thousands of teenagers complete suicide, making suicide the third leading cause of death for 15- to 24-year-olds. At least 25 attempts are made for every one completed teen suicide and nearly 60% of all adolescent suicides in the United States are committed with a gun, followed by drug overdose. Girls are reported to experience suicidal ideation and attempt suicide about twice as often as boys. Females: typically, complete suicide by overdosing or cutting. Males: typically, complete suicide by firearms, hanging, or jumping from heights.

Some teenagers experience intense feelings of pressure, misunderstanding, uncertainty, pressure to succeed, financial uncertainty, and other fears while growing up. For some teenagers, divorce, the formation of a new family with step-parents and step-siblings, or moving to a new community can be very unsettling and can intensify these self-doubts. A lot of these stressors are usually out of their control and thus they may experience feelings of sadness, hopelessness, helplessness, worthlessness, guilt, shame and other symptoms of depression and anxiety. Given this sense of helplessness or hopelessness about their current situation suicide may appear to be a solution to their problems and stress.

Suicide Risk Factors for Adolescents

There are several risk factors that are specific for adolescents. These risk factors should be monitored for the duration of treatment. Some of these risk factors include the presence of psychological disorders, especially depression, bipolar disorder, alcohol use as well as illicit and prescription drug abuse. Previous suicide attempts are associated with increased suicide risk. Some adolescents may present with sexuality or gender identity concerns, which is reported to be a risk factor. A history of physical, emotional, sexual and mental abuse may be present and should be assessed in addition to the adequacy of the social/family support network. The client may be experiencing disciplinary problems at school and in the home. And there could possibly be an extensive history of being the victim or perpetrator of bullying.

A teenager who is planning to commit suicide may also:

- Complain of being a bad person or feeling horrible and terrible on the inside.
- Provide verbal clues with statements such as: "I won't be a problem for you or anyone else for much longer," or "Nothing matters, I am useless," and "You don't have to worry about dealing with me anymore."
- They may give away favorite possessions, clean their room, throw away important belongings, etc.
- Suddenly become elated and happy following a period of depression.

Bullying

Bullying is defined as the demonstration of behaviors that make someone else feel inadequate, or focus on belittling someone else. Research has indicated that over 3.2 million students are victims of bullying each year. Approximately 160,000 teens skip school every day because of bullying and 7% of American student's report being bullied 2 to 3 times a month or more within a school semester.

Bullying can include harassment, physical harm, repeatedly demeaning speech and efforts to ostracize another person. Bullying is active, and is done with the intention of bringing another person down. It is important to realize that there are different kinds of bullying:

Physical bullying

This is the most obvious form of bullying. This type of bullying, involves the initiator attempting to physically control the other. This can look like kicking, punching and other physically abusive activities that are intended to impart terror in the one bullied, or to possibly pressure him or her to do something. Physical bullying increases in elementary school, peaks in middle school and declines in high school. Verbal abuse, on the other hand, remains constant.

Emotional bullying

This is a very subtle form of bullying. These methods aim at getting someone else to feel isolated, alone and may even prompt depression. This type of bullying is designed to get others to ostracize the person being bullied. This form of bullying typically involves females and has been conceptualized as female relational aggression.

Author, Rachel Simmons explores female relational aggression (also known as covert aggression or covert bullying) in her book *Odd Girl Out*. This is a type of aggression in which harm is caused to another by damaging their relationships or social status. It has long-lasting effects on relationships, self-esteem, self-worth, and the ability to navigate healthy relationships with others.

The peak of this type of bullying typically occurs during a sensitive period when intimate and close relationships involving trust, bonding, and self-image are forming.

Potential Components of Relational Aggression

- Being unexpectedly ousted from a "friend group"
- Being ignored by a group of friends
- Not being invited to a party that everyone else is attending
- Having rumors spread about you
- Someone posting derogatory images of you online
- No one liking your pictures on Instagram
- Having someone post negative or demeaning comments about you on a social media outlet

The cyber age has provided a breeding ground for this type of aggression, and our clients can be bombarded daily with negative comments, images or untruths about themselves.

For example, since being ostracized from her "friend group," a teenage client has been addicted to Instagram. She stated, "I know it's not good for me to look at it, but I can't help it. I can at least see what they are doing, and I can at least know if they are having fun or not. I look to make sure other people don't "like" their pics on there. I feel like if people don't like their pictures, it will make me feel better. And that's all I want; to feel better about what they did to me."

Another client taught me that her self-worth was associated with her "likes" on her Facebook page. She reported that her moods were contingent on these "likes," and when a post was not liked she would even make changes to her image or how she might word a comment.

Because this type of aggression is covert, others may be oblivious that it is happening. Some children may even deny being victimized due to embarrassment, their desire to preserve their friendship with the aggressor, or fear of reprisal.

There are various websites that promote these types of unhealthy behaviors and as treating clinicians we must be aware of these websites and the effects these sites have on our clients' well-being. Social media has allowed everyone, both brave and cowardly, to have a platform to denigrate and ostracize others. A list of some of the more popular websites has been provided below. Please remain aware that this list can change and in order to stay current on this information, we must engage in discussions with our clients and continue to educate ourselves about this platform of communication.

Social Websites Potentially Used as Bullying Forums

- Yik Yak
- Whisper
- Secrets
- Ask.Fm.com (can be linked to Instagram)
- ChatRoulette.com
- KIK (App for smartphone)
- KEEK (App for smartphone)
- Chat for Omegle (for smartphone)

Verbal bullying
Verbal bullying involves using demeaning language to tear down another's self-image. Bullies who use verbal techniques unreasonably tease others, make belittling statements and use a lot of mockery with the intent to hurt the other person's feelings or humiliate the person in front of other people.

Cyber-bullying
Electronic bullying, using social media outlets, is becoming a very real and chronic problem for adolescents. This type of bullying involves instant messaging, text messages and online social networks to embarrass and shame others. This type of bullying can lead to learned helplessness, as one feels that they are not safe at school or online!

Suicide Prevention and Adolescents: Systemic Approach

Working with adolescents requires working within the family system. At times many of our adolescent clients have been given the "scapegoat" role in their families. As our client's symptomology improves, the dynamics in the household will also change, thereby disrupting the family system. It is critical to involve family members as much as possible in the treatment of our clients to help ensure changes remain constant and continue to improve. Family and social support are important variables to include when working with clients and should be incorporated when possible. Suicide and other self-destructive behaviors can be scary situations for parents, caretakers and loved ones to manage. Part of our job is to provide hope and guidance to these family members and direct them accordingly when attempting to manage these behaviors.

Education and Accessibility to Mental Health Resources

Educating all of those who may have contact with an adolescent is another key component in prevention of suicide. We never know with whom an adolescent may connect. Teachers are with these youths on a recurring basis and need to have the ability to identify "red flags" and understand how to better assess for suicidal inclinations and how to refer to the appropriate resources. There are several formats in which this type of education/training can occur.

School gatekeeper training is a type of program that can be designed to help school staff (e.g., teachers, counselors, and coaches) identify and refer students at risk for suicide. These programs also impart school personnel with skills on how to respond to suicide or other crises in the school.

Education and Mental Health Resources for Adolescents

- **Community gatekeeper training** are programs that train individuals in the community who have frequent contact with adolescents and medical health care providers to recognize and refer persons in this age group who are at risk for suicide.
- **General suicide education** incorporates students learning about suicide, warning signs, and how to seek help for themselves or others. These programs often integrate an assortment of activities that help advance self-esteem and social capacity.
- **Screening programs** can also be incorporated wherein a questionnaire or other screening instruments can be adapted to help identify high-risk adolescents and provide further assessment and treatment. Recurring assessments can help measure variations in attitudes or behaviors over time, to confirm or disconfirm effectiveness of a prevention strategy, and to identify continuing suicidal behavior.
- **Peer support programs** can occur in or outside of a school and are intended to cultivate peer relations and know-how in social skills amid high-risk youths.
- **Crisis centers and hotlines** involve qualified volunteers and paid staff who provide mobile counseling and other services for persons articulating suicidal ideation, intent or plan. These programs may also offer a type of walk-in crisis center and referral to mental health services.
- **Suicide survivor groups** comprise programs that focus on friends and relatives of individuals who have completed suicide. These types of programs are two-fold. They are designed to help avert or contain suicide clusters from happening and to help youths efficiently manage feelings of loss that occur subsequent to the sudden death or suicide of a peer.

Support and Openness

Support and acceptance are critical factors to consider when working with this population. Support can look like various things including familial support, peer support, support from counselors, teachers and therapists.

We are functioning in an age wherein technology is used in every facet of our lives. Incorporating technology and the use of the internet into your client's treatment plan is not only allowing you to use the most up-to-date resources, but it also allows you to meet your client where they are functioning and to take advantage of using a modality of communication that is the most relevant. There are several online suicide support groups for teens and adolescents. These sites are typically managed by a site administrator who monitors the content of the site and approves newly created forums and discussion boards. The discussion boards and forums are typically run by the group members. These types of support websites tend to have a high utilization rate and have been proven to be effective in the prevention of suicide among this group. One of the more popular sites is "To Write Love on Her Arms" https://twloha.com/

When using online resources with your clients it is imperative to be familiar with the site, social media forum, or group that you recommend. You want to ensure that the group will be beneficial to your client and meet his or her current need. You may even consider researching and discovering these types of websites with your clients during session to cultivate their investment in treatment. This kind of teamwork allows the client to somewhat direct treatment, thus improving overall compliance and treatment outcomes.

Acceptance of Need for Help

Educating parents about the current issues affecting their children, typically assists in helping to prevent suicide. Parents oftentimes become overwhelmed, frantic and have no idea how to manage a suicidal child. The methods they choose are often counterproductive and at times may worsen communication between the parent and child. When parents are educated about depression, suicide or any other ailment affecting their child, they are empowered and can be more involved with treatment.

When providing this type of sensitive information, you must keep in mind the parents' instinct, fear, and confusion. Empathy will take you a long way when working with parents of a suicidal client. The parent needs to be made aware of the importance of treatment compliance in and out of the therapy and their role in the home with respect to management. This may include teaching parents about various disorders and how to use techniques that are DBT- and CBT-based with their children. It is imperative that they are made aware of how their behaviors can be negatively reinforcing in certain situations and how to better respond to prevent operant learning from occurring (e.g., a mother gives her son or daughter *excessive* attention and time (reinforcing stimulus) for acting out inappropriately or engaging in self-harm behavior (behavior)). Parents can also be educated on how to help reduce the possibility of a completed suicide by removing lethal means from the home.

Adolescent Suicide Risk Checklist

Directions: If your client answers yes to three or more concerns on this checklist (excluding social support question), a suicide inquiry (presence of any current ideation, intent or plan) and/or possible suicide risk assessment is advised.

_____ Has there been any prior diagnosis of depression, anxiety or other mental health condition? Are these symptoms currently active? Are these symptoms currently being treated with medication or therapy?

_____ Has the client been a victim of bullying (physical, verbal, cyberbullying)?

_____ Is the client experiencing concerns about sexual identity or sexual orientation?

_____ Have there been any significant changes in behavior (isolating themselves, withdrawn, acting-out behaviors, increased drug or alcohol use)?

_____ Any history of prior suicide attempts or NSSI behavior?

_____ Any history of drug and alcohol abuse? Any current drug or alcohol use?

_____ Does the client have a strong social support network?

_____ Does the client report familial pressures?

_____ Does the client report frequent disciplinary problems or poor academic performance?

_____ Does the client present with a history of physical, mental, emotional or sexual abuse?

Parental Notification Guidelines

Directions: Use this worksheet as an outline to follow when discussing a suicidal child with a parent or caretaker.

1. Inform the parents that you believe their adolescent is at risk for suicide and why you are making this assessment.

2. Suggest that parents/caretakers can reduce the risk of suicide by removing firearms from the house and restricting access to other lethal means (knives, prescription medications, sharp objects, material that could be fashioned into a noose, razor blades, cleaning supplies, etc.).

3. Educate parents about different ways to dispose of, or at the very least limit access to, a firearm (use of law enforcement in disposal/removal of firearms from the home).

4. Note significant changes in behavior (isolating themselves, withdrawn, acting-out behaviors, increased drug or alcohol use; or if usually sad, are they excited, energetic).

5. Suggest heightened observation of child/adolescent (check-ins periodically throughout the evening, encouraging engaging in family/social activities, increasing family quality time, not allowing locked doors, monitoring extended periods of time in the bathroom).

6. Discuss development of a safety plan and the importance of enforcing the safety plan (if warranted).

7. Provide parents/caretakers with community resources that admit and treat adolescents and children (hospitals that admit children/adolescents, intensive outpatient treatment centers, drug and alcohol inpatient/partial hospitalization programs).

8. Explain current diagnosis or dual diagnosis to parents and how these symptoms play a role in the child's/adolescent's current suicidal behavior.

9. Provide parent/caretaker with information about groups/resources which will provide support for the parents (National Alliance on Mental Illness, other online community resources).

Chapter 7 | Non-Suicidal Self-Injury (NSSI)

Non-Suicidal Self-Injury (NSSI) is the most recent term coined in research when referencing self-injurious/self-destructive behaviors. It has been defined as "any non-fatal, serious, deliberate, self-harm with or without suicidal intent." Research conducted by Milton Brown, suggests that NSSI behaviors typically occur during the first half of the life cycle (ages 15–44). These behaviors were historically viewed as "suicide attempts," but we have learned that individuals engaging in this type of behavior, do not necessarily have a desire to die. They are engaging in these actions for other motives, including self-punishment, establishing emotional/cognitive congruence, self-regulation, and even as a result of possible addiction.

Research has indicated that those who engage in these types of behaviors typically report relief from anxiety when performing NSSI and that the painful sensation typically returns minutes, hours or days following the injury. This is one reason as to why these individuals report difficulty extinguishing this activity. It has also been stated that the presence of blood is significant in tension reduction.

Individuals who engage in this behavior often view it as a coping strategy and self-mutilators are described as having higher levels of anger and aggression when compared to those who did not report NSSI as a coping mechanism.

NSSI behaviors not only reference cutting, but involve a multitude of behaviors including, but not limited to:

- Ingesting objects (batteries, pens, razor blades)
- Inserting objects into the skin (fingertips, toes, genitalia)
- Using hot objects (fire, curling irons, irons, etc.)
- Impact with objects to include punching walls or other objects (asphalt, rocks, concrete, trees, etc.)
- Impact with self (hitting, slapping, punching self)
- Carving words or symbols into the skin
- Rubbing sharp objects into the skin (glass)
- Ripping or tearing of the skin
- Scratching or pinching
- Smashing digits with hard objects (hammer, rocks, other heavy objects)
- Interference with wound healing (peeling off scabs, salt in wounds, keeping wounds infected)
- Self-induced vomiting (without any other symptoms indicative of an eating disorder)
- Falling down stairs or hurling oneself from various heights
- Allowing others, to include animals, to inflict physical pain

ETIOLOGY

There are several models and theories related to NSSI. In this section, we explore these various hypotheses. We will begin by exploring the medical model of NSSI, followed by the self-verification theory, the biosocial theory, the addiction model, the experiential avoidance model and the more recently developed stage model of NSSI.

Medical Model

The medical model is described as "a descriptive, phenomenological model of NSSI classification" and is centered on "atheoretical," descriptive observations. This model, which incorporates notions and terminology, is related to the field of psychiatry and takes into account those patients/clients who have co-morbid mental health disorders. In this classification, Nock and Favazza (2009) refer to NSSI *as "a symptom or associated feature of a specific mental health disorder even though it may occur in persons who do not meet diagnostic criteria of a mental illness—e.g., "copycat" cutting in high school students."*

Major NSSI

Major NSSI comprises infrequent acts that destroy substantial body tissue, such as eye removal and removal of body parts. They are sudden, disorganized, and often gory acts. 75% of this type of NSSI occurs during a psychotic episode, primarily schizophrenia. Approximately one-half occur during the first psychotic episode. The reasons patients typically report for such behavior often are not logical, for example, *"to enhance general well-being," most however, focus on religion, such as a concrete or literal interpretation of biblical texts referencing removal of an offending eye or hand or becoming one who has been castrated, or the focus may be related to sexuality, such as controlling troubling hypersexuality or fear of giving into homosexual urge"* (Nock and Favazza, 2009).

Related Diagnoses: Alcohol/drug intoxication, Schizophrenia and other psychotic disorders.

Treatment: Prevention is essential when managing major NSSI. Although there has not been any research indicating a specific psychotropic medication in the management of NSSI, literature recommends the possible use of atypical antipsychotics for psychotic patients who experience delusions and hallucinations related to religion, the Bible, or sexuality, as well as those who dramatically and suddenly change their appearance by cutting off their hair, engaging in extreme body modification practices, or wearing bizarre clothes. Research also suggests that these individuals may be at risk for recurring episodes as a result of the agitation related to these psychotic symptoms, and thus it is recommended that the agitation be managed and hospitalization guidelines be followed when attempting to address it.

Stereotypic NSSI

Stereotypic NSSI is most frequently associated with severe and profound mental retardation in addition to developmental disorders (e.g., autism). The behaviors can include, but are not limited to, repetitive head banging; eye extracting; biting lips, tongue, cheeks, or fingers; and face or head slapping. These behaviors may be monotonously repetitive, or have a rhythmic pattern. Afflicted individuals are believed to engage in these behaviors in order to self-soothe, and these behaviors are described as being ego syntonic, as they are often performed in the presence of others and without feelings of remorse, shame or guilt.

Related Diagnoses: Autism spectrum disorder, Tourette's syndrome, and intellectual disability (severe).

Treatment: Patients with this form of NSSI typically are unable to articulate what is causing them to experience distress. It is advised that information be gathered from caretakers about the specifics of the behavior (onset, duration, intensity) and it is advised to initially assess whether a patient/client is responding to some type of pain or a medical disorder such as an ear infection. Behavior therapy is the main modality of treatment when handling these behaviors. With respect to psychotropic medication management and referrals, it is advised that a combination of medications may be more effective than monotherapy in managing these behaviors.

Compulsive NSSI

Compulsive NSSI includes repetitive behaviors such as severe skin scraping and nail biting, hair pulling (trichotillomania), and skin digging (delusional parasitosis).

Related Diagnoses: Impulsive disorders.

Treatment: Research has shown that many compulsive NSSI patients/clients initially seek help from dermatologists or a family physician and are then referred to a psychiatrist, psychologist or other mental health professional when it is believed a mental health disorder exists rather than a particular skin condition. This type of NSSI is described to respond well to psychotherapy and although research on treatment is limited, it is advised that psychotropic medication may be effective.

Impulsive NSSI

Impulsive NSSI encompasses acts such as skin cutting, burning, and carving; sticking pins or other objects under the skin or into the chest or abdomen; interfering with wound healing; and smashing hand or foot bones. These behaviors usually are episodic and occur more frequently in females. The average age of onset in patients who engage in impulsive NSSI is 12 to 14, although it may occur throughout the life cycle.

Related Diagnoses: Anxiety disorders, cluster B personality disorders, somatoform and factitious disorders, dissociative identity and depersonalization disorders, eating disorders, mood disorders, and psychotic disorders.

Treatment: Patients who engage in episodic impulsive NSSI are described to respond well to various psychotherapies including dialectical behavioral therapy (DBT), cognitive-behavioral therapy (CBT), and interpersonal therapy. (These treatments will be further explored in subsequent sections of this workbook.) It also advised that a combination of psychotherapy and medication management may be even more effective than either modality alone when treating underlying psychiatric illnesses such as generalized anxiety disorder, posttraumatic stress disorder, or depression.

Self-Verification Theory

Self-verification theory posits that people have a commanding desire to confirm and stabilize their firmly held self-views. It has been long assumed that people form their self-views by observing how others treat them. As they obtain more evidence to support their self-views, people become progressively more sure of these views. Inflexibly held self-views enable people to make forecasts about their world, guide behavior, and preserve a sense of continuity, place, and coherence. Self-verification theory holds that people often desire self-confirming assessments even if their self-view is negative. For example, those who see themselves as unlovable, undesirable or as "bad" will prefer evidence that others also perceive them as such.

Persons who hate themselves will desire to harm themselves similar to how one might desire to harm any disliked person. NSSI behaviors can function as self-punishment, and the self-inflicted injuries viewed as deserved by the people who engage in this activity.

Biosocial Theory

Marsha Linehan proposed the biosocial theory to better understand the etiology and maintenance of self-harm behaviors. She hypothesizes that chronic negative emotions and self-invalidation are primary factors that predispose individuals with borderline personality disorder (BPD) to engage in self-mutilation and suicide attempts. The term "emotion dysregulation" refers to the combination of high sensitivity/reactivity to emotional stimuli and the inability appropriately regulate emotions (e.g., inability to distract, self-soothe; inability to tolerate frustration).

Those diagnosed with BPD often engage in impulsive and maladaptive behaviors (including NSSI) in response to intense and negative emotions. These maladaptive behaviors are either automatic, mood-dependent responses to emotions or attempts to temper or cope with negative emotions. These individuals also fluctuate between extremes of emotional experiencing (intense feelings of anger, frustration, sadness) and emotional inhibition (repressing negative affect).

Linehan (1993) notes that, "self-invalidation is learned from atmospheres that invalidate self-generated behaviors and communication of private experiences. These behaviors are often described as being punished, minimized, disregarded, pathologized or criticized by others. The exactitude of one's self-description is often rejected, and instead, these behaviors are attributed to negative traits such as languor, manipulation, negative attitude, and paranoia." Self-invalidation occurs when persons have learned to disregard, punish, and invalidate their emotions and themselves in ways similar to how others have treated them. In other words, they have internalized these undesirable messages and views about the self. In consequence, these persons may blame and judge themselves severely for their lack of control of behavior and emotions, and regard their ordinary responses as being unacceptable. Other forms of abuse that commonly occur in these settings may also explain their high emotional reactivity. As a result of predisposed biological susceptibility these traumatic experiences may sensitize them to react strongly to expressive stimuli and a variety of cues that become conditioned to early traumatic experiences.

According to Linehan's biosocial theory, negative emotions contribute to chronic NSSI behaviors in individuals diagnosed with BPD in three ways:

1. The reduction of emotional arousal following NSSI negatively reinforces the behavior.
2. Anger, contempt, and shame interfere with judgment, decision making and problem-solving ability, in addition to emotional processing.
3. Shame-related emotions immediately result in self-punishment, or strong desire to escape, hide or disappear (e.g., lose consciousness or die).

This emotion dysregulation model describes NSSI as an attempt to regulate negative emotions and is also referred to as the tension reduction model. This theory suggests that although these individuals achieve relief of escalating negative emotions this symptom relief unfortunately reinforces the self-harming behavior and thus these acts began to become sequential/stereotypical. If we were to develop a model of this process, it might look similar to the following:

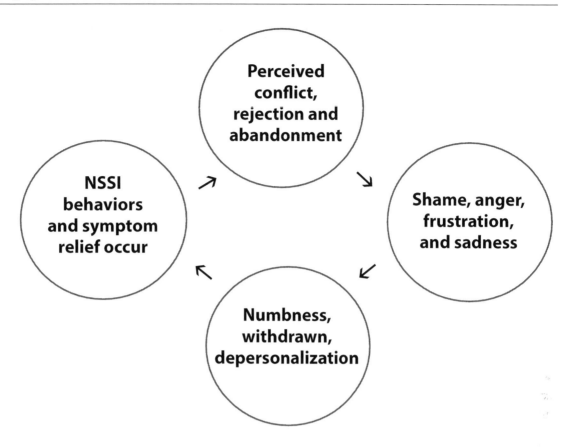

Addiction Model

The addiction hypothesis suggests that NSSI behaviors may engage the endogenous opioid system (EOS). Endogenous Opioids (endorphins) are created naturally in the body and target the brain's reward system by flooding the "circuit" with dopamine. Dopamine is a neurotransmitter located in areas of the brain that are responsible for reasoning, motivation, movement, emotion and feelings of pleasure. The overstimulation of this system, which rewards our everyday and natural behaviors, produces the euphoric effects sought after by those who abuse drugs or even engage in self-harm behaviors and, consequently, teaches them to repeat the behavior. The EOS regulates pain perception and levels of endogenous endorphins which result because of an injury. Over-stimulation of the EOS by repetitive self-injury can even lead to withdrawal symptoms when self-harm ceases which can lead in turn to more self-destructive behaviors to increase endorphin release.

Earlier studies of the EOS involved animal models, specifically primates. It was discovered, that not only were endogenous opioids responsible for the system's known role in modulating pain responses to physical and emotional stressors, but was also associated with attachment behavior deficits (approach avoidant, avoidant-avoidant) and anxiety-like responses. Additionally, research has also indicated that with respect to human beings, this system is involved in emotional regulation.

Regarding the animal models, it was observed that 1) monkeys engaged in grooming each other as a way to self-regulate and self-soothe; and 2) among these groups, there were several monkeys who continuously presented with agitation, irritation, were difficult to soothe and would often experience interpersonal problems with the other group members. Upon further research, it was discovered that those monkeys who presented with the inability to regulate emotions, presented with decreased levels of endogenous opioid receptors in the brain.

These receptors are related to emotion regulation and stress responses and help to facilitate normal social functioning. Opioids not only regulate or modulate pain, but when released also cause a feeling of euthymia and relief and at times may cause one to feel motivated and experience an increase in positive mood. This finding led to Prossin's (2010) research, in which he hypothesized similar mechanisms being involved in a human's inability to self-regulate and engagement in self-harm behaviors.

In 2010, Prossin, et al., *hypothesized neurochemical mechanisms in borderline personality disorder pathophysiology.* Upon inducing states of sadness in individuals diagnosed with BPD and using positron emission tomography and a selective μ-opioid receptor radiotracer, to scan brain functioning, they were able to identify differences in responsivity in the emotional processing regions of the brain when compared to those not diagnosed with BPD. Specifically, it was noted that those diagnosed with BPD showed chronic lower levels of opioid regulatory control with compensatory receptor up-regulation and they presented with an exaggerated response in these same areas, reflecting high sensitivity of BPD patients to emotional stimuli, with greater activation of the stress regulatory EOS and μ-opioid receptors.

With this study, they were able to provide initial evidence that individuals diagnosed with BPD, who frequently engage in NSSI, presented with regional alterations in the function of the EOS and μ-opioid receptors in brain regions involved in emotion and stress processing, decision making, and pain and neuroendocrine regulation. More research in this area is necessary in order to provide treatment guidelines and possible psychopharmological approaches to this issue.

Experiential Avoidance Model

Experiential avoidance is the phenomenon that occurs when a person is unwilling to remain in contact with certain (typically negative) internal experiences (e.g., bodily sensations, emotions, thoughts, memories, images, behavioral predispositions) and takes steps to modify the form and/or frequency of these experiences or the contexts that trigger these experiences, even when these forms of avoidance cause behavioral harm.

Experiential avoidance can be harmful because internal events (typically negative cognitions, affect, perceptions) are often unresponsive or are even ironically increased by deliberate control efforts. Because many forms of experiential avoidance are life distorting, sometimes difficult emotions are experientially important, and healthy behavioral changes often initially produce psychological discomfort. Thus, excessive experiential avoidance is likely to be associated with higher levels of psychopathology across the board and a lower quality of life.

This model purports that individuals engage in NSSI behaviors in order to avoid unwanted emotional states and that individuals with high levels of distress, of which they cannot regulate, will be more prone to engage in these behaviors due to automatic negative reinforcement (e.g., to stop bad feelings). The automatic negative reinforcement aspect of these behaviors may be related to poor emotion regulation skills.

Stage Model of NSSI

This model is reported to parallel the development of other addictive behaviors (drug, alcohol, gambling, pornography). Following this model allows clinicians to mutually understand NSSI behaviors, as well as develop effective treatment plans for their clients.

Stage 0: No Self-Harm Behavior
The lowest level of self-injury with no present or past self-injury.

Stage 1: Experimental NSSI

This stage involves the client's initial act(s) of self-harm behavior; this experience will contribute in determining whether or not they choose to repeat this behavior.

Adolescents in stage 1 are not yet committed to NSSI as a coping behavior, nor do they identify as one who self-injures. This stage is one of **experimentation** with the behavior.

Stage 2: Exploration

Self-injury is now perceived as a key method of dealing with daily stressors and negative internal states (cognitions/feelings). Adolescents may hide essential tools used to engage in the self-harm behavior (such as sharp instruments or gauze, Band-Aids, etc.) to ensure availability when the need arises to engage in the NSSI behavior.

During this stage, the client is **exploring** NSSI, they are discovering their physical and mental responses to the behavior. They may be actively engaged in seeking peer groups online or at school, as these groups can provide reinforcement to those who are self-harming. This camaraderie also intensifies the identification with NSSI behavior, which can make this behavior more difficult to extinguish.

Stage 3: Encapsulation

Clients are no longer experimenting or investigating the possibility of engaging in NSSI behavior. NSSI has become the primary (if not the only) method used to better manage negative affect.

These behaviors occur frequently and these clients may develop elaborate tactics regarding how, where and when self-injury will occur. In this stage, they begin to experience urges that are uncontrollable and intrusive, which makes it more difficult to conceal NSSI. This is the stage in which parents, guardians, friends, siblings, or school officials may become more aware of this behavior and a referral to a mental health provider may occur. As clinicians, this is typically the stage at which we intervene with most clients. These behaviors are typically not evident in the earlier stages (stages 0–2).

Stage 4: Pervasive Dysfunction

During this final stage, NSSI behavior is categorized by persistent self-injurious cognitions and behaviors.

At stage 4, these behaviors are hardly under an adolescent's control. Such extreme behavior is found almost exclusively in clinical populations and is not typical of the majority of adolescents who engage in NSSI. The probability of suicidal ideation, intent and plan is highest in stage 4.

NSSI BEHAVIOR AND RISK FACTORS FOR DEATH BY SUICIDE

Understanding and managing NSSI behavior is vital for several reasons. Primarily, research has demonstrated that individuals with a history of NSSI are nine times more likely to report suicide attempts, seven times more likely to report a suicide gesture and six times more likely to report a suicide plan.

The risk for suicide is increased when engaging in these behaviors:

Rehearsal

Suicide rehearsal is a behavioral portrayal, usually as part of a suicide plan, of choosing a preferred or undetermined suicide method. Suicide rehearsals may precede suicide attempts or suicide completions. Rehearsal of a suicide typically occurs much closer in time to the suicide attempt than preparations for suicide.

Rehearsals also weaken the protective factors against suicidal behavior and minimize the fear of pain and dying. Rehearsal ultimately impacts ambivalence related to suicidal behaviors.

Rehearsal provides presumptive evidence that the client is at acute, high risk for suicide and immediate clinical intervention is necessary. It also allows the clinician to explore the various methods of suicide that the client has considered, including prior rehearsals.

Rehearsal allows the client to:

- Overcome ambivalence about dying.
- Desensitize themselves to anxiety about performing the suicide act.
- Test or "perfect" the method of a planned suicide.
- Firm their resolve to complete suicide.

Preparation

Engaging in NSSI behaviors also allows for preparation of a suicide attempt. It allows an individual to choose a preferred method in completing a suicide attempt (cutting vs. hanging vs. handgun vs. overdose). When engaging in self-destructive behaviors, individuals can become habituated and pain tolerance increases, thus one may engage in more harmful behavior (e.g., cutting deeper) or choosing a more dangerous method in order to achieve symptom relief.

Also, when engaging in these behaviors, if others become aware (stages 3 and 4 in the stage model of NSSI) the client has the opportunity to assess the responsiveness of others. Is their behavior being positively reinforced (attention from others, procuring secondary gain)? Or does the behavior go unnoticed and ignored by others? For some individuals, the blatant disregard of their NSSI behavior may encourage more severe NSSI behaviors, thus causing habituation and the abatement of ambivalence.

Preparation also affords one the opportunity to determine the safest place to conduct NSSI behaviors or a suicide attempt. Continuously engaging in this behavior allows for mental preparation for a suicide attempt. Again decreasing ambivalence and increasing tolerance and habituation. Upon becoming desensitized to pain stimuli it is possible to habituate to pain and develop a high pain tolerance threshold. As a result, these behaviors may become more frequent and more severe, leading to a possible "accidental suicide."

Assessing for NSSI

What better way to acquire information **about** someone who self-injures than **from** someone who engages in these behaviors!

The following questionnaire was adapted from an interview form created by an administrator of a pro-injury/self-harm blog. It provides an abundance of information about triggers, frequency and duration of this behavior, in addition to information that would highlight the client's stage of change (pre-contemplation, contemplation, preparation, action or maintenance).

It also provides information about where the client may be functioning with respect to the stage model of non-suicidal self-injury (NSSI) behaviors (no self-harm behaviors, exploration, experimentation, encapsulation or pervasive dysfunction) and it gives additional information about the client's insight, awareness, and management of this condition. This checklist also provides information about family dynamics, interpersonal relationships, or lack thereof, and the client's willingness or unwillingness to share this information with others in their space.

NSSI Client Questionnaire

Directions: Use this worksheet when assessing for current self-harm behaviors and patterns. This worksheet can be used during an intake session or when warranted during treatment. These responses should be used to guide your treatment planning with the client.

1. Form of NSSI? (e.g., cutting, burning, inserting objects, etc.)

   _____

   _____

2. Why do you engage in NSSI behaviors? (e.g., emotion regulation, self-verification, symptom reduction, etc.)

   _____

   _____

3. When was the first time you engaged in NSSI?

   _____

   _____

4. Where do you most often engage in NSSI behaviors? (e.g., wrist, arms, stomach, thighs, etc.)

   _____

   _____

5. In what room/area do you most engage in these behaviors? (e.g., bedroom, bathroom, etc.)

   _____

   _____

6. What method/object do you use? (e.g., razor blades, lighters, needles, curling iron, etc.)

   _____

   _____

7. Do you hide it?

_____

_____

_____

8. Do you listen to music when you engage in NSSI? (This provides information about triggers—cognitive-affective relationships, mood states, etc.) If so, what type of music do you prefer? Why that choice?

_____

_____

_____

9. Have you shared this with anyone else? If so, who?

_____

_____

_____

10. Is there any diagnosable eating disorder, or symptoms of potential disordered eating habits?

_____

_____

_____

11. Any mental health diagnoses?

_____

_____

_____

12. How would you react if you discovered that your best friend was also engaging in these behaviors?

_____

_____

_____

Chapter 8 | Social Media, Trends and Peer Acceptance

Research has found that the effects of peer pressure and contagion can also influence people to engage in self-harm /NSSI behaviors. It has also been suggested that adolescent peer influence is a remarkably powerful phenomenon and that girls may be uniquely susceptible to the influence of their best friends' engagement in NSSI behaviors.

HOW DOES PEER INFLUENCE WORK?

Currently, there is no specific known mechanism. However, past research suggests that peers may influence one another through behavioral reinforcement of risky behaviors that are discussed within a social context (e.g., laughing or nodding affirmatively when discussing deviant acts). Peer conformity may also be the result of adolescents' attempts to adhere to perceived social norms and/or to manage their own sense of identity.

Research has indicated that NSSI behavior may be associated with high status and modeling of this behavior via observation of positive reinforcement associated with engaging in this behavior. For example, a research study showed that inpatient samples (adolescents hospitalized for suicide attempts/mild to moderate NSSI behaviors) were reported to have learned more progressive forms of NSSI behaviors while hospitalized through modeling and reinforcement as they observed how others' behavior was rewarded (attention) by staff.

INTERNET AND SOCIAL MEDIA AND NSSI

In general, researchers have found that the internet is becoming a major influence on the beliefs and perceptions of societal groups, specifically for those between the ages of 10–25. Approximately 75% of adolescents own a game console, an iPod/MP3 player, and/or a cell phone (Lenhart, 2009). American children and adolescents are exposed to 7 hours of entertainment media per day. Youth and young adults have daily internet access and engage in more online social networking and video sharing than any other age group.

More specifically, research has shown that the internet may represent a preferred means of communication and connection for otherwise isolated youth and young adults. One part of the internet's allure stems from the secret nature of the interaction it offers. Research indicates that anonymous e-communication may hold particular interest for those who experience many factors related to NSSI risk, to include psychological distress and other emotional difficulties.

The primary origin of these websites and e-communication communities began with the "Emo" subculture. The term "Emo" usually is depicted as originating from a melodic subgenre of punk rock music first called "emocore" or "emotional hardcore" and "has evolved to become a well-recognized slang term to describe a group with particular penchants in clothing, music and behaviors" (Lenhart, 2009). Emo music is characterized as emphasizing emotional or personal turmoil, behaviors, attitudes and values. Common themes include despair, depression, heart break, and self-loathing. Typical clothing includes black stovepipe jeans, body-hugging T-shirts, scarves, tartans, studded belts and black wristbands, black sneakers and skate shoes, males wearing heavy eyeliner, and some males also wear thick, black horn-rimmed glasses. And, with respect to hairstyle, the emphasis has been on long side-swept bangs, sometimes covering one or both eyes; hair may be straightened and dyed black, but some also adopt short, choppy layers; bright colors, such as blue, pink, red, or bleached blond also are typical.

"Emos" have been stereotyped as being emotional, sensitive, shy, introverted, or misery-ridden and prone to depression, self-injury, and suicide. Anorexia and other eating disorders are also believed to be ubiquitous in the Emo subculture. This group is also reported to exchange competitive messages on their websites about the scars on their wrists and how best to display them. On a more individual level, concern has been raised that members of this subgroup tend to be overly emotional, feel misjudged, and engage in self-harming behavior; often they are targets for bullies—including homophobic attacks because of the effeminate look of some in the subgroup. Individuals who are typically attracted to these online communities, are shunned by their peers, feel as if they do not belong or "fit in," have a limited social support network and have a strong desire to belong. They are seeking acceptance and relationships with others who are similar and can relate to their worldview. According to a number of websites related to the Emo culture, "Emo subculture is different from Gothic subculture (Goth) because Emo's only hate themselves; Goths hate everyone!"

As can be seen with the creation of the Emo subculture, the most commonly reported benefit associated with some online NSSI activity is that of social/peer support. Many adolescents and young adults who self-harm will seek others, online, to share their NSSI practices and connect with others who engage in this behavior; this may be mostly alluring to those who do not feel comfortable sharing their NSSI experiences with others in a face-to-face interaction. Furthermore, some research suggests that individuals involved in NSSI e-communities report decreases in NSSI behavior following the decision to join these groups. Thus, there seem to be some interpersonal benefits associated with some forms of online NSSI communication. Easy access to an abundance of NSSI-related content online may ultimately reinforce NSSI as an acceptable/normal behavior and perpetuate its occurrence in schools and other community settings as a means of group identification.

Since these age groups (ages 10–25 years) have the highest NSSI rates and adolescents who self-harm may engage in more online activity than those who do not self-harm, it makes sense that there has been a major increase in the NSSI content available online. To date, Facebook has been reported to contain over 500 groups relating to the Emo subculture promoting self-injury/pro-injury behaviors, lifestyle, culture, and context; and YouTube has been reported to contain, at a minimum, 5,000 videos dedicated to self-mutilation/pro-injury!

Many online media are reported to "normalize" this behavior as typical means for stress relief and often provide misinformation about para-suicidal behaviors.

In 2010, the International Society for the Study of Self-Injury recognized the burgeoning of NSSI activity occurring online and the importance of research in this area. The relationship between e-communication, internet use and the increase in NSSI behaviors, has also gained the attention of the media. It was reported that there were more than 400 news stories published worldwide, most of which focused on the impact these pro-injury sites and NSSI-encouraging websites have on those who use this modality of communication.

There are a substantial number of those who share their NSSI experiences with others via personal websites, discussion boards/blogs/forums, general e-communities (e.g., pro-injury or pro-ana (anorexia) websites,), and video-sharing websites (e.g., YouTube). Researchers have proposed that the way by which some share their NSSI experiences online may positively reinforce their behavior. This strengthening may also occur through virtual communication amid those who self-harm. Interactive websites (e.g., discussion forums, blogs, pro-injury chat rooms, video-sharing websites) allow users to access information about NSSI and to engage with fellow self-harmers about NSSI, thereby receiving validation that their behaviors are normal, acceptable and not maladaptive.

When sharing these experiences with others online, many disclosures contain detailed descriptions of NSSI that highlight emotional pain and suffering and they lack recovery-oriented messages about prognosis (1). Typically, NSSI is presented as an effective means to cope with distress and internal pain. These online disclosures do not typically address the pain associated with this method of coping, nor do they address the addiction component of this behavior. It may also be justified and glamorized which may impede one's desire to seek out mental health treatment.

Video sharing online, has been described as one of the most pertinent reinforcing internet activities, as these images are often triggering and suggestive to those who engage in these para-suicidal behaviors.

Here are a few links to popular pro-injury and pro-ana websites, as they are both highly utilized by those who engage in NSSI behaviors: When navigating these websites, please note the "therapy lingo" utilized by those who are attempting to join these sites. Also note the language used on the pro-ana websites, as it self-deprecating, while at the same time comforting and protective for those who are seeking belonging and acceptance. Take notice of the ages of these individuals, as well as the cult-like undertones of the site administrators.

- http://pro-si.livejournal.com
- http://bonesnotbeauty.livejournal.com
- http://anabootcamp.weebly.com/red-bracelet---rbc.html

Assessing Online Activity
Related to NSSI Behavior

Directions: Use this worksheet to assess your client's current on-line activity. This can be completed during an intake with the client or when warranted during treatment.

Activity Type

What type(s) of online activities do you engage in concerning NSSI (informational, interactive, social networking, and video viewing/sharing/posting)?

_____

_____

Online Community

What are the resources available?

_____

_____

Is this website professionally or peer driven? Moderated?

_____

_____

What specific activities do you engage in on these websites (live chat, posting, information seeking)?

_____

_____

Social Networking

What social networking websites are you affiliated with?

_____

_____

Do you have friendships/connections with other people who engage in NSSI?

_____

If yes, what is the nature of the relationship(s)?

_____

If no, what is the nature of the relationship(s)

_____

_____

Are you a member of any online group related to NSSI?

_____

_____

If yes, what are the themes surrounding that group (recovering from NSSI, pro-injury, pro-ana)?

_____

_____

If yes, is this group public or private?

_____

_____

If yes, is it moderated or supervised?

_____

_____

Are there any images/videos of NSSI among these groups?

_____

_____

What specific activities do you engage in on these websites (live chat, messaging, posting, information seeking)?

_____

_____

Video/Picture Sharing

What specific websites do you visit?

_____

_____

Do you create videos/photos related to NSSI?

_____

_____

If yes, discuss themes/content of videos created.

_____

_____

If yes, are these videos character (people) or non-character (stories) videos?

_____

_____

If yes, why are you choosing to create these videos (creative outlet)?

_____

_____

What types of videos/photos do you watch?

_____

_____

Are these character or non-character videos?

_____

_____

What are the general themes in these videos (recovering from, pro-injury, pro-ana)?

_____

_____

Do these videos present visual presentations of NSSI?

_____

_____

If yes, are these visual presentations accompanied by a warning?

_____

_____

Are these visual images of NSSI triggering?

_____

_____

If yes, discuss nature, intensity and degree of triggering material.

_____

_____

What other specific activities do you engage in on these websites (messaging, commenting, following channels)?

_____

_____

Frequency of Activity

Discuss frequency of NSSI online activities (explore usage, during week and weekend).

_____

_____

Functional Assessment of NSSI Activity in Relation to Internet Activities

When/why did you first start engaging in NSSI online activities? Explore first episode.

_____

_____

Has your behavior increased/decreased/remained the same since you began engaging in NSSI online activities?

_____

_____

What are events/interactions, thoughts, and feelings that preceded/occur during/follow the online activity?

_____

_____

Do you self-injure before/after engaging in NSSI online activities?

_____

_____

If yes, explore online activities that may confer/reduce NSSI risk.

_____

_____

Adapted from Lewis, S. et, al 2012

STAGES OF CHANGE AND NSSI BEHAVIORS

The transtheoretical model of change (TTM) (Prochaska & DiClemente, 1993) addressed how people modify a problem behavior or acquire a positive behavior. This is a model of intentional change. This model focuses on the decision making of the individual and may help to explain differences in persons' success during treatment for a range of mental health and physical health concerns. This model helps to provide information about treatment compliance, resistance, and the motivation in treatment. It allows the therapist to better gage the client's capacity for change and is informative when developing specific treatment plans.

This model has been adapted in explaining the treatment course of NSSI behaviors and provides guidelines about the client's perspective and the course of treatment contingent on these stages. Keep in mind that this model is non-linear and our clients can waffle between stages and even regress dependent on their distress tolerance and ability to manage in a crisis. The model is as follows:

Pre-contemplation Stage

During this stage, there is a lack of knowledge or failure with previous attempts to change; behavior is minimized, consequences of these behaviors are not important enough to change; client may avoid discussion about this behavior and denial may be present. The benefits of ceasing this behavior outweigh the costs at this stage. The client is oblivious to the detrimental nature of this behavior and may be defensive and hostile when engaged about this issue. Clients may also present with a distorted view of their coping abilities and remain unaware of the addictive component of their behavior.

Treatment implications

At this stage of change, contemplating future consequences is not enough motivation to change the client's current behavior. Therefore, strategies such as motivational interviewing could be used during this period. Motivational interviewing a technique in which you become a helper in the change process and express acceptance of your client. Ambivalence about the maladaptive behavior (and change) is normal and constitutes an important motivational obstacle in recovery. This ambivalence has the ability to be resolved by working with your client's intrinsic motivations and values.

When engaging in this type of technique, the therapist approach should be empathic, supportive, and yet directive, as you want to create a safe environment wherein changes can occur (direct and aggressive confrontation may tend to intensify client defensiveness and lessen the likelihood of behavioral change).

Contemplation Stage

During this stage of change, the client has more of a cognitive awareness that NSSI behaviors are dangerous. They may be contemplating change, but remain "on the fence" or ambivalent about changing their behavior. They are not considering change within the next month.

Treatment implications

During this stage, transient emotional gains provided by the behavior outweigh the desire to change. Treatment strategies may include increasing the client's pleasurable activities and building meaningful relationships. You may want to encourage the evaluation of pros and cons of behavioral changes and help to identify and promote novel and positive outcome expectations.

Preparation Stage

During this stage of change, your client may be committed to attempting to reduce NSSI behaviors and begin to experiment with small changes. They plan to at least make changes within the next month and may be more comfortable with suggestions of progressive changes (e.g., actually discussing their NSSI behaviors in session or agreeing to keep record of how often they engage in NSSI). During this stage, they are more active in self-exploration and will be responsive to feedback.

Treatment implications

When your clients experience change, confidence is bolstered and they are more inclined to make bigger changes. Do not be discouraged if episodic NSSI occurs, as you are attempting to extinguish and replace a behavior which has been "successful" in assisting your client's mood dysregulation. Making lifestyle changes is a difficult process and may involve more of a "step-down" approach for various clients. Introduction to the use of impulse control logs could be implemented, as well as having active discussions on successes and relapses.

Identify and promote new and positive outcome expectations in your client. It is always important to reinforce positive changes by way of applause and acknowledgment of successes, no matter how small or big! The individual needs encouragement to evaluate pros and cons of behavior change. The therapist needs to identify and promote new, positive outcome expectations in the individual and encourage small initial steps. Typically, these clients have taken some actions in the past year such as joining a NSSI recovery group (online or in vivo), consulting with a therapist, investing in self-help books or phone applications, or trusting in a self-change approach. These clients are appropriate for action-oriented programs, such as a peer group or being involved in volunteer activities.

Action Stage

During this stage of change, the client is actively engaged in new and healthy behaviors. The active work toward desired behavioral change including modification of environment (removing stressors, removing objects that can be used to self-harm), experiences, or behavior have been made. At this stage, your client has made specific obvious modifications in their lifestyle within the past six months and precautions should be taken to prevent relapse.

Treatment implications

During this stage, you are encouraged to help the client restructure external and internal cues and strengthen social support. You should help enhance and promote self-efficacy for dealing with stressors and conflict and help to defend against feelings of loss and frustration. You could incorporate the technique of a functional behavioral analysis (which will be discussed in detail in the upcoming chapters) or complete impulse control logs regularly and highlight and share therapeutic gains. It is helpful to assist your clients in working through urges and using alternative coping strategies. It is also advised to introduce new behaviors such as grounding techniques, stress inoculation, distress tolerance, breathing exercises and internal distraction methods (mindfulness).

Maintenance Stage

During this stage of change, clients begin to present with stronger levels of self-confidence at being able to manage NSSI urges. They are maintaining the changes made in the action stage and are insightful about their triggers, growth edges, and strengths. These clients are actively involved in their treatment planning and have become well versed about their issue. Here, the focus is on ongoing, active work to maintain changes made and relapse prevention. At this stage people are less tempted to relapse and become more confident that they can continue their behavioral changes.

Treatment implications

During this stage, there is less need for external support, as the client is able to rely on internal motivation to remain NSSI-free. You are moving toward more infrequent sessions and can move to a "booster session" model, meaning, instead of seeing the client weekly or bi-weekly, they may be seen once per month and a natural termination of treatment occurs. You can assist your client in planning for follow-up support and be certain to reinforce internal rewards and process coping with relapse.

Chapter 9 | Treatment of Non-Suicidal Self-Injury Behaviors

WHEN ARE CLIENTS TYPICALLY REFERRED FOR TREATMENT?

Clients are typically referred for therapeutic services when the NSSI behaviors have become the primary method to control negative affect (encapsulation stage). As previously stated, during this stage, the urges to engage in these behaviors are more difficult to control and the NSSI behaviors may come into the awareness of a loved one or other authority figure. Similar to drug and alcohol addictions, the ability to continue functioning at a high level dwindles and these behaviors begin to affect various areas of life including social, academic and occupational. These behaviors interfere with the ability to manage stressful events and when experiencing duress, the individual may impulsively and automatically "need" to engage in these behaviors. Clients are also typically referred to treatment when they construct elaborate plans involving self-injurious behaviors and present with a morbid preoccupation with cutting.

Research has indicated that the average length of outpatient treatment for NSSI behaviors is 6–9 months and is followed by periodic booster sessions to solidify gains and reinforce new strategies.

Process group treatment is contra-indicated with individuals who engage in NSSI during the initial phase of treatment, as they are more likely to reinforce each other's maladaptive behaviors than to make treatment gains. The potential for triggering memories and affective reactivity is very high if a psychotherapy process group is conducted. Research has also suggested that it is vital to remain aware of the clients' stage of change when contemplating group therapy and, if group therapy is warranted, then a skills-based group (frustration tolerance, emotional regulation, mindfulness) would most be appropriate. These types of groups are structured, time-limited, task-oriented and focus on a specific skill that will assist in extinguishing NSSI behaviors.

DIALECTICAL BEHAVIORAL THERAPY (DBT)

One of the main tenets of DBT involves the reconciliation of apparent opposites (e.g., good vs. bad, black vs. white, love vs. hate). According to Charles H. Elliott (2010), "*Dialectics breaks down our concepts into their seemingly opposite parts–viewed another way, as thesis, antithesis, and synthesis. Dialectics are one of the important unifying concepts that reflect how the mind fundamentally understands and perceives most core concepts and ideas. And the field of psychology contains an abundance of such concepts, including self-esteem, trust, courage, honesty, rage, passivity, withdrawal, impulsivity, inhibition, blameworthiness, guilt, risk taking, and on and on. Dialectics are based in part on the fact that we cannot fully understand any of these abstract concepts without appreciating that they consist of bipolar opposites with a higher level of integration somewhere in between them.*"

It functions as a frame for therapy by providing a worldview, a theory of disorder, a style of persuasive communication and it involves offering both acceptance and change-focused solutions for client's problems. It also seeks to increase patients' comfort with inconsistency, ambiguity, and change. For example, when conducting DBT with a client with NSSI, self-mutilation may be viewed as helping them cope with their painful emotions (e.g., valid or understandable), while also treated as a destructive act that contributes to long-term suffering and needs to be changed.

The primary goal of DBT is to reduce the effects of emotional dysregulation and help clients to avoid events that trigger para-suicidal impulses (e.g., stimulus control) and blocking access to lethal means by way of involving others in treatment and increased supervision of the client. It involves using external controls to assist in the management of these self-destructive behaviors while therapy and skill building is taking place.

Standard DBT involves a 1-year commitment of outpatient treatment including weekly primary individual psychotherapy sessions and skills-training sessions. Primary therapists work on the major maladaptive behaviors targeted in DBT (e.g., self-harm behaviors). The individual psychotherapy in DBT provides the relationship and context in which patients use new skills to gain control over self-harm and suicidal behaviors. Whereas the skills training follows a structured psycho-educational format (typically in a group) to address deficits in the ability to regulate emotions, tolerate distress, and interact effectively with others.

Core Strategies of DBT

Cognitive–behavioral therapy procedures are the main methods of change in DBT. This therapy also incorporates acceptance strategies which assist in the development of self-validation and acceptance. Skills training is a major component of this treatment and include skills such as mindfulness, emotion regulation, distress tolerance, and interpersonal effectiveness. The modules utilized in DBT are building blocks (in other words, one skill must be mastered before moving on to the next skill set). These modules have been listed below, in that order, with mindfulness being the first skill to be learned, and interpersonal effectiveness being the last skill, as it requires mastery of the other three skills in order to be the most effective.

Mindfulness

Mindfulness is defined as: *The ability to attend to the present moment without being judgmental or reacting to it based on previous experiences.* Simply stated, mindfulness is the ability to live in the present while experiencing the emotions that the current situation invokes totally and with perspective. This is considered to be a foundation skill on which the other three skills of DBT are established. It assists your client to acclimate to new situations without being overwhelmed by the intense feelings.

Distress Tolerance

Distress tolerance skills help your client to accept and manage stressful situations steadily, non-judgmentally and rationally, so that he/she is able make good and effective decisions instead of panicking when faced with distress or stressful encounters with others.

Emotion Regulation

Emotion regulation training aids the client in better managing negative affect, increases awareness of their current state of mind and vulnerability to certain emotions, and it helps to increase more positive affect. This training assists your client to pinpoint certain obstacles that impede their ability to change adverse emotions.

Interpersonal Effectiveness

During interpersonal effectiveness training, your clients are educated on how to communicate effectively with others. The approaches utilized in this module are comparable to those incorporated in assertiveness and interpersonal skills training. These skills are targeted at assisting your client in avoiding interpersonal conflicts and feeling more comfortable in exercising their boundaries by way of telling others "No!" This training is developed to help your client navigate situations wherein the objective of the interaction is to change or to resist any attempts made by others to change the person in question.

Communication Strategies

Communication strategies are described as irreverent and reciprocal in DBT. This does not imply that we are aggressively confrontational and tell our clients whatever we are thinking! But it does refer to the genuineness of this communication in that it should be open, honest, and model two-way interactions between the client and the therapist. This type of communication involves straightforward responsiveness and explicit discussion about what is occurring in the room with the therapist. It involves providing the client with honest feedback about their behaviors and more importantly it allows the client to present this way with the therapist, thus showing a mutual respect.

Example 1

Client: "So, are you mad at me for cutting myself last week? I really tried hard to do better and I only did it twice."

Therapist: "Yes, I am bothered that you chose to cut yourself instead of using the skills I know you have learned and I am also glad that you were honest with me and forthcoming about this. I appreciate the fact that you only cut twice last week instead of the usual 10–20 times! That's great! So what do you think we need to do in order to get you to once a week? Tell me what was happening for you during those periods."

Example 2

Client: "I know that you hate me like everybody else does. I can feel it when I am sitting here with you. I can see it in your body and face. It's OK, you can tell me. I don't care!"

Therapist: "I sense that you are angry about something today. I am uncertain about what, but it sounds like you are feeling defensive, sad, and perhaps vulnerable. Almost as if you are attempting to push me away. It is true, at times you say things that are offensive and I don't know what to make of them and it's also true that I know this is the way you navigate the world and the people in your space, so today isn't special for me. Tell me what is really going on?"

Case Management

Case management strategies involve the encouragement of your client, with appropriate help and support, to deal with their own problems in the environment in which they occur. These strategies are listed following.

Consultation-to-the-patient

This strategy allows communication to occur as needed when the client may be experiencing duress about their relationship with another medical/mental health professional or any other person with whom she/he may be having difficulty. This involves assisting your client to process their issue and to directly address the issue with this person. It is a strategy that helps to minimize splitting behaviors that may occur when treating this individual in conjunction with other medical/mental health providers.

Environmental intervention

This is acceptable but only in very specific circumstances where a particular outcome seems essential and the client does not have the power, rights or capability to produce this outcome. This intervention should only be utilized when no other options are available.

For example, your client informs you that s/he has been unable to procure an appointment with a specific social worker of whom **YOU** referred and you are aware that this social worker's case load is full and she/he is often difficult to locate. You have more access to this social worker than your client and have daily contact with this individual, thus you may choose to consult with the social worker about your client and attempt to schedule an appointment time.

Supervision/consultation

Consultation with other therapists is intended to be *therapy for the therapists* and to support DBT providers in their work with those who often have severe, complex, difficult-to-treat disorders. The consultation team is designed to assists therapists in staying motivated and competent to manage/treat their client in order to provide the best treatment possible. Traditional DBT involves developing teams that typically meet weekly and consist of individual therapists and group leaders who share accountability for each of their client's care. Although, most settings are not designed to allow for this in-depth and consistent practice, it is important to consult, when possible, with colleagues and other practitioners involved with your client's care.

Managing clients who present with NSSI or suicidal behavior can become mentally and emotionally overwhelming. Countertransference can and will occur with these clients, and it is important to remain aware when this dynamic is occurring in the room. Research has shown that the phenomenon of "countertransference hate" does in fact exist and can present in various forms. You may find yourself desiring to challenge the client in a non-therapeutic way, as they may trigger defensiveness in session or you may look forward to the client canceling or being a no-show for a session. You may find yourself becoming exasperated or even becoming physically ill when anticipating the client session.

Countertransference hate can also look like feeling forced to "take care" of the client or feeling responsible for their well-being. You may be overly involved in their treatment, inside and outside the therapy room. These responses are typical and are a normal part of the therapy process. The danger comes when the clinician ignores these issues or mitigates these feelings and thoughts and they continue unaddressed. Consultation needs to occur in order to better navigate these issues in treatment and to help the therapist remain objective and effective.

Countertransference is often discussed in terms of experiencing negative emotions toward a client.

However, a clinician can also experience positive countertransference toward a client. It is very possible to experience feelings of elation or joy when working with certain clients; you may be overly concerned or become "too" invested in their well-being and progress in treatment. You may worry about the client when they do not show for sessions or ruminate about them while out of the office.

These feelings are not inappropriate, but you may be having countertransference with this client and you really need to discuss these feelings with a trusted a colleague. These feelings can become detrimental to treatment and taint your judgment when they are ignored, mitigated or kept secret. These feelings can interfere with your decision-making processes about this client and your ability to remain objective in treatment or even about your own behavior.

Following is an example of my personal experience with this type of countertransference with a client.

Case Study

Countertransference Example

Ruth* was a 75-year-old, single female, who resided alone. She had never been married and had no children. Her parents died approximately 10 years ago and she maintained limited contact with her remaining living, immediate family (two brothers and one sister) who lived in various states across the country. These relationships remained strained and almost nonexistent. She had few friends in the area and would often engage in petty arguments with these friends wherein she would have no contact with these individuals for several months.

She claimed to "be just fine" with her relationship(s) with others, but would often become depressed during holidays and other occasions (birthdays, anniversaries) when no one contacted her or returned her phone calls or Facebook messages. Her only "family" were six cats, two dogs and one bird of whom she referred to as "children." She was very attached to her animals and three of these animals died during our work together. These deaths were difficult for her and she would often spend considerable amounts of money to ensure their longevity and health. At times, she would incur excessive amounts of debt, of which she could not afford, as she was retired and lived on a fixed income. Nevertheless, no amount of money was too much for their livelihoods.

Caring Too Much?

I had the privilege of working with Ruth for approximately five years. During this time period, I came to learn more about who she was as a woman and learn how she became the woman who presented before me. She shared intimate and often sad details of her childhood, her adolescence, her adventurous twenties and surviving her tumultuous adulthood. She shared her life with me, every week, for five years! And I grew to admire her strength and resiliency. I admired her life experiences and her worldliness. I had grown to care about Ruth.

Initially, I did not think anything of my positive regard for her. I looked forward to our therapy sessions and would find myself thoroughly engaged in treatment. This was how it should look, right? I should care about my clients and look forward to hearing about their progress. I should be invested in their well-being. Right? I mean that's what this job is all about!

No. . .no, no, no! I was responding to my countertransference with Ruth.

This became evident for me when she invited me on an outing, outside of the office, and I ACTUALLY CONSIDERED this possibility. I even tried to justify it! I said to myself, "This would be OK! I mean I would have a chance to observe her outside of the therapy room in her natural environment and then I would learn more about her to be even more effective in therapy. I am not breaking any ethical rules, it's not a sexual relationship or harmful. Why can't I go?"

Losing Your Objectivity

And then, I stopped myself! "Come on, Meagan! You would never consider this with another client. You would have immediately addressed this in session and explained the boundaries of treatment. You are treating her differently. You are responding to her much differently than with other clients. You are losing your objectivity. You know you can't engage in any personal activities with this client. It may not be unethical, but you don't know how she may interpret this interaction and how this would ultimately impact treatment, which is why she is here for treatment."

Upon having this epiphany, I consulted with a good friend and trusted colleague about this experience. I was honest with her about my feelings and my thoughts concerning this client and she confirmed my hypothesis regarding my countertransference. She processed this in-depth with me and acknowledged this very real and emotional occurrence as being a human response. I had developed a relationship with this client; I knew her innermost thoughts, shared her pain, her joy, her sadness, and even her loneliness. Her loneliness was the root of my countertransference, that was about "my stuff." To know she had no one in this world that shared their love and time with her. And that she may even die alone in her home, really resonated with me. These were facts of her life that I needed to accept and remain objective about my role in her life. My role was to remain her mental health care provider and to meet her needs in the therapy room. She sought me out to assist her with better navigating her life. This was my assigned role and I was OK with that.

Understanding And Explaining My Feelings

After this consultation and gaining a better understanding of my feelings, I was able to process with my client and explain to her why I would be unable to join her on this outing. She thanked me for this feedback and exclaimed, "Well, I guess we won't ever hang out outside of this room, because I have got too much to work on! I much rather have that!" We were good! I was able to deal with the countertransference and address this issue with my client. But I had to, first, BE AWARE that this was occurring.

Pay attention to your emotional reactions while in session. Always question yourself if you are doing things that are atypical or if you think your actions would be questioned by your colleagues. We are one of the primary tools in the room and we need to remain vigilant!

*Client name and actual details have been changed for confidentiality purposes

Clinician Worksheet

Countertransference Checklist

If you are experiencing any of the following, please be advised that consultation may be warranted. Check if you are doing or feeling any of the following:

_____ Strong feelings of avoidance toward the client

_____ Feelings of anger, hostility, or frustration toward the client

_____ Frequent contemplation of transferring the client

_____ Aversive physiological response when anticipating client session

_____ Desire to "take care of" the client or "save" the client

_____ Excitement or feelings of euphoria when client cancels session

_____ Being inauthentic in therapy sessions with your client or defensive

_____ Feelings of guilt following a session in which boundaries needed to be reinforced

_____ Strong negative affective response to client while in session or when consulting

_____ Spending an excessive amount of time with this client's case (more than typically warranted) and attempting to justify why this client requires special or different treatment

_____ Becoming anxious or uncomfortable during a therapy session with this client and this anxiety, at times, interferes with therapy

_____ Enforcing stricter boundaries with this client than with other clients that present with similar issues

STAGES OF TREATMENT IN DBT

DBT is divided into four stages of treatment. These stages are defined by the severity of the client's behaviors, and therapists work with their clients to reach the goals of each stage in their progress toward having a life that they experience as worthy of living.

Stage 1

During this stage, the client presents as overwhelmed and their behavior is typically out of control. This can look like various behaviors, as they may be trying to attempt suicide, engaging in NSSI, drug and alcohol abuse and/or engaging in other types of self-destructive behaviors. When clients initially begin DBT treatment, they often describe their experience of their mental well-being as painful, hopeless and out of control. The goals for this stage are to hopefully assist the client to move from being out of control and overwhelmed to achieving more appropriate behavioral control.

Stage 2

During this stage, your client may be living a life of silent fear and anxiety. Their behavior is better managed, but they continue to suffer emotionally and mentally, often due to past physical, psychological, and emotional trauma and invalidation. Their emotional experience is typically inhibited and repressed. The goals of this stage help the client move from a state of discreet desperation to that of being able to experience a wide range of emotionality. If warranted, posttraumatic stress disorder (PTSD) can be specifically addressed during this stage of treatment.

Stage 3

During this stage, the client's task is to learn to how live. To learn how to define their life goals, develop self-respect, and attain peace and congruence. The primary goal in this stage is that your client is able to lead a life of "typical" happiness and unhappiness.

Stage 4

When engaging in stage 4, your clients may seek to find a deeper meaning through a spiritual existence. Marsha Linehan has suggested a fourth stage specifically for those clients for whom a life of commonplace happiness and unhappiness fails to meet a further goal of spiritual fulfillment or a sense of connectedness to a greater whole. During this stage, the objective of treatment is for your client to move away from a sense of incompleteness toward an ongoing capacity for experiences of hope, joy and freedom (holistic and complete congruence and self-acceptance).

TREATMENT AND DBT

Establishing Therapeutic Alliance

Your clients have to trust that you have their best interest in mind and that you are being genuine. Being authentic with your clients is a key component of establishing a therapeutic relationship. If they do not trust you, therapy will not be productive and non-compliance may become problematic. Genuineness involves being open to feedback from your client and providing honest feedback. It involves establishing boundaries with your client and remaining consistent in treatment.

Functional Behavioral Analysis

Functional behavioral analysis is generally considered to be a problem-solving process for addressing problem behavior. It relies on a variety of techniques and strategies to identify the purposes of specific behavior. A functional behavioral analysis looks beyond the behavior itself. It attempts to identify significant, client-specific social, affective, cognitive, and/or environmental factors associated with the occurrence (and non-occurrence) of specific behaviors. Behavioral intervention plans based on an understanding of "why" one engages in self-destructive behaviors can be extremely useful.

A Functional Behavioral Analysis worksheet has been provided in this chapter to utilize this intervention with your client.

Cognitive Restructuring

Cognitive restructuring is a useful technique for understanding aversive feelings and moods, and for challenging the at-times wrong "automatic beliefs" that can underlie them. Bad moods are unpleasant, they can reduce the quality of your client's performance, and they can undermine your client's relationships with others. Cognitive restructuring helps your client to change their negative or distorted thinking that often negatively affects their mood states and affect.

A Cognitive Restructuring worksheet has been provided in this chapter. This worksheet should be introduced to the client, by you, during the therapy session. Discuss the purpose of cognitive restructuring with your client and how this intervention will assist in developing more adaptive thinking patterns. The worksheet can be used by the clinician and client.

Functional Behavioral Analysis

Directions: Use this worksheet to guide the assessment of your client's target behavioral problem. This worksheet can also be utilized in the development of a treatment plan for your client. An example of a completed functional behavioral analysis can be found on the following pages.

Stage 1: Hypothesis Development

Identify the behavior & define it in terms that are:

specific

observable

measurable

Identify times when the client:

is most likely to engage in the behavior

is least likely to engage in the behavior

factors or events that seem to contribute to the self-destructive behavior

specific immediate events/triggers (the stimulus that sparked the behavior)

"setting events" (events that happened before the behavior of concern, and lowered the client's ability to handle the situation…e.g., argument with a spouse or loved one)

Stage 2: Hypothesis Testing (optional and at times, questionable)

Conduct experiments. This would occur by interviewing your client about certain experiences or analyzing recent occurrences in their everyday life.

Verify/revise the hypotheses (regarding which variables maintain the undesirable behavior) by controlling (Q & A with clients, what ifs? Or discuss what occurs in the absence of the variable) circumstances & events:

present client with different degrees and types of the hypothetical stimuli (setting event and/or originator)

prevention of the occurrence of the hypothetical stimulus (setting event and/or antecedent)

present/explore other stimuli that might have an effect on the behavior

promote the demonstration of a new, replacement behavior that you suspect would meet the client's needs and thus replace the inappropriate behavior. (Remember that the replacement behavior must meet the needs/desires of the client to at least the same extent as the inappropriate action. Otherwise, why would your client consider changing to the new behavior?)

Stage 3: Behavioral Intervention Plan (BIP)

Develop a realistic plan of action in the BIP part of the client's treatment plan:

set goals and objectives

describe direct interventions

identify prescribed responses to displays of the self-destructive behaviors

list replacement behaviors and how they will be taught to the client

note any changes in services provided (e.g., group therapy, medication management)

Stage 4: Implementation of the Plan

Teach positive (or less negative) alternative behaviors that will serve the same purpose(s) as the inappropriate behaviors, and hopefully promote the use of the positive behaviors.

Modify events/circumstances associated with problem behaviors so that inappropriate behaviors are no longer prompted or rewarded.

Functional Behavioral Analysis

Date: June 12, 2015

Client: Ida Client

Antecedents (A)	Behavior (B)	Consequences (C)
1. Engaged in an argument with her parents. They asked her why she couldn't be as good as her sister and told me that if she were then maybe they wouldn't punish her as much.	2. Client stated that she become enraged, felt shame, embarrassment and that she wasn't good enough. Felt like her parents did not accept her.	3. Client stated that she locked herself in the upstairs bathroom and began to cut her torso and upper thighs. After seeing the blood, she stated that she felt "relief" and stopped the cutting.
4. Got in trouble at school and met with vice principal who asked her why she was having so many difficulties. He then stated that he knew her sister and continued to "rave" about her being "such a good student."	5. Client became "enraged" and felt hate for her sister and then felt guilt for feeling hate toward her. Stated she felt overwhelmed and alone.	6. Upon returning home, client locked herself in bedroom and proceeded to cut her thighs. Stated that when this occurred she "felt better" and no longer felt guilty since she "punished herself."
7. Client stated that she got into an argument with her best friend and that she informed client she did not want to be her friend anymore.	8. Client reported feeling abandoned and alone and empty. Client reported that "she was just one more person who didn't love me because I am not worthy of it."	9. Client stated that she did not wait to cut herself at home and chose to go to the girl's bathroom at school and used a staple to scratch her arms and thighs. She stated, "after a while I felt OK enough to go back to class and it wasn't so bad."
10. Client stated that she observed that her best friend was with someone else on Instagram and lied to her about going to a party.	11. Client reported feeling rejected, sad and empty.	12. Client stated that she didn't cut herself, but did have suicidal ideation. She stated that she didn't "do it because I am too scared to do it." She then stated that she chose to cut herself later that evening and immediately experienced symptom relief.

Hypothesis (based on the assumption that other ABCs showed a similar pattern)

Engaging in NSSI when interactions with important people (parents, friends, authority figures) are perceived as negative or minimizing. She experiences aversive affect when being compared to sister, provokes feelings of not being good enough and unimportant. Client does not express feelings during these interactions and internalizes her anger, and frustration. When she is able to express these emotions via cutting, she experiences symptom relief. Client has now associated symptom relief with the cutting behaviors and has now chosen this behavior to manage negative affect.

Plan

Highlight this pattern in treatment with client in order to help her remain aware of the triggers in her environment. Help client to learn healthier forms of expressing negative affect, by way of incorporating DBT skills of mindfulness, emotion regulation, distress tolerance and interpersonal effectiveness. Assist client with lessening these behaviors and highlight when she has decreased this behavior. Recognize gains and efforts made toward the above goals. Explore alternative behaviors in which to replace the NSSI with client. Incorporate client's feedback into the treatment plan in order to facilitate compliance and investment in her treatment. Explore client's relationships with significant others and use psychoeducation to empower client in better understanding the nature of relationships and the "gray areas" in relationships.

Behavior Chain Analysis

Directions: This form should be completed with the guidance of your clinician. This worksheet will be used to identify triggers and patterns that lead to problem behavior. Please be honest and candid when providing responses.

1. Describe the specific **problem behavior** (flashback, cutting, dissociation, hiding, closeting, panic attack, etc.).

   A. Be very specific and detailed. No vague terms.

   _____

   _____

   _____

   B. Identify exactly what you did, said, thought or felt (if feelings are the targeted problem behavior).

   _____

   _____

   _____

   C. Describe the intensity of the behavior and other characteristics of the behavior that are important.

   _____

   _____

   _____

   D. Describe the problem behavior in enough detail that an actor in a play or movie could recreate the behavior exactly.

   _____

   _____

   _____

2. Describe the specific **precipitating event** that started the whole chain of behavior. Start with the environmental event that started the chain. Always start with some event in your environment, even if it doesn't seem to you that the environmental event "caused" the problem behavior. Possible questions to get at this are:

   What exact event precipitated the start of the chain reaction?

   _____

   _____

   _____

When did the sequence of events that led to the problem behavior begin? When did the problem start?

_____

_____

_____

What was going on the moment the problem started?

_____

_____

_____

What were you doing, thinking, feeling, imagining at that time?

_____

_____

_____

Why did the problem behavior happen on that day instead of the day before?

_____

_____

_____

3. Describe in general, **exposure factors** happening before the precipitating event. What factors or events made you more vulnerable to a problematic chain? Areas to examine are:

A. Physical illness; unbalanced eating or sleeping; injury

_____

_____

_____

B. Use of drugs or alcohol; misuse of prescription drugs

_____

_____

_____

C. Stressful events in the environment (either positive or negative)

_____

_____

_____

D. Intense emotions, such as sadness, anger, fear, loneliness

_____

_____

_____

E. Previous behaviors of your own that you found stressful

_____

_____

_____

4. Describe, in candid detail the **chain of events** that led up to the problem behavior. What next? Imagine that your problem behavior is chained to the precipitating event in the environment. How long is the chain? Where does it go? What are the links? Write out all links in the chain of events, no matter how small. Be very specific, as if you are writing a script for a play.

A. What exact thoughts (or beliefs), feelings, or actions followed the precipitating event? What thought, feeling, or action followed that? What next?

_____

_____

_____

B. Look at each link in the chain after you write it. Was there another thought, feeling, or action that could have occurred? Could someone else have thought, felt, or acted differently at that point? If so, explain how that certain thought, feeling, or action came to be.

_____

_____

_____

C. For each link in the chain, is there is a smaller link you could describe.

_____

_____

_____

5. The links can be thoughts, emotions, sensations and behaviors. What are the **consequences** of this behavior? Be specific.

A. How did other people react immediately and later?

_____

_____

_____

B. How did you feel immediately following the behavior? Later?

_____

_____

_____

6. What effect did the behavior have on you and your environment. Describe, in detail, various **solutions** to the problem.

A. Go back to the chain of your behaviors following the prompting event. Circle each point or link indicating that if you had done something different, you would have avoided the problem behavior.

_____

_____

_____

B. What could you have done differently at each link in the chain of events to avoid the problem behavior? What coping behaviors or skillful behaviors could you have used?

_____

_____

_____

7. Describe in detail the **prevention strategy.** How could you have kept the chain from starting by reducing your vulnerability? Describe what you are going to do to REPAIR important or significant consequences of the problem behavior.

_____

_____

_____

Sample Worksheet

Cognitive Restructuring

Directions: Use this worksheet as an example of how to complete the following "Cognitive Restructuring Exercise."

Step 1: Calm Yourself

If you're still upset or stressed by the thoughts you want to explore, you may find it hard to concentrate on using the tool. Use meditation or deep breathing to calm yourself down if you feel particularly stressed or upset.

Step 2: Identify the Situation

Begin by describing the situation that triggered your negative mood, and write this here.

_____

_____

Step 3: Analyze Your Mood

Next, jot down the mood, or moods, that you felt during the situation. Here, moods are the primary feelings that we have, but they are not thoughts about the situation. An easy way to discriminate moods from thoughts, is to think about it like this: Moods can typically be described using one word, whereas thoughts are more complex.

For example, "She embarrassed me in front of all of my friends" would be a thought, while the associated moods might be frustration, embarrassment, anger, or agitated.

_____

_____

_____

Step 4: Identify Automatic Thoughts

Write down the natural reactions, or "automatic thoughts," you experienced when you felt the mood. In the example above, your thoughts might be:

- "Maybe she doesn't like me or she is jealous of me."
- "She hates me."
- "I knew it. . . they always talk about me."
- "She is such a (fill in the blank)!"
- "No one likes me."

In this example, the most disturbing thoughts (the "hot thoughts") are likely to be "She hates me" or "No one likes me."

_____

_____

Step 5: Find Objective Supportive Evidence

Identify the evidence that objectively supports your automatic thoughts. In our example, you might write the following:

- "She made a derogatory statement about me."
- "She said it in front of other people."

Your goal is to look objectively at what happened, and then to write down certain events or comments that steered your automatic thoughts.

_____

_____

_____

Step 6: Find Objective Contradictory Evidence

Identify and write down evidence that opposes the automatic thought. In our example, this might be:

- "What she said wasn't true."
- "No one else has ever said this about me."
- "My other friends did not respond to her."

If you notice, the above statements are reasonable and more rational than the initial reactive thoughts.

_____

_____

_____

Step 7: Identify Fair and Balanced Thoughts

At this step, you have considered both sides of the situation. Now, you should be equipped with the information you need to make a fair, balanced interpretation of what occurred.

If you still feel uneasy, process the situation with other people, or assess the question in some other way.

When you come to a well-adjusted conclusion, jot down these thoughts. The sensible thoughts in this example might now include:

- "No one else has said this about me. Other people have said more positive things."
- "She may be mad about something else and it's not about me."
- "There was an argument, but we are still friends."
- "The way she handled the situation was inappropriate."
- "My other friends were shocked about what she said and ALL of my friends weren't there."

_____

_____

Step 8: Evaluate Your Present Mood

You should now have a better understanding of the situation, and more than likely your mood has improved. Write down how you feel currently.

Reflect on what you can do or could have done about the situation. (When looking at the situation using the above steps, the issue may be of lesser importance, and you may determine that nothing needs to be done about it.)

Finally, create some positive affirmations that you can use to counter any similar automatic thoughts in the future. And keep these affirmations handy. For example, use Post-it notes, and stick them in various places (e.g., bathroom mirror, in your closet, sun visor in your car, in a drawer) in order to remind yourself about the "good things and true things" about who you are.

_____

_____

_____

_____

_____

_____

_____

_____

Client Worksheet

Cognitive Restructuring Exercise

Directions: Use this worksheet to identify, analyze and restructure your thoughts about an event that you perceived as distressing.

Situation: Describe what triggered your negative mood. Be as specific as possible.

_____

_____

Analyze Your Mood: Describe how you felt about in the situation and how are you feeling now (e.g., angry, frustrated, sad).

_____

_____

Identify Automatic Thoughts: List the automatic thoughts that you had about this issue.

_____

_____

Find Objective Supportive Evidence: Jot down any evidence you can find that supports the automatic thoughts that you identified above.

_____

_____

Find Objective Opposing Evidence: Look at your automatic thoughts and write down the objective evidence that opposes these thoughts. Take into consideration others' perspectives and jot these down as well. Compose your new perspective below:

_____

_____

Identify Reasonable and Sensible Thoughts: Take a look at the cognitions you listed above in the previous two sections. Now, look at these issues from a more balanced perspective and jot down these new more rational thoughts.

_____

_____

Evaluate Your Current Mood: Take a few moments to monitor your current mood. How do you feel? Have your feelings gotten better or improved? Is there anything you need to do about this issue that would improve the situation?

_____

_____

I would like you to keep in mind that it is DIFFICULT if not IMPOSSIBLE to perform DBT in its purest form in most settings. Many agencies, practices, hospitals and other settings, do not allot time to see a client weekly, conduct skills groups with the client, and allow you to leave work to attend weekly supervision regarding the client.

There are other principles of DBT that may also conflict with agency policies and standards of practice. For example, one position of DBT encourages the clinician to avoid reinforcing maladaptive behavior. If a client acts out (suicidal/NSSI gesture) it is advised that you do not immediately tend to the client, as we do not want to positively reinforce this behavior with attention and excessive doting. Well, in some agencies, policy may require you to respond immediately to any client that engages in suicidal behavior or self-harm activities. We must be creative in the way we implement the practice of DBT and incorporate this type of treatment into our agency policies, thereby effectively treating the client and meeting the needs of your employer.

Here are a couple of case examples illustrating how I have, creatively, incorporated DBT methodology into treatment and practicing within the scope of my employment.

Case Study

DBT Into Treatment

While working for the federal prison system, there were several clients that presented with cluster B personality disorders (Borderline, Narcissistic, and Antisocial) and would engage in a multitude of acting-out behaviors to include, but not limited to cutting themselves, swallowing objects, threatening suicide (daily), feigning suicide attempts, and even ingesting cleaning agents at times.

There was one client, specifically, who learned that when engaging in any of the above actions, Psychology Services had to respond immediately. Really, we were allowed 24 hours, per policy, to respond to these gestures, but typically we were quick to respond to these incidences at the request of other staff who were not trained in DBT. They did not understand that this immediate responsiveness reinforced this behavior and was not helpful to assisting the client in learning better impulse control and frustration tolerance skills. These staff members only knew what policy stated, and they wanted us to respond immediately to all of these cases.

Clinically, I was aware that this way of working would be to the client's detriment as well as remain disruptive to the daily functioning of the institution, and I needed to figure out a way to incorporate the DBT tenets that would be helpful with this case, while meeting the demands of my employers.

A Phone Call

During one of my "on-call tours", I received a phone call about this specific client. He threatened to kill himself due to "disliking the food on his tray." He refused to obey directives provided by the officer and thus Psychology Services (namely, me) needed to report to the institution to "handle this guy." I was very familiar with him and knew that he did not present with any suicidal ideation, intent or plan; but we have to check out any report of suicide as circumstances can easily change. An accidental suicide remains a suicide, regardless of the client's motives.

Agency policy allotted a 24-hour response time to these behaviors. During this period, the client is removed from his cell and placed under the observation of staff until the psychologist arrives on site. He is placed under this observation with no objects, clothing, or items of which can be used to engage in self-harm and he is not allowed to leave this observation area until I arrive.

History Of Malingering

I was aware that the client was safe and under the supervision of other staff, I was also aware of this client's manipulative behaviors and history of malingering in order to procure various requests, such as cell changes, phone privileges, or additional food items. Prior suicide assessments conducted with the client indicated that he was a low risk candidate for suicide. I was able to use all of this information in addition to my clinical judgment and consultation with a colleague to make the clinically-informed choice to report to the institution on the 23rd hour of my 24-hour time frame.

Upon arriving to the institution to assess the client, he was no longer reporting suicidal ideation and stated, "I am fine doc, I just had a moment. I don't need to see you, just put me back in my cell. I am fine. I am not going to do anything to myself, I just wanted you to make them fix my food. I am good though. I am tired and I just want to go back to my cell. Please. I am sorry."

Reinforce DBT Skills

He was then informed that this author had driven a 2-hour distance, one-way, to tend to his concerns and that my job was to ensure his safety and reinforce the DBT skills of which he learned in prior weeks. Frustration tolerance and impulse control skills were discussed at-length with the client and he professed understanding and the willingness to utilize these skills "next time I don't like something." He was provided feedback about his cooperation and released to return to his cell. I did not receive another phone call about his maladaptive behavior during his tenure at the institution.

Case Study

Incorporating Tenets of DBT

While employed at a different agency, I acquired a client who was diagnosed with borderline personality disorder. She had been able to manage her reactivity, for the most part, but was currently being triggered by her husband's dismissive behavior and emotional neglect. She had become emotionally volatile and reactive when feeling slighted or when her husband remained non-responsive to her concerns. She would become emotionally overwhelmed and had difficulty managing these emotions and feelings. This had become disruptive to her everyday functioning. She was unable to focus and/or concentrate, had difficulty performing tasks at work, would often ruminate and began to become paranoid about others' intentions toward her.

Therapy involved addressing her concerns about her relationship, past relational trauma and the incorporation of DBT skills concepts to include frustration tolerance, impulse control and emotion regulation. These skills were warranted to assist with her ability to become more responsive to situations rather than reactionary in her environment. They were incorporated to assist her in managing this whirlwind of emotions, while navigating her everyday life encounters, to include her work, social, academic and family life. She responded well in treatment. She completed all of the work in treatment and was always ready to discuss all that she learned about a skill concept or other bibliotherapy of which was assigned.

Emergency Call

But, she was not applying these skills during volatile interactions with her spouse. One evening, at approximately 11:30 pm, following a verbal altercation with her husband, she called the on-call emergency line seeking my assistance. See, at this agency, if a client contacted the on-call services, we were required to respond, immediately. . .no matter what. . .each and every time. . .we must respond.

Following this phone call, my client began to contact this on-call service at least 2-3 times per week for several weeks. Each call would reference a verbal altercation with her spouse, or his non-responsiveness to a text or phone call. Each call occurred after 10 pm, to include weekdays and weekends. This was becoming a problem, not only for me, but for the on-call service as well, as they began to become desensitized to her phone calls and would, sometimes, forget to contact me for several hours following a phone call. This was not good.

Strengthen Boundaries In Treatment

I would address this issue during sessions and each session she reported that she would attempt to apply the skills learned in therapy, but this did not happen. After consultation with my supervisor, I determined that I needed to strengthen boundaries in treatment and not reinforce my client's behavior.

This led to the development of "guidelines" referencing the "appropriate and inappropriate" uses of the on-call services. These uses were delineated and discussed in detail with my client. She was informed that I would ALWAYS respond to any calls she made to the on-call service, as this was the agency's policy. However, if her reasons were not of those delineated as being appropriate during this meeting, she would forfeit her next in-person session. She exclaimed, "What! So, if I see you in person on a Friday and call you on a Sunday, I won't see you that upcoming Friday, it will be the following Friday! So, that would be two weeks!"

Agreeing To The Guidelines

I again explained the reasons for choosing to utilize the on-call services and emphasized the importance of her incorporating the DBT skills practiced during weekly sessions. Her discomfort with these skills was acknowledged and processed with her. She was encouraged to use these skills during her conflicts in order to get better, to be better, to respond better, and feel better. She was also informed that I would be doing her a disservice by reinforcing the very behaviors of which we are attempting to extinguish and/or better manage. She, ultimately, agreed to the terms of these "guidelines" and only contacted the on-call service on one other occasion; however, her reason was legitimate and appropriate. She was provided positive feedback about utilizing the services appropriately and she responded well to this feedback.

These examples illustrate incorporating principles of DBT that are effective when implemented appropriately, while continuing to meet the demands of the agency.

- The client's maladaptive behaviors were **not** positively reinforced.
- Learned DBT skills and their ability to implement these skills were reinforced which resulted in reduction of their behavior.
- Application of these skills increased their ability to manage frustration and conflict.

USING ONLINE RESOURCES IN TREATMENT WITH YOUR CLIENTS

Most of our clients are using the internet and are engaging in online activity daily. A recent study indicated that those armed with smartphones or tablets check these devices approximately 100 times per day! 100 times per day! That is amazing! Even as early as first grade, children are being exposed to computer use in schools and in the home. We have Wi-Fi capability in our cars, on airplanes, when visiting other countries, restaurants, and even in church! I can't tell you how many smartphones I see being pulled out when the pastor asks the church members to follow along for Bible passage readings! With that being said, I have no doubt that the age of the "paper/pencil homework assignment" will soon be dated and antiquated. They have an "App" for everything these days, including therapeutic interventions.

In the NSSI chapter of this workbook, we addressed NSSI behaviors and how the use of internet and online blogs/message boards/forums and groups have fueled contagion of this behavior with certain groups. We are also aware that learning theory teaches us that it is easier to extinguish a behavior if we can replace the behavior with something similar, but less harmful to our clients. Which is why incorporating the use of these devices into treatment is so essential when we are attempting to work with NSSI behaviors. Especially, if our clients are using the internet as a support forum or way to gather information and/or validation about this behavior.

I have had much more success with treatment compliance when I am able to use online resources and therapy applications in session with my clients who engage in self-injurious behaviors. Of course there are guidelines that should be followed when using this modality of communication and/or treatment with your clients.

Informed Consent

If you are going to incorporate online activities you need to delineate the use of this activity in your informed consent form. When discussing the use, you should be specific in how it will be used, what applications may be utilized, and how often will it be used. You can also provide information about any specific support groups to which you may refer or any specific message/boards or forums you may incorporate in treatment. You may want to delineate the costs and benefits of using this type of method (power outages, emergency situations, inability to guarantee confidentiality or who else may be using this site, loss of data, etc.).

Educate Yourself on the Site!

NEVER refer a client to a website or direct them to use a phone application with which you have not had personal experience. Using the internet as a resource is no different than referring a book to a client or referring a client to a treatment provider. You want to make sure you are familiar with the nuances of the site and it is even advised that you contact the site administrator if you have specific questions not immediately available on the site. This is specifically important when referring clients to NSSI recovery websites or support groups for various mental health concerns including suicide.

Introduce the Site or Phone Application During a Therapy Session

You can use the session to navigate the site with the client, familiarize them with the site or phone application and answer any questions that may arise. This way you are able to ensure that they are following treatment guidelines and it allows the client to take some ownership of their treatment. It also demonstrates your investment in the client's use of the site/phone application.

Discuss Any Concerns

Discuss any concerns the client or guardian may have about an application or website. Be able to answer difficult questions and be ready to provide strong rationale about the use of this technology in treatment. If the child is "on punishment" or phone restriction this should be discussed with the parent in order to consult about treatment exceptions, to ensure continuity of care.

Below, I have provided a list of the most up-to-date NSSI chat rooms, forums, support groups and message boards. Some of these sites are excellent for use with your client, in addition to their family members. At times, we all know that parents can be sensitive about this topic and have difficulty comprehending these concepts. Taking a systemic approach in managing this issue is vital, as we need the support of guardians/caretakers/parents when working with their children. The more they know, the more they are open to feedback and understanding this behavior. Some of these sites have outstanding resources for parents, siblings and loved ones that are dealing with someone engaging in NSSI behavior, thus these resources can be invaluable when working within a family system.

These sites are designed to be informative and supportive and provide your client with a healthier outlet to get their needs met. Instead of seeking belongingness and acceptance needs from an unhealthy and self-destructive forum, they are able to have these same needs met, within the same modality with more positive messages. Please note that these sites were up-to-date at the time this workbook was being developed. Given the ever changing nature of on-line data/resources, some of these sites may be renamed or no longer currently active. These sites are being used to illustrate the availability of resources.

Online NSSI Resources

- Recover Your life (http://www.recoveryourlife.com/)
- Self-injury.net Safe Haven (http://gabrielle.self-injury.net/)
- Teen Line Online (http://teenlineonline.org/)
- Healthy Place Self-Injury Forum (http://www.healthyplace.com/forum/self-injury/)
- Self-Harm: Recovery, Advice, and Support (http://www.thesite.org/healthandwellbeing/mentalhealth/selfharm)
- Kids Help Phone (http://www.kidshelpphone.ca/Teens/home.aspx)
- Holding of Wrist (http://holdingofwrist.com)
- Reach-Out.com (http://reachout.com/)
- Scar-Tissue.net (http://www.scar-tissue.net/)
- Fort Refuge (http://www.fortrefuge.com/forum/)
- Bodies Under Siege Forum (http://buslist.org/phpBB/)
- Bodies Under Siege (BUS) Chat (http://buschat.info/)
- Virtual Teen Cutting and Self-Harm Forum (http://www.virtualteen.org/forums/forumdisplay.php?f=16)
- Removing Chains (http://www.removingchains.org/rooms/under-18-depression-mental-health-chat-room)

CBT/DBT and Other Intervention Applications for Smartphone Devices

Please familiarize yourself with each application prior to making a referral for a client. If you are going to incorporate technology in your therapy sessions, please have this highlighted in your informed consent form.

iPhone, iTouch, iPad	Android Phone Apps
1. SAM—Self-Help App for Anxiety	1. SAM—Self-Help App for Anxiety
2. Virtual hope box	2. Virtual hope box
3. MindQuire for iPad	3. Cognitive Diary CBT self-help
4. The CBT App	4. Depression CBT self-help guide
5. Happify	5. The Worry Box
6. MyCBT	6. Fig—personal wellness guide
7. Anxiety Coach	7. Happy Life
8. Thought Diary	8. Happy Habits: Choose Happiness
9. Mood & Anxiety Diary	9. Irrational Thinking CBT Test
10. Mood Diary—the Phobic Trust	10. Stop Panic & Anxiety
11. Mind Shift for Anxiety	11. Mind Shift for Anxiety
12. eCBT	12. Deeds Journal
13. iCBT	13. CBT Referee
14. CBT Referee	14. Suicide Safety Plan
15. iStress	15. Re-motivate Activity Tracker
16. Gratitude Journal	16. Depression Aid
17. Journal Diary	17. CBT Thought Record Diary
18. Live Happy	18. Journal
19. My Thoughts	19. I Journal
20. Smart Goals	20. This Journal
21. LifeTick (values & goals)	21. Alura Cognitive Therapy
22. Beat Panic	22. PTSD Coach
23. DBT Self-Help	23. T2 Mood Tracker
24. MoodKit	24. Pacifica

25. Pacifica	25. Mood Journal Plus
26. Affirmations	26. Mood Sentry
27. Music for Refreshment	27. Habit Factor (goals)
28. MoodPanda	28. MyChain (maintaining goals)
29. MoodJournal	29. LifeTick (values & goals)
30. Mood Sentry	30. Music for Refreshment
31. EFT Clinic	31. Private Diary
32. Panic Aid	32. Exploring EFT
33. Thought Box	33. Self-Esteem Blackboard
34. Fig—personal wellness guide	34. Confidence Quotes
35. Master Fear of Flying	35. Mindfulness bell—set reminders!
36. Headspace	36. Insight Timer - meditation
37. Calm (mindfulness)	37. OCD
38. Breathe 2 Relax	38. Breathe 2 Relax
39. Omvana	39. Headspace
	40. Calm—Meditate, Sleep, Relax

Windows Phone 7	Blackberry
1. Feel Good Tracker	1. Mood Journal
2. Smart Goals	2. Dear Diary
3. CBT Diary	3. LifeTick (values & goals)
4. What Now	

Chapter 10 | Teletherapy and Suicidal Clients

TELEMENTAL HEALTH

Telemental health has become more widely utilized in the last five years. Also referred to as "telebehaviorial health," "e-counseling," "e-therapy," "online therapy," "cybercounseling," or "online counseling," telemental health has been defined as: *the provision of remote mental health care services (using modalities including videoconferencing, computer programs, and mobile applications) by a variety of different mental health providers, such as psychiatrists, psychologists, social workers, counselors, and marriage and family therapists.* Behavioral health care models have incorporated technology to include hospitals establishing telepsychiatric assessment programs in their emergency departments as well as the development of virtual networks of mental health professionals providing services to underserved geographic areas. "Telemental health" has been found to be equivalent to face-to-face treatment.

Remote assessment of suicidality involves complex legal issues including:

- Licensing requirements for remote delivery of care
- Legal procedures for involuntary detainment
- Commitment of potentially harmful patients
- Liability questions related to the remote nature of the mental health service

BENEFITS OF TELETHERAPY

The use of telecommunications to provide mental health services to isolated or underserved populations has received increasing attention in the past decade This modality of treatment can be used to assist disabled clients who can't leave their homes, remote, rural patients without access to health care, or some cases of severe anxiety or OCD. It can also be useful in situations in which commuting to therapy proves to be an insurmountable barrier. The Department of Veterans Affairs (VA) has been successful in implementing this modality of treatment to veterans in rural areas or those who are unable to be physically present at the main VAMC in their city and state.

Research has also found that face-to-face contact, or even a video image, is not required for successful mental health care intervention and some patients would be more comfortable given some physical and emotional space.

CONCERNS ABOUT TELETHERAPY

Although teletherapy can be useful, there remain concerns about implementing this form of treatment. Distractions can detract from the computerized experience (e.g., your client may check email during a session, or text). Conversations can be more easily recorded and later made public and you have to know the rules and regulations of the state in which you are providing services to the client. It is illegal to conduct ongoing, long-term therapy in a state where you are not licensed. Another concern is that the commitment that is made to personal care (scheduling appointments, taking time away from other activity, going to a private, special place for therapy) does not happen as readily online and a client who is suicidal may require much more active and intensive services than teletherapy can provide.

GUIDELINES FOR THE USE OF TELETHERAPY

There is little consistent guidance across states on how mental health professionals should use these and other forms of electronic communication such as email, Skype and various forms of videoconferencing. (FYI: Skype is NOT compliant with the Health Insurance Portability and Accountability Act [HIPAA] and should be used with caution. Several states have agencies that will provide an encrypted service to conduct this modality of treatment.) You should contact your malpractice insurance carrier to confirm that telehealth services— both in-state and across jurisdictional lines—are covered under your malpractice policy. In addition, the Association of State and Provincial Psychology Boards has created a credential called the *Interjurisdictional Practice Certificate* that facilitates temporary practice in other jurisdictions.

The American Psychological Association (APA) Task Force, which developed telepsychology guidelines for psychologists, recently published Guidelines for the Practice of Telepsychology (September, 2013) and conducted a 50-state review (October, 2013) in order to assess each state's readiness to conduct or implement teletherapy. These findings can be located on the webpage below.

http://www.apapracticecentral.org/advocacy/state/telehealth-slides.pdf.

The National Association of Social Workers and the Association of Social Work Boards *Standards for Technology and Social Work Practice* was developed in 2005. This document can be located with the provided link below.

https://www.socialworkers.org/practice/standards/naswtechnologystandards.pdf.

It is advised that each clinician check whether your state licensing board has issued any policies related to telehealth/telepsychology/teletherapy.

For illustration purposes, we will highlight "telepsychology" guidelines as issued by the APA. We will use these guidelines as our frame of reference, as we discuss them in relation to conducting teletherapy with your suicidal clients.

These guidelines were designed to address the burgeoning area of teletherapy. Telepsychology is defined, for the purpose of these guidelines, *as the provision of psychological services using telecommunication technologies as expounded in the "Definition of Telepsychology."*

The current guidelines are informed by relevant APA standards and guidelines, including the following: Ethical Principles of Psychologists and Code of Conduct ("APA Ethics Code") (APA, 2002a, 2010), and the Record Keeping Guidelines (APA, 2007). In addition, the assumptions and principles that guide the APA's "Guidelines on Multicultural Training, Research, Practice, and Organizational Change for Psychologists" (APA, 2003) are infused throughout the rationale and application describing each of the guidelines. Therefore, these guidelines are informed by professional theories, evidence-based practices and definitions in an effort to offer the best guidance in the practice of telepsychology.

APA delineates that these guidelines reference statements that infer or recommend specific professional behaviors, endeavors or conduct for psychologists or any mental health professional. These guidelines contrast from standards, in that standards are mandated and may include an enforcement piece. As a result, these guidelines are described as aspirational in intent. These guidelines are meant to guide mental health professionals as they apply updated and recent standards of professional practice when applying telecommunication technologies as a means of delivering their professional services.

Guideline 1: Competence of the Psychologist

"Psychologists who provide telepsychology services strive to take reasonable steps to ensure their competence with both the technologies used and the potential impact of the technologies on clients/patients, supervisees or other professionals."

In Other Words

If you have not received adequate training in using the hardware required to perform telehealth services, then it would be unethical to perform this modality of treatment. You must familiarize yourself with the program, software, data system, and equipment that will be used in providing services. You must understand the costs and benefits of this type of therapy and be able to articulate these to your client. As the treating clinician you are also expected to exercise clinical judgment when assessing a client expressing suicidal ideation. There should be a specific protocol established in managing these types of clients and it is advised that you consult with your board and/or mental health professionals prior to developing your protocol.

Guideline 2: Standards of Care in the Delivery of Telepsychology Services

"Psychologists make every effort to ensure that ethical and professional standards of care and practice are met at the outset and throughout the duration of the telepsychology services they provide."

In Other Words

Conducting teletherapy doesn't involve providing lowered professional standards of care to your client. You must conduct therapy in an appropriate setting. Your licensure information needs to be visible, whether you develop a separate icon, or have this displayed on your webpage, in the background. Whatever you choose, it again, needs to be easily located by the client. Your client should still be afforded the confidentiality and privacy that you would provide to an in-person client.

Guideline 3: Informed Consent

"Psychologists strive to obtain and document informed consent that specifically address the unique concerns related to the telepsychology services they provide. When doing so, psychologists are cognizant of the applicable laws and regulations, as well as organizational requirements that govern informed consent in this area."

In Other Words

The informed consent is a cornerstone when choosing to provide this type of service to your clients. This allows you to delineate the benefits and costs to utilizing teletherapy, discuss alternatives when the client is experiencing a crisis, put in place safety plans, advise contacting others, discuss your suicide protocol, and communication risk. You would also need to include information about data and technology risk, the inability to control for confounding variables including power outages, loss of connection or equipment failure. You can include any back-up plans, if warranted, due to machinery malfunction. Your clients should be advised of emergency clinics or nearest ER's in case of suicidal ideation. Remember, we have to demonstrate "due diligence" when providing treatment services to our clients. When developing your informed consent, review this document through "due diligence" lenses.

Guideline 4: Confidentiality of Data and Information

"Psychologists who provide telepsychology services make reasonable effort to protect and maintain the confidentiality of the data and information relating to their clients/patients and inform them of the potentially increased risks to loss of confidentiality inherent in the use of the telecommunication technologies, if any."

In Other Words

Again, in order to meet the above guideline, you must familiarize yourself with the equipment and programming being implemented. You need to also be able to educate your clients about the risk of losing data and the possibilities of their files, records, or e-files being compromised and the procedures that have been established to address such instances.

Guideline 5: Security and Transmission of Data and Information

"Psychologists who provide telepsychology services should take reasonable steps to ensure that security measures are in place to protect data and information related to their clients/patients from unintended access or disclosure."

In Other Words

You need to be familiar with the computer programs you choose to use with your clients. These systems should be HIPAA compliant and meet the law requirements in your state. It is also important that the companies you choose to contract your services (telehealth site providers) meet certain standards. These standards include meeting federal government standards that require that you to be HIPAA compliant as a "covered entity" and have signed the "Business Associate Agreement" (BAA) which is also required by law, as per the HIPAA Omnibus Act (January, 2013).

Video service providers are **NOT** obligated to inform health providers about their professional obligations or related mandates. As HIPAA "covered entities;" however, clinicians serving US citizens must utilize technology that remains compliant with all applicable state, provincial and federal laws. Providers in other countries must be compliant with relevant laws in the countries whose citizens they serve.

Following is a compilation of companies that claim to meet either both or one of the standards listed above. It is advised that you educate yourself about any company you are choosing with respect to providing this type of service.

Company Name	HIPAA "Compliance" or BAA
CarePaths Reports	HIPAA compliance
Chiron Health Reports	HIPAA compliance and BAA
Choruscall Reports	HIPAA compliance and BAA
CloudVisit Reports	HIPAA compliance and BAA
CNOW, Inc. Reports	HIPAA compliance
Counsel Reports	HIPAA compliance
Doxy.me Reports	HIPAA compliance and BAA
eVisit Company Reports	HIPAA compliance and BAA
Influxis Reports	HIPAA compliance and BAA
Interactive Care Reports	HIPAA compliance and BAA
MedWeb Reports	HIPAA compliance
OmniJoin by Brother Reports	HIPAA compliance
ReachHealth Reports	HIPAA compliance and BAA
Revation Reports	HIPAA compliance
SBR Health Company Reports	HIPAA compliance and BAA
Secure Telehealth Reports	HIPAA compliance and BAA
Secure Video Reports	HIPAA compliance and BAA
Soltrite Reports	HIPAA compliance
TeleHealth365, Inc. Reports	HIPAA compliance and BAA
thera-LINK Reports	HIPAA compliance and BAA
V2VIP Reports	HIPAA compliant "encryption"
VIA3 Reports	HIPAA compliance and BAA
Vidyo Company Reports	HIPAA compliance and BAA
Virtual Therapy Connect Reports	HIPAA compliance and BAA
Vitel Net Reports	HIPAA compliance
Vsee Reports	HIPAA compliance and BAA
WeCounsel Company Reports	HIPAA compliance and BAA

Guideline 6: Disposal of Data and Information and Technologies

"Psychologists who provide teletherapy services make reasonable efforts to dispose of data and information and the technologies used in a manner that facilitates protection from unauthorized access and accounts for safe and appropriate disposal."

In Other Words

You have to treat this information similarly to a paper file. What happens to this information should you close the practice or leave the agency? What arrangements have you made to dispose of the information should you die or become ill? What safeguards have been established to discretely manage this "cyber information"?

Guideline 7: Testing and Assessment

"Psychologists are encouraged to consider the unique issues that may arise with test instruments and assessment approaches designed for in-person implementation when providing telepsychology services."

In Other Words

What testing instruments would be the most appropriate to use with a client? If you choose to engage in testing using this treatment modality how are you able to control for confounding variables (room temperature, noise level, distractions in the area)? Does this affect the validity of testing, particularly if providing a standardized assessment? These are all questions that one must consider when exploring the issue of testing and assessment.

Guideline 8: Interjurisdictional Practice

"Psychologists are encouraged to be familiar with and comply with all relevant laws and regulations when providing telepsychology services to clients/patients across jurisdictional and international borders."

In Other Words

You must be familiar with the laws in your state and the state of which your client resides. There are often fines and sanctions for failing to follow these standards.

> ### IGNORANCE IS NO EXCUSE AND NO DEFENSE!

Chapter 11 | Ethical and Legal Implications

Confidentiality is defined as the ethical duty to fulfill the promise that client information received during therapy will not be disclosed without authorization. Section B.1.c (APA Ethics Code) outlines the exceptions to confidentiality including the fact that confidentiality does not apply "when disclosure is required to prevent clear and imminent danger to the client." Any decision to breach confidentiality should be made with careful consideration. Determining that a client is at risk of committing suicide leads to actions that can be exceptionally disruptive to the client's life. When a decision is made that the client is a danger to self, a clinician must take whatever steps are necessary to prevent the harm. Actions to prevent this harm must be the least intrusive to accomplish that result, However, this is not always possible, specifically in cases where involuntary hospitalization occurs or when law enforcement/legal system becomes involved.

When working with suicidal clients, there is always a fear of the client completing suicide, but there are also litigation concerns. During these instances, families are in mourning and at times, unfortunately, can be blaming and looking at the clinician as being negligent in caring for their loved one.

We may be employed by agencies who have policies and procedures in place and if we perform our jobs "within the scope of employment" we "should" be safe from litigation. This is not always the case, which is why it is pertinent to remain knowledgeable about your responsibilities and duties to your clients.

REASONABLE DUTY AND NEGLIGENCE

The following are considered **reasonable duty** for clinicians in terms of suicide prevention (Remley & Herlihy, 2001):

- Clinicians must know how to make assessments of a client's risk for suicide and must be able to defend their decisions

- When a decision is made that the client is a danger to self, the clinician must take whatever steps are necessary to prevent the harm

- Actions to prevent harm must be the least intrusive to accomplish that result

"As long as mental health and health professionals have been able to show prudent and responsible care (through assessment of risk and tailored intervention planning), the courts have tended to rule in favor of the practitioner." (Brems, 2001, p. 166) (22)

Typically when a lawsuit is launched against a clinician it is in the context of negligence. Let's delineate negligence:

Negligence

- A duty was owed by the clinician to the client
- The duty owed was breached
- There is sufficient legal causal connection between the breach of duty and the client's injury
- Some injury or damages were suffered by the client

Clinician Worksheet

Were you Negligent?

Directions: Use these questions to guide your decision making when negligence is being considered.

_____ Was the clinician aware, or should have been aware, of the risk?

_____ Was the clinician thorough in assessment of the client's suicide risk?

_____ Did the clinician make "reasonable and prudent efforts" to collect sufficient and necessary data to assess risk?

_____ Was the assessment data misused, thus leading to a misdiagnosis where the same data would have resulted in appropriate diagnosis by another mental health professional?

_____ Did the clinician mismanage the case, being either "unavailable or unresponsive to the client's emergency situation"?

MINOR CLIENTS

When working with children and adolescents, it is important to remain educated about the limits of confidentiality and the rights to privacy as determined by the laws in your respective states. When working with minors who are suicidal the following guidelines can be helpful to follow.

Working With Minors

- It is typically best practice to make parents/guardians aware of the suicide risk for their children.

- Technically, the clinician's legal liability ends when parents have been notified that their child is at risk for suicide and preventive actions have been recommended.

- It is always recommended to document any recommendations or referrals made to the parents about their children. If a parent refuses to follow the clinician's recommendations, it is advised to have the parents sign documentation stating that they are aware of the risk involved in choosing to dismiss the mental health provider's concerns and recommendations.

- Clinicians have an obligation to follow up with a child, if parents or other significant others fail to act on prevention recommendations. This follow-up should be well documented in the client file.

Release of Suicidal Client to Parent or Other Authorized Official

Name:_____

Age: _____ Gender: _____

Presenting issue/threat of suicide:

_____

_____

Current means (gun, knife, pills, etc.):

_____

_____

Prior Attempts (Y/N): If yes, when and how:

_____

_____

Name and who (identify relationship) will accompany client to hospital?

_____

_____

Reliable transportation or do police need to be called (Y/N)? If no, call 911. Provide the caretaker a copy of directions to the hospital, behind this sheet.

_____

_____

He/she will be referred and admitted to:

_____

_____

WHAT GETS IN THE WAY OF PROVIDING ADEQUATE CARE?

Therapist Discomfort

Therapists tend to feel uncomfortable with the subject of NSSI and suicide. We must appreciate that each client is a unique person. At times, clinicians have a tendency to approach clients as a "diagnosis" or category and fail to keep in mind that each client presents with a personal set of experiences and needs. Thus clients require interventions that are tailored to their specific needs and issues. We tend to forget the preventive factors. When working with these type of clients, it may be in an immediate or crisis-oriented setting. Thus our goal is to assist the client returning to their "status quo" level of functioning. However, we still need to provide clients with skill sets that will be more preventive in nature and effective in helping the client manage these issues **BEFORE** suicidal intent or plan develop.

Failure to Consult

At times, we become accustomed to doing things in a certain way or we may not have accessibility to other mental health providers in the community. It is always imperative to consult with other health care providers when managing a suicidal client. This type of work can cause clinicians to experience duress which could cloud judgment or compromise problem-solving abilities. It is responsible to consult with others and be proactive in being aware of your available resources.

Inadequate Training

When I teach the psychology portion of the Intermediate Use of Force class with police officers, I stress the importance of "**Train How You Fight and Fight like You Train**" to demonstrate the importance of taking all of their training experiences seriously and to use these opportunities to enhance their skills to better prepare themselves for any scenario that may occur while on duty.

The same concept holds true for us as mental health professionals. We have to understand and learn more about suicidal behavior! We need to attend all of the trainings provided to us and take advantage of any learning opportunities related to the assessment and treatment of suicidal behaviors. We need to be aware of the most recent research, screening tools, assessment techniques, and treatment techniques to be as effective as possible when working to prevent suicides or when working with clients to better manage suicidal behavior. The more we train, the better equipped we are to help our clients "fight" the clinical issues that cause them daily suffering and agony.

Fears of Legal Liability

Fear of litigation often cloud therapists' abilities to focus on the welfare of the client. Clinicians may even avoid addressing this issue or recognizing subtle red flags in efforts to avoid litigation. **IGNORANCE IS NOT A LEGAL DEFENSE.** Remember the negligence checklist? How could avoidance be construed as negligence?

Chapter 12 | **Consultation and Self-Care**

ALWAYS, ALWAYS, ALWAYS CONSULT!

It is important to look for consensus when assessing for suicide and follow the advice in making decisions. Consultation can occur with other healthcare professionals or others involved with the patient's care. Other resources include family members, medical records, prior treatment providers and significant others.

LOSING A CLIENT TO SUICIDE

Studies show that one in five psychologists and counselors and one in two psychiatrists lose a client to suicide in the course of their careers. Losing a client to suicide can be jolting, disheartening, shocking and surreal. This is probably one of the most dreaded events that could happen to a mental health professional in their career.

Many times, the clinician can develop PTSD symptoms, or acute stress disorder symptoms, in addition to experiencing feelings of grief and bereavement. This grief can become complicated, as you are not only grieving the loss of the client, but you are grieving for their family members, and you are grieving for your own loss. You may experience disillusionment with the profession, you may lose security in your clinical abilities and trust that therapy is effective. You may question your clinical judgment and ability to discern, in addition to losing confidence in the entire process!

Losing a client to suicide can also lead to personal growth, improvement of therapy skills, and empathy toward other colleagues. But too often, mental health care providers do not respond effectively to these feelings and may minimize or attempt to normalize their responses. Awareness, acknowledgment, and action (the three A's) are vital when attempting to manage the death of a client.

Awareness

A client suicide is likely to impact clinicians' professional identities, their relationships with colleagues, and their clinical work. It is true that these feelings can be a normal reaction; however, when they begin to interfere with your daily functioning or pertinent areas of your life (e.g., work or interpersonal relationships) then a problem exists. You have to recognize these reactions and process them accordingly in order to successfully survive a client's completed suicide.

Acknowledgment

Reactions typically include initial shock, denial, numbness, intense sadness, anxiety, anger, and intense distress. Survivors (clinicians) also are likely to experience posttraumatic stress disorder symptoms such as intrusive thoughts, experiences of detachment, and dissociation. Clinicians may question their clinical competence and ability to provide therapeutic services to future clients. This may lead to countertransference issues in therapy and can lead to the clinician avoiding the topic of suicide or being overzealous about the topic of suicide. Grief reaction for clinicians may also include feelings of guilt, loss of self-esteem, and self-doubts about one's skills and clinical competence. They may be fearful of being blamed for the suicide, or fear of relatives' reactions (e.g., litigation).

Action

Seeking therapy services, support and consultation are vital in surviving and even thriving, when losing a client to suicide. Many clinicians avoid seeking services for this occurrence for various reasons and some have reported a pattern of isolation and interpersonal discomfort with their colleagues, who implicitly or explicitly expressed judgment about their competence. You **CANNOT** allow these fears to impede your work in treatment, as many of your clients can be better assisted by what is learned from the experience.

As mental health providers we are requested to provide "due diligence" when serving clients. We can try to be as preventive and therapeutic as possible, but ultimately, the final decision to stay alive and prosper will be the client's. Upon examination of this loss, if you know and are certain that you provided the best care possible for your client, please don't give up. You chose this profession for a reason or it chose you. Stay diligent and steadfast when completing this work. It is worth it!

BURNOUT

Burnout has been defined a number of ways, but most researchers favor a multifaceted definition developed by Maslach and colleagues (1993; 1996) that encompasses three dimensions:

- Emotional exhaustion
- Depersonalization
- Reduced personal accomplishment

The dimension of emotional exhaustion references feelings of being worn-out, overextended, and drained. Depersonalization (also referred to as cynicism) denotes negative and cynical attitudes toward one's consumers (our clients) or work in general (agencies, hospitals, insurance companies). A reduced sense of personal accomplishment (or efficacy) includes negative self-evaluation of your work with consumers (our clients) or overall job effectiveness.

Many researchers consider burnout to be a job-related stress condition or even a "work-related mental health impairment." Although burnout is correlated with other mental health conditions, such as anxiety and depression, research also demonstrates that burnout is a concept separate from these other mental health disorders.

Several studies have shown that more than half of mental health workers may be experiencing high levels of burnout. Burnout has been associated with a large number of negative conditions affecting different types of employees, their organizations, and the clients they serve. Professionals who experience burnout often report impaired emotional and physical health and a diminished sense of well-being. Burnout has also been associated with increased rates of depression, anxiety, sleep problems, memory deficits, neck and back pain, and excessive alcohol consumption. Burnout has been correlated with a number of negative organizational outcomes including reduced commitment to the organization, negative attitudes, and often absenteeism and high turnover.

Burnout can affect the way that mental health services are provided to our clients, and we may not be as cognizant about mistakes and make poor decisions regarding client care. Research has shown that burnout has been positively correlated with poor ethical decisions and impaired judgment about client care. As a clinician, you may notice yourself canceling clients, being consistently late for work or for client appointments, forgetting about scheduled appointments, having difficulty with completing client notes or mismanagement of administrative duties. You may even begin to have difficulty recognizing and maintaining appropriate client/clinician boundaries.

Vacation or time off **WILL NOT** fix burnout! This is an issue that may require therapeutic intervention and consistent consultation or even supervision. We have to remain aware when we begin to experience burnout. The earlier you are able to recognize it, the sooner you can address it. As mental health professionals, we have to do a better job practicing what we preach to clients. What have you done to take care of yourself lately? If it takes longer than 30 seconds to answer this question, DO BETTER! Take care of yourselves, so you can continue to provide these mental health services with the same passion and enthusiasm as you may have had 2, 5, 10, or 20 years ago.

References

Acker, G. (2010). The challenges in providing services to clients with mental illness: Managed care, burnout and somatic symptoms among social workers. *Community Mental Health Journal, 46*(6), 591–600.

Adler, P. A., & Adler, P. (2008). The cyber worlds of self-injurers: Deviant communities, relationships, and selves. *Symbolic Interaction, 3,* 33–56.

American Association of Suicidology. (1994). *Suicide prevention guidelines.* Washington, DC: American Association of Suicidology.

American Association of Suicidology. (2001). *Therapists as survivors of suicide: Basic information.* Washington, DC: American Association of Suicidology.

American Psychiatric Association. (2003). Practice guideline for the assessment and treatment of patients with suicidal behaviors [Supplemental material]. *American Journal of Psychiatry, 160*(11), 1–60.

American Psychiatric Association. (2013). *Diagnostic and statistical manual of mental disorders* (5th ed.). Washington, DC: American Psychiatric Association.

American Psychological Association Practice Organization. (2012). Guidelines for the Practice of Telepsychology. Retrieved February 18, 2017, From http://www.apa.org/practice/guidelines/telepsychology.aspx (accessed on February 18, 2017).

American Psychological Association Practice Organization. (2012b). Social media: What's your policy? *Good Practice, spring/summer,* 10–18.

American Psychological Association. (2015). *Telepsychology: 50-state review.* Retrieved October 27, 2016, from http://apapracticecentral.org/advocacy/state/telehealth-slides.pdf

Anderson, M. (1999). Waiting for harm: Deliberate self-harm and suicide in young people—A review of the literature. *Journal of Psychiatric and Mental Health Nursing, 6*(2), 91–100.

Andrews, B. (1995). Bodily shame as a mediator between abusive experiences and depression. *Journal of Abnormal Psychology, 104*(2), 277–285.

Andrews, G., & Slade, T. (2001). Interpreting scores on the Kessler Psychological Distress Scale (K10). *Australian and New Zealand Journal of Public Health, 25,* 494–497.

Asarnow, J. R., Jaycox, C., Duan, N., LaBorde, A. P., Rea, M. M., Murray, P., Wells, K. B. (2005). Effectiveness of a quality improvement intervention for adolescent depression in primary care clinics. *Journal of the American Medical Association, 293,* 311–319.

Awa, W. L., Plaumann, W., & Walter, U. (2010). Burnout prevention: A review of intervention programs. *ClientEducation and Counselling, 78*(2), 184–190.

Bancroft, J., Skrimshire, A., & Simkins, S. (1976). The reasons people give for taking overdoses. *British Journal of Psychiatry, 128*, 538–548.

Baraff, L. J., Janowicz, N., & Asarnow, J. R. (2006). Survey of California emergency departments about practice for management of suicidal client and resources available for their care. *Annals of Emergency Medicine, 48*, 452–458.

Barnes, S. M., Walter, K. H., & Chard, K. M. (2012). Does a history of mild traumatic brain injury increase suicide risk in veterans with PTSD? *Rehabilitation Psychology, 57*(1), 18–26.

Baumeister, R. F. (1990). Suicide as escape from self. *Psychological Review, 87*(1), 90–113.

Beck, A. T. (1986). Hopelessness as a predictor of eventual suicide. *Annals of the New York Academy of Sciences, 487*, 90–96.

Beck, A. T., Brown, B. K., Berchick, R. J., Stewart, B. L., & Steer, R. A. (1990). Relationship between hopelessness and ultimate suicide: A replication with psychiatric outpatients. *American Journal of Psychiatry, 147*(2), 190–195.

Beck, A. T., Brown, G., & Steer, R. A. (1989). Prediction of eventual suicide in psychiatric inpatients by clinical rating of hopelessness. *Journal of Consulting and Clinical Psychology, 57*(2), 309–310.

Beck, A. T., Rush, A. J., Shaw, B. F., & Emery, G. (1979). *Cognitive therapy of depression.* New York, NY: Guildford Press.

Beck, A. T., Steer, R. A., Kovacs, M., & Garrison, B. (1985). Hopelessness and eventual suicide: A 10-year prospective study of patients hospitalized with suicidal ideation. *American Journal of Psychiatry, 142*, 559–563.

Beck, A. T., & Weishaar, W. E. (1990). Suicide risk assessment and prediction. *Crisis, 11*(2), 22–30.

Beck, J. (2005). *Cognitive therapy for challenging problems: What to do when the basics don't work.* New York, NY: Guilford Press.

Berman, A., & Cohen-Sandler, R. (1983). Suicide and malpractice: Expert testimony and the standard of care. *Professional Psychology: Research and Practice, 14*(1), 6–19.

Bohnert, A. S., Valenstein, M., Bair, M. J., Ganoczy, D., McCarthy, J. F., Ilgen, M. A., & Blow, F. C. (2011). Association between opioid prescribing patients and opioid overdose related deaths. *Journal of the American Medical Association, 305*, 1315–1321.

Bongar, B. (1992). Guidelines for risk management in the care of the suicidal patient. In B. Bongar (Ed.), *Suicide: Guidelines for assessment, management, and treatment* (pp. 268–282). New York, NY: Oxford University Press.

Bongar, B. (2002). *The suicidal patient: Clinical and legal standards of care* (2nd ed.). Washington, DC: American Psychological Association.

Brems, C. (2000). *Basic skills in psychotherapy and counseling.* Pacific Grove, CA: Brooks/Cole.

Brenner, L. A., Homaifar, B. Y., Adler, L. E., Wolfman, J.H., & Kemp, J. (2009). Suicidality and Veterans with a History of Traumatic Brain Injury: Precipitating Factors, Protective Factors, and Prevention Strategies. *Rehabilitation Psychology, 54*(4) 390–397.

Brent, D. A., Emslie, G., Clarke, G., Wagner, D.W., Rosenbaum, J., Asarnow, J., & Keller, M., et. al, (2008). Switching to another SSRI or to venlafaxine with or without cognitive behavioral therapy for adolescents with SSRI-persistent depression. *Journal of the American Medical Association, 299,* 901–913.

Brown, G. K. (2002). *A review of suicide assessment measures for intervention research in adults and older adults.* Retrieved August 2, 2016 from http://www.sprc.org/sites/default/files/migrate/library/BrownReviewAssessmentMeasuresAdultsOlderAdults.pdf

Brown, M. (July 22, 1998). The behavioral treatment of self-mutilation. Paper presented at the Self-Mutilation, Treatment & Research Symposium, 16th Congress of the World Association for Social Psychiatry, Vancouver, BC.

Brown, M. (2006). Linehan's theory of suicidal behavior: Theory, research, and dialectical behavior therapy. In T. Ellis (Ed.), *Cognition and suicide: Theory, research, and practice* (pp. 91-117). Washington, DC: American Psychological Association.

Brown, M. Z. (2007). Cognitive behavior therapy for chronically para-suicidal patients. *San Diego Psychologist, 22*(2), 9–10.

Brown, M. Z., & Chapman, A. L. (2007). Stopping self-harm once and for all: Relapse prevention in Dialectical Behavior Therapy. Therapist Guide to Evidence Based Relapse Prevention. *Practical Resources for the Mental Health Professional, 9,* 191–213.

Brown, S. D., Perez, R. M., & Reeder, B. L. (2007). The costs and benefits of merging counseling centers with student health services: Perceptions of the experienced. *Journal of College Student Psychotherapy, 22*(1), 3–16.

Bullying Statistics. (n.d.). Retrieved October 27, 2016, from http://www.bullyingstatistics.org

Caine, E. D. (2004, February 22–26). Population based approaches to suicide prevention in later life. Paper presented at the annual meeting of the American Association of Geriatric Psychiatry, Baltimore, MD.

Caruso, K. (n.d.b). Eating disorders and suicide. Retrieved October 27, 2016, from http://www.suicide.org/eating-disorders-and-suicide.html

Caruson, K. (n.d.a). Elderly suicide. Retrieved October 27, 2016, from http://www.suicide.org/elderly-suicide.html

Cavanagh, J. T., Carson, A. J., Sharpe, M., & Lawrie, S. M. (2003). Psychological autopsy studies of suicide: A systemic review. *Psychological Medicine, 33,* 395–405.

Center for Mental Health in Schools at UCLA. (2009). About emo youth subculture. Retrieved October 27, 2016, from http://smhp.psych.ucla.edu/pdfdocs/youth/emo.pdf

Center for Substance Abuse Treatment. (2008). *Substance abuse and suicide prevention: Evidence and implications—A white paper* (DHHS Pub. No. SMA-08-4352). Rockville, MD: Substance Abuse and Mental Health Services Administration.

Centers for Disease Control and Prevention. (2015). *Suicide: Facts at a glance.* Retrieved from https://www.cdc.gov/violenceprevention/pdf/suicide-datasheet-a.pdf

Centers for Disease Control and Prevention, National Center for Injury Prevention and Control. (2007). National Suicide Statistics. Retrieved May 7, 2016 from https://www.cdc.gov/violenceprevention/suicide/statistics/index.html

Cheatle, M. D. (2014). Assessing suicide risk in patients with chronic pain and depression [Supplemental material]. *Current Pain Perspectives, 63*(6), 6–11.

Chemiss, C. (1980). *Staff burnout: Job stress in the human services.* Beverly Hills, CA: Sage.

Chiles, J. A., & Strosahl, K. D. (1995). *The suicidal patient: Principles of assessment, treatment, and case management.* Washington, DC: American Psychiatric Press.

Chiles, J. A., & Strosahl, K. D. (2005). *Clinical manual for assessment and treatment of suicidal patients.* Washington, DC: American Psychiatric Press.

Comtois, K. A., & Linehan, M. M. (2006). Psychosocial treatments of suicidal behaviors: A practice-friendly review. *Journal of Clinical Psychology: In Session, 62,* 161–170.

Conwell, Y. (1995). Suicide among elderly persons. *Psychiatric Services, 46*(6), 563–564.

Crook, T., Raskin, A., & Davis, D. (1975). Factors associated with attempted suicide among hospitalized depressed patients. *Psychological Medicine, 5,* 381–388.

Dhal, Eldon. Dr. (2014). Suicide in the Elderly: A Disturbing Trend that is Underreported! Retrieved February 16, 2017, from http://lifechoicevitamins.blogspot.com/2014/08/suicide-in-elderly-distrurbing-trend.html

DeLeo, D., & Ormskerk, S. C. (1991). Suicide in the elderly: General characteristics. *Crisis, 12*(2), 3–17.

Deutsch, C. J. (1984). Self-reported sources of stress among psychotherapists. *Professional Psychology, 15,* 833–845.

Dilsaver, S. (2007). Suicide attempts and completion in patients with bipolar disorder. *Psychiatric Times.* Retrieved October 27, 2016, from http://www.psychiatrictimes.com/articles/suicide-attempts-and-completions-patients-bipolar-disorder

Do Something. (n.d.). 11 facts about bullying. Retrieved October 27, 2016, from https://www.dosomething.org/us/facts/11-facts-about-bullying

Doyle, B. B. (1990). Crisis management of the suicidal patient. In S. J. Blumenthal & D. J. Kupfer (Eds.), *Suicide over the life cycle: Risk factors, assessment, and treatment of suicidal patients* (pp. 381–423). Washington, DC: American Psychiatric Press.

Duggan, J., & Whitlock, J. (2012). Self-injurious behaviors in cyber space. *Encyclopedia of Cyber Behavior* (pp. 768–781). Hershey, PA: IGI Global.

Elliott, C. H. (2010). What Does Dialectical Mean? Anxiety and OCD Exposed. With Laura L. Smith, Ph.D. and Charles G. Elliott, Ph.D. PsychCentral. Retrieved March 30, 2017, from https://blogs.psychcentral.com/anxiety/2010/02/what-does-dialectical-mean/

Ellis, T. E. (1990). Strategies for helping suicidal clients, Part I: Crisis management. In W. F. Fremouw, M. dePerczel, & T. E. Ellis (Eds.), *Suicide risk: Assessment and response guidelines* (pp. 98–129). New York, NY: Allyn & Bacon.

Ellis, T. E. (2006). *Cognition and suicide: Theory, research and practice.* Washington, DC: American Psychological Association.

Favazza, A. R. (2012). Nonsuicidal self-injury: How categorization guides treatment. Retrieved May 6, 2015 https://www.researchgate.net/publication/267561838_Nonsuicidal_self-injury_How_categorization_guides_treatment

Favazza, A. R., & Conterio, K. (1989). Female habitual self-mutilators. *Acta Psychiatrica Scandinavica, 79,* 283–289.

Favazza, A. R., & Rosenthal, R. J. (1993). Diagnostic issues in self-mutilation. *Hospital Community Psychiatry, 44,* 134–140.

Fiske, H. (1998). Applications of solution-focused therapy in suicide prevention. In D. Deleo, A., Schmidtke, & R. Diekstra (Eds.), *Suicide prevention: A holistic approach* (20)185-197. Dordrecht, Netherlands: Kluwer.

Franko, D. L., Dorer, D. J., Keel, P. K., Jackson, S., Manzo, M. P., & Herzog, D. B. (2005). How do eating disorders and alcohol use disorder influence each other? *International Journal of Eating Disorders, 38,* 200-207.

Franko, D. L., Keel, P. K., Dorer, D. J., Blais, M. A., Delinsky, S. S., Eddy, K. T., Charat, V., Renn, R., and Herzog, D. B. (2004). What predicts suicide attempts in women with eating disorders? *Psychological Medicine, 34,* 843–853.

Friedman, M., Glasser, M., Laufer, E., Laufer, M., & Whol, M. (1972). Attempted suicide and self-mutilation in adolescence. *International Journal of Psychoanalysis, 53,* 179–183.

Gallagher-Thompson, D., & Osgood, N. (1997). Suicide in later life. *Behavior Therapy, 28*(1), 23–41.

Garman, A. N., Corrigan, P. W., & Morris, S. (2002). Staff burnout and client satisfaction: Evidence of relationships at the care unit level. *Journal of Occupational Health Psychology, 7*(3), 235–241.

Gibbons, R. D., Brown, C. H., Hur, K., Marcus, S. M., Bhaumik, D. K., Erkens, J. A., et al. (2007). Early evidence of regulators' suicidality warnings in SSRI prescriptions and suicide in children and adolescents. *American Journal of Psychiatry, 164,* 1356–1363.

Gilliland, B., & James, R. (1993). *Crisis intervention strategies* (2nd ed.). Pacific Grove, CA: Brooks/Cole.

Gliatto, M. F., & Rai, A. K. (1999). Evaluation and treatment of patients with suicidal ideation. *American Family Physician, 59*(6), 1500–1506.

Goldston, D. B., Molock, S. D., Whitbeck, L. B., Murakami, J. L., & Zayas, L. H. (2008). Cultural considerations in adolescent suicide prevention and psychosocial treatment. *American Psychologist, 63,* 14–31.

Gould, M. S., King, R., Greenwald, S., Fisher, M., Kramer, R., & Flisher, A. J. (1998). Psychopathology Associated With Suicidal Ideation and Attempts Among Children and Adolescents. *Journal of the American Academy of Child and Adolescent Psychiatry, 37*(9) 915–923.

Gould, M. S., Munfakh, J. L., Lubell, K., Kleinman, M., & Parker, S. (2002). Seeking help from the internet during adolescence. *Journal of the American Academy of Child and Adolescent Psychiatry, 41*, 1182–1189.

Griffith, J. (2012). Correlates of suicide among army national guard soldiers. *Military Psychology, 24*, 568–591.

Grunberg, P. H., & Lewis, S. P. (2014). Self-injury and readiness to recover: Preliminary examination of components of the stage model of change. *Counseling Psychology Quarterly, 28*(4), 361–371.

Gupta, S. (2013, February 8). The risk of suicide among people suffering from bulimia. *Binge Eating and Bulimia*. Retrieved October 27, 2016, from http://www.bingeeatingbulimia.com/blog/2013/2/8/the-risk-of-suicide-among-people-suffering-from-bulimia.html

Gupta, S., Black, D. W., Arndt, S., Hubbard, W. C., & Andreasen, N. (1998). Factors associated with suicide attempts among patients with schizophrenia. *Psychiatric Services, 49*(10), 1353–1355.

Gutheil, T. (1999). Liability issues and liability prevention in suicide. In D. Jacobs (Ed.), *The Harvard Medical School guide to suicide assessment & intervention* (pp. 561–578). San Francisco, CA: Jossey-Bass.

Haines, J., Williams, C., Brain, K., & Wilson, G. (1996). The psychophysiology of self-mutilation. *Journal of Abnormal Psychology, 104*(3), 479–489.

Hatzenbuehler, M. L. (2011). The social environment and suicide attempts in lesbian, gay and bisexual youth. *Official Journal of the American Academy of Pediatrics*. Retrieved October 27, 2016, from http://pediatrics.aappublications.org/content/early/2011/04/18/peds.2010-3020

Heilbron, N., & Prinstein, M. J. (2008). Peer influence and non-suicidal self-injury: A theoretical view of mechanisms and moderators. *Applied and Preventive Psychology, 2*(4), 169–177.

Hendin, H., Lipschitz, A., Maltsberger, J. T., Haas, A. P., & Wynecoop, S. (2000). Therapists' reactions to patients' suicides. *American Journal of Psychiatry, 157*(123), 2002–2027.

Homafir, B. Y., Brenner, L. A., Forster, J. E., & Nagamtoto, H. (2012). Traumatic brain injury, executive functioning and suicidal behavior: A brief report. *Rehabilitation Psychology, 57*, 337–341.

Hufford, M. R. (2001). Alcohol and suicidal behavior. *Clinical Psychology Review, 21*(5), 797–811.

Ilgen, M. A., McCarthy, J. F., Ignacio, R. V., Bohnert, A. S., Valenstein, M., Blow, F. C., & Katz, I. R. (2012). Psychopathology, Iraq, Afghanistan service, and suicide among Veterans Health Administration patients. *Journal of Consulting and Clinical Psychology, 80*(3), 323–330.

Jacobs, D., & Brewer, M. (2004). APA guidelines provides recommendations for assessing and treating patients with suicidal behaviors. *Psychiatric Annals, 34*, 373–380.

James, L. C. (2012). Introduction to special section on suicide prevention. *Military Psychology, 24*, 565–567.

Jamison Redfield, K. (2007). *Manic-depressive illness: Bipolar disorders and recurrent depression.* Oxford, UK: Oxford University Press.

Jobes, D. A., & Drozd, J. F. (2004). The CAMS approach to working with suicidal patients. *Journal of Contemporary Psychotherapy, 34*, 73–85.

Joiner, T. (2005). *Why people die by suicide.* Cambridge, MA: Harvard University Press.

Joiner, T. E., Walker, R. L., Rudd, M. D., & Jobes, D. A. (1999). Scientizing and routinizing the assessment of suicidality in outpatient practice. *Professional Psychology*: Research and Practice, 30, 447– 453.

Jones, I. H., Congiu, L., Stevenson, J., Strauss, N., & Frei, D. Z. (1979). A biological approach to two forms of human self-injury. *Journal of Nervous and Mental Disease, 167*, 74–78.

Kamath, P., Reddy, Y. C., & Kandavel, T. (2007). Suicidal behavior in obsessive–compulsive disorder. *Journal of Clinical Psychiatry, 68*(11), 1741–1750.

Kemperman, I., Russ, M. J., & Shearin, E. (1997). Self-injurious behavior and mood regulation in borderline personality disorder patients. *Journal of Personality Disorders, 11*(2), 146–157.

Kennedy, S., Koeppe, R. A., Young, E. A., & Zubieta, J. K. (2006). Dysregulation of endogenous opioid emotion regulation circuitry in major depression in women. *Archives of General Psychiatry, 63*, 1199–1208.

Kessler, R. C., Andrews, G., Colpe, L. J., Hiripi, E., Mroczek, D. K., T. Normand, S.-L., Walters, E. E., & Zaslavsky A.M. (2002). Short screening scales to monitor population prevalences and trends in non-specific psychological distress. *Psychological Medicine, 32,* 959–956.

Khan, A., Leventhal, R., Khan, S., & Brown, W. (2000). Suicide risk in patients with anxiety disorders: A meta-analysis of the FDA's database. Retrieved April 2013, from https://www. researchgate.net/publication/11560275_Khan_A_Leventhal_RM_Khan_SR_Brown_WA_ Severity_of_depression_and_response_to_antidepressants_and_placebo_an_analysis_of_the_ Food_and_Drug_Administration_Database_J_Clin_Psychopharmacol_22_40-45.

Kleespies, P. M. (2011). A study of self-injurious and suicidal behavior in a veteran population. *Psychological Services, 8*(3), 236–250.

Kovacs, M., Beck, A. T., Weismann, A. (1975). Hopelessness: An indicator of suicide risk. *Suicide, 5*(2), 98–103.

Krasner, M. S., Epstein, R. M., Beckman, H., Suchman, A. L., Chapman, B., Mooney, C. J., & Quill, T. E. (2009). Association of an educational program in mindful communication with burnout, empathy, and attitudes among primary care physicians. *Journal of the American Medical Association, 302*(12), 1284–1293.

Kreitman, N. (1977). *Para suicide.* Chichester, UK: John Wiley & Sons.

Kress, V. E., Bario-Minton, C. A., Adamson, N. A., Paylo, M. J., & Pope, V. (2014). The removal of the multiaxial system in the DSM-5®: Implications and practice suggestions for counselors. *Professional Counselor.* Retrieved October 27, 2016, from http://tpcjournal. nbcc.org/the-removal-of-the-multiaxial-system-in-the-dsm-5-implications-and-practice-suggestions-for-counselors

Kress, V. E., & Paylo, M. J. (2014). *Treating those with mental disorders: A comprehensive approach to case conceptualization and treatment.* Columbus, OH: Pearson.

LaFemey, M. C. (2005). Suicidal threats in long-term care: While at risk, older adults are not likely to attempt suicide in a nursing home. *Advance for Nurses, 7*, 25.

Langlois, S., & Morrison, P. (2002). Suicide deaths and suicide attempts. *Health Reports, 13*(2), 9–22.

Lenhart, A. (2009). Teens and social media: An overview. *New York Department of Health and Mental Hygiene.* Retrieved October 27, 2016, from http://isites.harvard.edu/fs/docs/ icb.topic786630.files/Teens%20Social%20Media%20and%20Health%20-%20NYPH%20 Dept%20Pew%20Internet.pdf

Lester, D. (1997). The role of shame in suicide. *Suicide Life Threat Behavior, 27*(4), 352–361.

Lewis, S. P., Heath, N. L., Michael, N. J., & Duggan, J. M. (2012). Non-suicidal self-injury, youth, and the internet: What mental health professionals need to know. *Child and Adolescent Psychiatry and Mental Health, 6*(1), 13.

Linehan, M. M., Armstrong, H. E., Suarez, A., Allmon, D., & Heard, H. L. (1991). Cognitive–behavioral treatment of chronically parasuicidal borderline patients. *Archives of General Psychiatry, 48*, 1060–1064.

Linehan, M. M., Comtois, K. A., Murray, A. M., Brown, M. Z., Gallop, R. J., Heard, H. L. et. al. (2006). Two year randomized controlled trial and following of dialectical behavior therapy vs. therapy by experts for suicidal behaviors and borderline personality disorders. *Archives of General Psychiatry, 63*, 757–766.

Linehan, M. M., Tutek, D. A., Heard, H. L., & Armstrong, H. E. (1994). Interpersonal outcome of cognitive behavioral treatment for chronically suicidal borderline patients. *American Journal of Psychiatry, 151*, 1771–1776.

Loebel, J. P. (2005). Completed suicide in late life. *Psychiatric Services, 56*(3), 260–262.

Lordache, L., & Low, N. C. (2010). The advantages of bipolar disorder. *Journal of Psychiatry & Neuroscience, 35*(3), E3–E4.

Maguen, S., Luxton, D. D., Skopp, N. A., & Madden, E. (2012). Gender differences in traumatic experiences and mental health in active duty soldiers redeployed from Iraq and Afghanistan. *Journal of Psychiatric Research, 46*(3), 311–316.

Malone, K. M. (1997). Pharmacotherapy of affectively ill suicidal patients. *Psychiatry Clinics of North America, 20*, 613–624.

Maltsberger, J. T., & Buie, D. H. (1974). Countertransference: Hate in the treatment of suicidal patients. *Archives of General Psychology, 30*(5), 625–633.

Marlatt, G. A., & Witkiewitz, K. (Eds.). (2007). *Therapist's guide to evidence-based relapse prevention*. Amsterdam, Netherlands: Academic Press.

Maslach, C., Jackson, S. E., & Leiter, M. P. (1996). *Maslach Burnout Inventory manual* (3rd ed.). Palo Alto, CA: Consulting Psychologists Press.

Maslach, C., & Pines, A. (1979). Burn-out: The loss of human caring. In A. Pines & C. Maslach (Eds.), *Experiencing social psychology: Readings and projects* (pp. 246-252). New York, NY: A. A. Knopf.

Maslach, C., Schaufeli, W. B., & Leiter, M. P. (2001). Job burnout. *Annual Review of Psychology, 52*, 397–422.

McCarty, D., & Clancy, C. (2002). Telehealth: Implications for social work. *Social Work, 47*(2), 153–161.

Meichenbaum, D. (2005). 35 years of working with suicidal patients: Lessons learned. *Canadian Psychologist, 46*, 64–72.

Moscicki, E. K. (1997). Identification of suicide risk factors using epidemiologic studies. *Psychiatry Clinics of North America, 20*, 499–517.

Murphy, G. E. (1997). The physician's responsibility for suicide. II. Errors of omission. *Annals of Internal Medicine, 82*(3), 305–309.

National Institute of Mental Health. (1998). *Priorities for prevention research at NIMH: A report by the National Advisory Mental Health Council Workgroup on Mental Disorders Prevention Research* (NIH Pub. No. 98-4321). Rockville, MD: National Institutes of Health.

Neuringer, C. (1964). Rigid thinking in suicidal individuals. *Journal of Consulting Psychology, 28*, 54–58.

Neuringer, C. (1974). Attitudes toward self in suicidal individuals. *Life-Threatening Behavior, 4*(2), 96–106.

Nock, M., Prinstein, M. J., & Sterba, S. K. (2010). Revealing the form and function of self-injurious thoughts and behaviors: A real-time ecological assessment study among adolescents and young adults. *Psychology of Violence, 1*, 36–52.

Paykel, E. S., & Dienelt, M. N. (1971). Suicide attempts following acute depression. *Journal of Nervous and Mental Disease, 153*(4), 234–243.

Peterson, E. M., Louma, J. B., & Dunne, E. (2002). Suicide survivors' perceptions of the treating clinician. *Suicide and Life-Threatening Behavior, 32*(2), 158–166.

Pratt, D., Piper, M., Appleby, L., Webb, R., & Shaw, J. (2006). Suicide in recently released prisoners: A population-based cohort study. *Lancet, 368* (9530), 119–123.

Prossin, A., Love, T. M., Koeppe, R. A., Zubieta, J.-K., & Silk, K. R. (2010). Dysregulation of regional endogenous opioid function in borderline personality disorder. *American Journal of Psychiatry, 167*, 925–933.

Quek, T. (n.d.). Understanding chronic pain. Retrieved October 27, 2016, from http://www.webhome.idirect.com/~readon/pain.html

RAND National Defense Research Institute. (2014). *Sexual assault and sexual harassment in the US military.* Retrieved October 27, 2016, from http://www.rand.org/pubs/research_reports/RR870.html

Remley, T. P., Jr., & Herlihy, B. (2001). *Ethical, legal, and professional issues in counseling.* Upper Saddle River, NJ: Pearson.

Roberts-Dobie, S., & Donatelle, R. J. (2007). School counselors and student self-injury. *Journal of School Health, 77*(5), 257–264.

Robins, E., Murphy, G., Wilkinson, R. H., Jr., Gassner, S., & Kayes, J. (1950). Some clinical considerations in the prevention of suicide based on 134 successful suicides. *American Journal Public Health, 49*, 888–889.

Rudd, M. D. (1989). The prevalence of suicide ideation among college students. *Suicide and Life-Threatening Behavior, 19*, 173–183.

Rudd, M. D. (1998). An integrative conceptual and organization approach to treating suicidality. *Psychotherapy, 335*, 346–360.

Rudd, M. D. (2004). Cognitive therapy for suicidology: An integrative comprehensive and practical approach to conceptualization. *Journal of Contemporary Psychotherapy, 34*, 59–72.

Rudd, M. D., Joiner, T. E., & Rajab, M. H. (2001). *Treating suicidal behavior: An effective, time-limited approach.* New York, NY: Guilford Press.

Salkovskis, P., Atha, C., & Storer, D. (1990). Cognitive–behavioral problem-solving in the treatment of patients who repeatedly attempt suicide: A controlled trial. *British Journal of Psychiatry, 157*, 871–876.

Seigel, K. (1982). Rational suicide: Considerations for the clinician. *Psychiatric Quarterly, 54*, 77–83.

Seigel, K., & Tuckel, P. (1984). Rational suicide and the terminally ill cancer patient. *Omega, 15*, 263–269.

Self-Injury and Eating Disorders. Retrieved June 10, 2013, from https://www.eatingdisorderhope.com/treatment-for-eating-disorders/ o-occurring-dual-diagnosis/self-injury

Serna, P. (2011). *Adolescent suicide prevention program manual.* Newton, MA: Suicide Prevention Resource Center.

Shaffer, D., & Peffer, C. R., (2001). Practice parameters for the assessment and treatment of children and adolescents with suicidal behavior. *Journal of the American Academy of Child and Adolescent Psychiatry, 40*, 24–51.

Simeon, D., Stanley, B., Frances, A., Mann, J. J., Winchel, R., & Stanley, M. (1992). Self-mutilation in personality disorders: Psychological and biological correlates. *American Journal of Psychiatry, 149*, 221–226.

Simmons, R. (2011). *Odd girl out revised and updated: The hidden culture of aggression in girls.* Wilmington, MA: Mariner Books.

Simpson, G., & Tate, R. (2002). Suicidality and traumatic brain injury: Demographic, injury and clinical correlates. *Psychological Medicine, 32,* 687–698.

Simpson, M. (1975). The phenomenology of self-mutilation in a general hospital setting. *Canadian Psychiatry Association Journal, 20,* 429–434.

Some Facts About Suicide and Depression. Retrieved May 28, 2014 from https://www.cga.ct.gov/asaferconnecticut/tmy/0129/Some%20Facts%20About%20Suicide%20and%20Depression%20-%20Article.pdf

Stop Bullying. (n.d.). Facts about bullying. Retrieved October 27, 2016, from http://www.stopbullying.gov/kids/facts/index.html

"Suicide." (2015). *Merriam-Webster.* Retrieved October 27, 2016, from http://www.merriam-webster.com/dictionary/suicide

Suicide: Facts at a Glance. Retrieved June 1, 2013 from https://www.cdc.gov/violenceprevention/pdf/suicide-data sheet-a.pdf.

Suicide and, LGBT People: How to talk about it. Retrieved May 12, 2013 from http://www.lgbtmap.org/file/talking-about-suicide-and-lgbt-populations.pdf

Suicide Prevention Resource Center. (2008). Risk and Protective Factors for Suicide. Retrieved May 21, 2013 from http://www.sprc.org/sites/default/files/migrate/library/RiskProtectiveFactorsPrimer.pdf.

Tangney, J. P., Wagner, P., & Gramzow, R. (1992). Proneness to shame, proneness to guilt, and psychopathology [Erratum]. *Journal of Abnormal Psychology, 101*(4), 738.

Tanney, B. (1995). After a suicide: A helper's handbook. In B. Mishara (Ed.), *The impact of suicide* (pp. 100–120). New York, NY: Springer.

Telch, C. F. (1997). Skills training treatment for adaptive affect regulation in a woman with binge-eating disorder. *International Journal of Eating Disorders, 22,* 77–81.

U.S. Department of Defense. (2013). *Suicide event report calendar year 2013.* Retrieved March 12, 2014 from http://t2health.dcoe.mil/sites/default/files/DoDSER-2013-Jan-13-2015-Final.pdf

U.S. Department of Defense, Sexual Assault Prevention and Response Office. (2014). *Annual report on sexual assault in the military, fiscal year 2014.* Retrieved June, 2015, from http://sapr.mil/public/docs/reports/FY14_Annual/FY14_DoD_SAPRO_Annual_Report_on_Sexual_Assault.pdf

U.S. Department of Health and Human Services Office of the Surgeon General & National Action Alliance for Suicide Prevention. (2012). *National strategy for suicide prevention: Goals and objectives for action.* Washington, DC: Department of Health and Human Services.

US Department of Veterans Affairs. (2015). *Profile of women veterans.* Retrieved May, 2017 from https://www.va.gov/vetdata/docs/SpecialReports/Women_Veterans_Profile_12_22_2016.pdf

U.S. Department of Veterans Affairs Office of Inspector Gender. (2010). *Review of combat stress in women veterans receiving VA health care and disability benefits.* Retrieved October 27, 2016, from http://va.gov/oig/52/reports/2011/VAOIG-10-01640-45.pdf

Valente, S. M. (1994). Suicide and elderly people: Assessment and intervention. *Omega, 28*(4), 317–331.

Van Heeringen, C., James, S., Buylaert, W., Remoortel, J.V. (1995). The management of non-compliance with referral to out-patient-after-care among attempted suicide patients: A controlled intervention study. *Psychological Medicine, 25*, 963–970.

Whitlock, J. (2010). Self-injurious behavior in adolescents. *Public Library of Science, 7*(5), e1000240.

Wiklander, M., Samuelsson, M., Jokinen, J., Nilsonne, A., Wilczek, A., Rylander, G., Asberg, M. (2012). Shame-proneness in attempted suicide patients. *BMC Psychiatry, 12*, 50.

Williams, E. C., Moriarty Daley, A., & Lennaco, J. (2010). Assessing non-suicidal self-injurious behaviors in adolescents. *American Journal for Nurse Practitioners, 14*(6), 18-20, 23-26.

Yaeger, D., Himmelfrab, N., Cammack, A., Mintz, J. (2006). DSM-IV: Diagnosed posttraumatic stress disorder in women veterans with and without military sexual trauma. *Journal of General Internal Medicine, 21*(3), 65–69.

Zottarelli, M. (2015). *Women veteran screening guide: For providers and advocates to identify women veterans in their programs.* Swords to Plowshares. Retrieved October 27, 2016, from https://www.swords-to-plowshares.org/wp-content/uploads/Women-Veteran-Screening-Guide-2015.pdf

---

**For your convenience, purchasers can download and print
worksheets and exercises from www.pesi.com/suicide**

Websites

American Association of Suicidology
http://www.suicidology.org/

American Foundation for Suicide Prevention
http://www.afsp.org/

American Psychiatric Association Practice Guidelines for the Assessment and Treatment of Patients with Suicidal Behaviors
www.psych.org/psych_pract/treat/pg/suicidalbehavior_05–15–06.pdf

APA Guidelines Assessing and Treating Patients with Suicidal Behaviors
http://stopsuicide.org/downloads.Sltes/Docs/APASuicideguidelinesReviewArticle.pdf

Aeschi Working Groups
www.aeschiconferenceunibe.ch/

Getselfhelp.co.uk (CBT Self-help site)
https://www.getselfhelp.co.uk/index.html

Joint Commission National Client Safety Goals
http://www.jointcommission.org/PatientSafety/NationalPatientSafetyGoals

National Institute of Mental Health (NIMH) Suicide Fact Sheet
http://www.nimh.nih.gov/research/suicide.cfm

NIMH Frequently Asked Questions About Suicide
http://www.nimh.nih.gov/research/suicidefaq.cfm

Resource Guide for Implementing (JCAHO) 2007 Client Safety Goals On Suicide
www.mentalhealthscreening.org/events/ndsd/JCAHO.aspx

Review of Suicide Measures for Adults
http://www.nimh.nih.gov/research/adultsuicide.pdf

Review of Suicide Measures for Children
http://www.nimh.nih.gov/research/measures.pdf

Selected Bibliographies on Suicide Research-1999
http://www.nimh.nih.gov/research/suibib99.cfm

Suicide Prevention Resource Center: Best Practices Registry for Suicide Prevention
http://www.sprc.org

Suicide Statistics from CDC's National Center for Health Statistics
http://www.cdc.gov/nchs/fastats/suicide.cfm

The Surgeon General's Call to Action to Prevent Suicide
http://www.surgeongeneral.gov/library/calltoaction/default.htm

U.S. Department of Health and Human Services
http://www.afsp.org/

Made in the USA
Coppell, TX
11 August 2022

81303024R00129